Haeckel

His life and work

Wilhelm Bölsche

Alpha Editions

This edition published in 2020

ISBN : 9789354004803

Design and Setting By
Alpha Editions
email - alphaedis@gmail.com

As per information held with us this book is in Public Domain.
This book is a reproduction of an important historical work. Alpha Editions
uses the best technology to reproduce historical work in the same manner
it was first published to preserve its original nature. Any marks or number
seen are left intentionally to preserve its true form.

HAECKEL

HIS LIFE AND WORK

BY

WILHELM BÖLSCHE

WITH INTRODUCTION AND SUPPLEMENTARY CHAPTER BY THE
TRANSLATOR,

JOSEPH McCABE

WITH THIRTEEN ILLUSTRATIONS

PHILADELPHIA
GEORGE W. JACOBS & CO.
PUBLISHERS

Contents

	PAGE
INTRODUCTION	9

CHAPTER I
EARLY YOUTH 15

CHAPTER II
AT THE UNIVERSITY 51

CHAPTER III
THE RADIOLARIA 82

CHAPTER IV
DARWIN 102

CHAPTER V
THE SCIENTIFIC CONGRESS OF 1863 . . . 144

CONTENTS

CHAPTER VI
THE "GENERAL MORPHOLOGY" 172

CHAPTER VII
GROWTH OF IDEAS 252

CHAPTER VIII
THE CROWNING YEARS 294

BIBLIOGRAPHY 323

INDEX 329

List of Illustrations

HAECKEL . . . . . . *Frontispiece*
    From the painting by Franz von Lenbach.

JENA . . . . . . *Facing p.* 42

A FISHING PARTY IN HELIGOLAND IN 1865 . ,, 70
    Ernst Haeckel, Anton Dohrn, Richard Greef, Max Salverda, Pietro Marchi.

A RADIOLARIAN . . . . . ,, 94

HAECKEL . . . . . . ,, 128
    From the bust by G. Herold.

HAECKEL IN 1880. . . . . ,, 154

HAECKEL IN 1890 . . . . ,, 178
    From a relief by Kopf.

HAECKEL'S VILLA AT JENA . . . ,, 216

HAECKEL AND HIS ASSISTANT MIKLUCHO-MACLAY
    AT LANZAROTE, IN THE CANARIES, 1867 . ,, 244

LIST OF ILLUSTRATIONS

A Siphonophore. . . . . Facing p. 248

Haeckel in 1874 . . . . ,, 272

Haeckel in 1896 . . . . ,, 292
    From a photograph by Gabriel Max.

Haeckel and a Group of Italian Professors
    at Genoa, 1904 . . . . ,, 300

Introduction

ONE of the admirable maxims that crystallises the better sense or experience of men reminds us that we must "say nothing but good of the dead." Unhappily, we have taken the words of our sage fathers in too large a sense. A feeling has grown amongst us that we should "say nothing good except of the dead," at least as regards those who differ from us. So has many a man gone from the world with little suspicion of the appreciation that might have warmed him in the last chill years; many a man sunk into the grave with the harsh echo of dishonouring words still rumbling in his ears. It may be that our ideas, our truths, would not suffer greatly if we could patiently endeavour to trace the community of humane feeling that lies beneath the wide gulfs that often separate us intellectually from each other.

Professor Ernst Haeckel is one of those combative figures of all time who take misunderstanding as a part of their romantic career. If he had shut himself within the laboratory, as some of his gifted colleagues did, all the world would honour him to-day. His vast range of biological knowledge, almost without parallel in our specialist days, fitted him for great scientific achievements. His superb special contributions to biology—his studies of radiolaria, sponges, medusæ, &c.—give ample evidence of it. As things are, he has, Professor Hertwig says, "written his name in letters of light in the history of science." He holds four gold medals for scientific research (Cothenius, Swammerdam, Darwin, and Challenger), four doctorates (Berlin, Jena, Edinburgh, and Cambridge), and about eighty diplomas from so many universities and academic bodies. But he was one of those who cannot but look out of the windows of the laboratory. His intense idealism, his sense of what he felt to be wrong and untrue, inflamed by incessant travel and communion with men, drove him into the field of battle. In the din and roar of a great conflict his name has passed on to a million lips and become the varied war-cry of fiercely contending parties. A hundred Haeckels, grotesque in their unlikeness to each other, circulate in our midst to-day.

The present work is a plain study of the personality of Haeckel and the growth of his ideas. The character of Haeckel was forged amid circumstances that have largely passed away from the scientific world of our time. The features, even, of the world he has worked in of recent years in Germany are so different from our own that no

Englishman can understand him without sober study of his life. He has often been called "the Darwin of Germany." The phrase is most misleading. It suggests a comparison that is bound to end in untruth and injustice. In the same year that Haeckel opened his Darwinian campaign in Germany he won the prize for the long jump—a record jump. It is the note of much in his character. He was no quiet recluse, to shrink from opposition and hard names, but a lusty, healthy, impetuous, intrepid youth, even when his hair had worn to grey. A story is told of how, not many years ago, the Grand Duke of Weimar playfully rallied him, in the midst of a brilliant company, on his belief in evolution. To the horror of the guests, he slapped the powerful noble on the shoulder, and told him to come to Jena and see the proofs of it. In his seventy-first year we find him severely censuring his Emperor—the emperor of many fortresses—in a public lecture at Berlin.

How his vigour and his resentment arose as barrier after barrier was raised before him: how his scorn of compromise was engendered and fed: how he accumulated mountains of knowledge in obscure, technical works before he formulated his sharp didactic conclusions: all this is told in the following story. For good or ill he has won an influence in this country, and his story should be read. It is, in itself, one of rare and varied interest, and it is told by one of the most brilliant penmen of modern Germany, his former pupil, now a distinguished biologist, Professor Wilhelm Bölsche.

The time seems to have come in England for the publication of some authoritative picture of the great biologist and controversialist. One work of his circulates by the hundred thousand amongst us, and has had a deep and lasting influence on the thoughts of large classes of men. His influence is hardly less in France and Italy, as well as in Germany; his doctrines have, in fact, been translated into fifteen different tongues. The deep, sometimes bitter, controversy that they have engendered must have led to a desire to know more of the man and his making. The attempts that have been made here and there to "construct" him from his ideas and literary manner are, as the reader will see, very far removed from the reality. Behind all the strained inferences from doctrines, behind all the dishonouring epithets, there is a genial, warm, deeply artistic, intensely idealist nature, sung with enthusiasm by poets who have known him. Once, in playful scientific mood, Haeckel tried to explain his own character in his familiar terms of heredity and environment. He came of a line of lawyers, straight, orderly, inexorable men. He had lived and worked in quiet Jena, in the beautiful valley of the Saale. But he did not speak of that larger environment—the field of battle, stretching far away, beyond the calm Thuringian hills, to the ends of Europe. We must place Haeckel's ardent and high-minded nature in that field, face to face with his opponents, if we would understand him.

For the supplementary chapter I have drawn

freely on another biographical sketch by one of Haeckel's pupils, Dr. Breitenbach, and other sources. For the illustrations I am indebted chiefly to Professor Haeckel himself, and can only offer him in return this grateful effort to lift his inspiring and impressive personality above the dust and cloud of a great controversy.

JOSEPH McCABE.

CHAPTER I

EARLY YOUTH

"I AM wholly a child of the nineteenth century, and with its close I would draw the line under my life's work." Thus does Professor Haeckel speak of himself. There is a note of gentle resignation in the words, but the time is coming when men will give them a different meaning. Whatever greater achievements may be wrought by a future generation in the service of truth and human welfare, their work will be but a continuation of the truth of our time, as long as humanity breathes. On the intrepid, outstanding figures of the nineteenth century will shine a light that is peculiarly theirs, an illumination that men will dwell on for ever—as we look back, in personal life, on the young days of love. It was a strong love that brought our century to birth.

The soul of humanity has for four centuries been passing through a grim crisis.

Let us imagine ourselves for a moment before the noble painting by Michael Angelo in the Sixtine

Chapel at Rome. What art! What utter revelation of the power of man's mind! But, we ask, what material did the genius of humanity choose in those days for the manifestation of its giant power? The last judgment: the Christ descending at the blare of the last trumpet, to reward the faithful and banish the sinner into everlasting pain: the Almighty, breathing His spirit into Adam, or mystically upbuilding Eve from the rib of the man. There was no "symbolic" intention in the picture; the deepest feeling of hundreds —nay, thousands—of years was embodied in it. The artist merely gave an imperishable external form to the most treasured truth of his time.

Yet, slowly and gradually, what a mighty change has come about!

Columbus has sailed over the blue seas, and a new side of the earth lies in the violet haze of the dawn. Copernicus sees the ball of the earth roll round the sun through space, by force of some mysterious law. Kepler dreams of the world-harmony that will replace the ever-acting Deity, and discovers at length an unsuspected regularity in the framework of the heavens. Galileo turns his new optic tube to the stars, and at once the heavens are changed, not only for the calculating, mathematical mind, but even for the eye of sense: there are jagged peaks on the moon, satellites circling about Jupiter, a wilderness of stars lying across the Milky Way, spots on the sun, rings round Saturn. Giordano Bruno shatters the ancient crystalline vault of the firmament; every "fixed star" in the Milky Way is to him a flaming sun, the pulsing heart of a whole world, in which, perchance, human hearts like ours throb and leap on a hundred planets. The red, murderous flames of hate close over Bruno, but they cannot dim the light of the new stars. It is in the eye and the brain of the new men that arise, and will nevermore fade from them.

The seventeenth century, opening amid the last glare of the martyr-fires, quickens with a vague yearning and expectation.

In the eighteenth century the old world breaks up. From the new stars, from the new world, new ideas come. On all sides is the crash and roar of conflict. Dread flames break out in the social, moral, and æsthetic life of men. But the century ends in the birth of a greater artist than Michael Angelo.

Goethe, on the morn of the nineteenth century, paints a new Sixtine Chapel in his poetry. But he no longer depicts the old ideas. He speaks of God-Nature. To him God is the eternal force of the All. His thoughts turn no longer on Creation and the Last Judgment. An eternal evolution is the source of his inspiration. He regards the whole universe as a single, immeasurable revelation of spirit. But this spirit is the rhythmic outflow of infinite developments. It becomes Milky Way and sun and planet, blue lotus-flowers and gay butterfly. At last it takes the form of man, and reads the stars as an open book. In Homer and Goethe it directs the style and the pen; in Michael Angelo and Raphael it guides the pencil and the brush.

All this unfolds in Goethe, as in a vision with yet half-opened eyes.

Then the nineteenth century begins. Nature is its salvation, the salvation of its most practical, most real need. It must struggle for its existence, like any other century, but it has new and improved weapons for the struggle. All the earlier ages were but poor blunderers. The lightning flashed on the naked savage, and he fell on his knees and prayed, powerless as he was. In the eighteenth century it dawned on men's minds that this might be some force of nature. The nineteenth century sets its foot on the neck of the demon of this force, presses him into its service, plays with him. Its thoughts and words flash along the lightning current, as if along new nerve-tracks, that begin to circle the globe. Man becomes lord of the earth, from the uppermost azure down into the dark, cold abysses of the ocean, from the icy pole to the burning tropical desert. And at length man turns his thoughts upon himself.

Man, his arm resting on the splendid instruments of modern research, raises his hand to his brow, and turns philosopher. He becomes at once more bold and more modest than ever.

What Goethe had seen in vision rises before him now in sharp, almost hard outline from his own real life-work. He has succeeded in bringing nature and its forces to his feet, because it was flesh of his flesh and blood of his blood. He is its child. A thousand tongues proclaim the truth to him, a naïve, almost simple, revelation of reality. He digs in the earth, and ancient bones and skulls tell him vaguely of the past. Such once was he, devoid of civilisation, at the verge of the animal world. He searches his frame through and through for further light. There is the brain, where the thoughts crowd together. There is the cell, that builds up the whole body, the cell that so closely resembles the lowest of all living things, not yet distinct enough to be either animal or plant. Here are the forms that he successively assumes in his mother's body, before he is born—forms that can hardly be distinguished from those of the animal at the same stage of development. From almost divine heights he has sunk down to the beast, to the primitive cell—nay, deeper still, to the elementary, force-impelled matter of the universe.

But this early picture dissolves at once in an ennobling and inspiring truth. Nature becomes man. In this he presses once more to the heart of the most-high. Nature is God. Goethe sang of God-Nature. The new God pulses in every wave of man's blood. In Michael Angelo's picture God breathes his spirit into Adam. The new Adam of the nineteenth century is God's spirit, in body and soul, from the very first, for he is Nature. He needs no more. When he looks up to the shining stars, he looks into the eyes of God and his own. He has come down from those stars like the bright dew in which they are now mirrored. He belongs to them, but they also are in him. All-Nature: and he is a part of Nature. All-development: and he is a phase of the development.

That is the great philosophical dream of the nineteenth-century worker. His hand is black with labour, but his spirit is full of light, the light of the stars and of the world.

No one can understand the greatness of a man like Ernst Haeckel who has not learned this melody. Nature is not a flat surface: it is an ocean. When Columbus crossed the seas in his three frail barques long ago to seek a new world in the distant haze, he little dreamed that the gray waters buried other new worlds a thousand yards beneath his keel—worlds of the deep-sea, into which our age has slowly dipped with its dredges. So we in turn may run our eye over the blue surface of nature, and think of its mysterious gold-lands and spice-islands, without suspicion of all that outspreads beneath our keel. Yet that glorious day on which Columbus found "his land" is an inspiration to us, his remote grandchildren. The life we are going to examine will bring before us such a morning of discovery. Columbus went in quest of Zipangu (as he called Japan), and he found America. Not one of us, however gifted he be, can be quite sure that, in leading humanity, he is not sailing into another such heroic error. Let us say that at once to all, friends and opponents. America or Zipangu—let it be so. Perhaps any man might have found Zipangu, while only the genius could reach America.

. . . . .

When Gustav Freytag, who had a most happy quality for writing memoirs, was composing his admirable *Pictures from the Past of Germany*, he sought in each period some prominent man of plain and downright character, yet who had something typical of his age in his sentiments, as if the time-spirit spoke through him. In this quest he twice (in the fourth volume, for the period from the close of the eighteenth century to the Wars of Freedom) lit upon earlier members of Haeckel's family. The first was Haeckel's grandfather on the mother's side, Christoph Sethe; the second was his father, Councillor Haeckel.

This simple fact shows the stuff of Haeckel's race. The older Sethe was an important man in his time. He left to his children manuscript memoirs of his eventful life, which have, unfortunately, been only sparsely used by Freytag, though the whole deserved to be regarded as a source of history. The general facts in relation to him were collected by Hermann Hüffer, who was not merely interested in the jurist because he was one himself, but was brought into touch with him as a result of his brilliant study of Heine. Sethe's eldest son, Christian, the uncle of Ernst Haeckel, is the well-known friend of Heine's youth to whom the poet dedicated the "Fresco-sonnets" in his *Book of Songs* and wrote the finest of his early letters. This Christian Sethe (he died on May 31, 1857, being then Provincial Director of Revenue at Stettin), was a lawyer, like his father, and the father himself came of a legal family. Haeckel's own father, moreover, the husband of one of Christian's sisters, was a State Councillor at the time of his death, and his elder brother was a Provincial Councillor. Thus Haeckel's genealogical tree spreads into the legal profession in a curiously complex way.

We naturally reflect for a moment if we could fancy Haeckel himself as a lawyer. It is hardly possible. He would at least have been a very rebellious member of the profession, and have been sadly lacking in respect for the venerable traditions and powdered wigs of the court—assuming, of course (which a mere layman has no right to question), that there ought still to be such traditions and costumes in the profession. In his vigorous *Riddle of the Universe* he has, from his scientific point of view, brought strictures against the legal profession that leave nothing to be desired in the way of candour, when we recollect the long tradition of his family. In its lingering in the rear of the progress of the times the whole science of law seemed to him to be a "riddle of the universe." The jurist is apt to be respected as an embodiment of our highest culture. In reality that is not the case. The distinctive object of his concern, man and his soul, is only superficially studied in the preparation for the law, and so we still find amongst jurists the most extraordinary views as to the freedom of the will, responsibility, and so on. "Most of our legal students pay no attention to anthropology, psychology, and evolution, the first requisites for a correct appreciation of human nature. They 'have no time' for it. It is unfortunately all absorbed in a profound study of beer and wine and the 'noble art' of fencing; and the rest of their valuable time is taken up in learning some hundreds of paragraphs from the books of law, the knowledge of which is supposed to qualify the jurist to fill any position whatever in the State."

The student of psychology, however, cannot fail to see that the disposition that led so many members of Haeckel's family into the legal profession was also developed in himself to some extent. There is perhaps no other scientist of his time with such an imperious craving for clearness, for clean lines and systematic arrangement. At least in the whole of the Darwinian period no other has made so great an effort to convert the scattered flight of phenomena in the realm of life into the even course of so many fixed "laws." In many of his writings this tendency to formulate laws is so pronounced that the layman instinctively has an impression of dogmatism on the part of the author. This has been grossly misunderstood, and made to play an important part in the controversial work of his opponents. The truth is that this sharp outlook and pronounced tendency to formulate clear and unambiguous "laws" in the animal and plant worlds is a matter of temperament as much as of judgment. It is very possible that we have here an hereditary trait, an innate aversion for disorder and confusion—for a thoughtless rushing ahead without clear ideas and plan. The trait was the more important and helpful as a man of Haeckel's type was sure to be one of the most active revolutionaries in his science, even apart from Darwinian ideas. It would be difficult to find another reformer in any great province of thought who, immediately after effecting a complete overthrow of the older ideas, has hastened so quickly to build up the new, to devise a nomenclature and a classification down to the smallest details, and hand on at once to his successors a splendid order once more. Zoology, which seemed to crumble into chaos after Darwin's victory and the collapse of the old framework, came out of Haeckel's hands, after barely two years' work, in the shape of a new and graceful Darwinistic structure—not, indeed, perfect and finally completed, but entirely habitable for the young generation. They could add new stones as they thought fit, or pierce new windows, and so on; but at all events the chaos was terminated at a critical moment by this iron man of order. I will only add, to complete the picture, that one of the three doctorates that Haeckel holds to-day is that of law (an honorary degree), in addition to his qualifications in philosophy and medicine. He now only lacks the theological degree, but I fear that he will neither take the trouble to secure it nor have it conferred on him as an honorary distinction for his merit in that department.

The Sethes and Haeckels of the earlier generation were not merely zealous jurists, but also characteristic figures of Napoleonic and post-Napoleonic Prussia. Christoph Sethe, the patriarch of the maternal line, was Privy Councillor of the Prussian Government at Cleve at the beginning of the last decade of the eighteenth century, though he was then young. When the French occupied the country he accompanied the Government to Münster, in 1802, which had become a Prussian town. But the stalwart German was pursued even there by the detested Napoleonists. He was sent to Düsseldorf as General Procurator in 1808, and came into dangerous conflict with the French authorities shortly before the Emperor's fall. The mobilisation of the troops for the campaign of 1812 had led to a disturbance amongst the workers. Sethe's sense of patriotism and justice was affronted by the arbitrary proceedings of the French. He was summoned to give an account at Paris, the chief object being to retain him—the most powerful official in the Rhine district and not a very safe man—as a hostage during the crisis. It was at Paris that he made the finest phrase of his life. Roederer, the minister, tried to intimidate him with the threat that the Emperor might have a dangerous man like him shot at any moment. "You will have to shoot the law first," replied Sethe. We are often reminded of this saying in the biography of Sethe's grandson. If Haeckel had been burned at the stake like Giordano Bruno, he would have thought of nothing but the "law"—the law of truth and freedom that they would burn with him.

Christoph Sethe continued to play an important part in the service of Prussia, to which, of course, he returned, together with the Rhinelands, after Napoleon's fall. He was destined to live through the terrible reaction under Frederic William the Third, and the fiery outburst under his successor. After the early death of his wife their youngest daughter, Bertha, managed his house and large family.

She lived until her death (April 1, 1904) in her quiet, unpretentious home in one of the large empty streets behind the Tiergarten at Berlin, reaching the age of ninety-two, but never losing her freshness of mind and memory. In my many happy talks with the aged lady the succeeding periods seemed to melt together. The small, old furniture and the ancient, ever-ticking clock made me forget, in dreamy twilight hours, that the red glare in the sky above the houses beyond, that faintly lit up the old-time room, was the reflection from the twentieth century of the electric flames that flashed on the great modern city. On the table lay the latest part of Haeckel's (her nephew) fine illustrated work for artistically minded scientists and scientifically minded artists —the *Art-forms in Nature*. The dear old lady spoke with pride of her knowledge of the "radiolaria," the mysterious unicellular ocean-dwellers, described in Haeckel's splendid monograph, the flinty shells of which are amongst the finest artistic treasures of nature. She called them the "dear radiolaria" with all the tenderness of the emotional man of science who had felt a sort of psychic relation, a living affinity, to the tiny microscopic strangers he had been the first to arrange and describe in their thousands. Smiling, with quiet pride, she told me how her nephew visited her, when he came to Berlin; how, with the unassuming ways of this sound stock, he chose to sleep in the clothes-drying loft; how he invited his friends to come and hear of his voyages and work, bringing thirty of them to share a single dish of herring-salad in his naïve way, and how, as they continued to pour in, he made seats for them of boards and tubs, and fed them with his wonderful genius for anecdote so that none went away fasting. She dwelt with entire satisfaction on the last, the "zoological" phase, of the Haeckel-Sethe house. Yet it all blended softly with the old and the past of nearly a century ago. Over the patriarchal furniture hung the oil painting of Christoph Sethe, with the large Roman nose that runs through the family down to Ernst Haeckel himself, and gives the chief feature to his otherwise soft profile. Under a glass shade, in the old fashion of our grandfathers that we perhaps do not sufficiently appreciate, was a fine bust of Schleiermacher. He was a friend of the Sethes. Bertha Sethe was confirmed by him. He died four days before Ernst Haeckel was born, on February 12, 1834. The sister came from the grave to attend the mother of the new-born child. A little fact of that character seems to pour out a broad stream of light. The religious sense was strong in the Sethes, but it was not of the rigid conventional character. It came from the depths of human destinies, of individual experience. In those depths it is always found associated with that other fundamental quality of human experience and inner life—a zeal for the truth. Schleiermacher, the Good, had endeavoured within the limits of his time (if not of our time) to erect a new and firmer Christendom. Darwinism might very well have adjusted itself to this new Christendom, that needed no record of miracles from disputed historical works to support it, but sought the holiest ideal prophetically in the symbolic conception and the development of the true, the good, and the beautiful. Had Schleiermacher read the *Natural History of Creation*, or later theologians shared his temper, one wonders how much exaggeration and bitterness might have been spared on either side. But religion was not prepared to dissociate itself from "the Church," and with the Church there could be no compromise. Thus one's thoughts travelled from the radiolaria in Haeckel's latest publication and the old bust of Schleiermacher, which was protected by its glass shade, in this home of old-world piety, from the wicked flies of the twentieth century.

An elder sister of Bertha Sethe and daughter of the old Christoph Sethe had married the much older lawyer, Karl Haeckel, in the twenties. The first-fruit of this marriage was Ernst Haeckel's elder brother, the Provincial Councillor Haeckel who died a few years ago, a high-minded and sensitive man. He remained throughout life faithful to the strict traditional forms of religious experience, in spite of all his admiration for his gifted zoological brother.

The second and last child did not appear until ten years later. Ernst Haeckel was born on the 16th of February, 1834, shortly after the death of Schleiermacher, as I have explained. Most of what I know of his earliest years was told me by his venerable aunt Bertha.

His father died long ago, in 1871. Gustav Freytag has pointed out how eagerly he drank in the morning air of the dawning freedom before 1813. For many years he was at a later date a very close friend of Gneisenau. He was an earnest, conscientious, upright man, with no particular artistic arabesques to his life, and at the same time no errors. The victories of 1870 lit up the red sunset of his days. He was one of those happy folk who thought that *all* was accomplished in the great achievements of those days, and had little suspicion of what was still to come. The mother survived him for many years. Her son's *Indian Travels* was dedicated to her on her eighty-fourth birthday, November 22, 1882. The dedication ran: "Thou it was who from early childhood fostered in me a sense for the infinite beauties of nature: thou hast ever watched my changeful career with all the ceaseless care and thought that we compress in the one phrase—a mother's love."

Ernst Haeckel was born at Potsdam, but in the same year the father was transferred to Merseburg, where the child was brought up. It was not his destiny to be a child of Berlin. Saxony remained essentially his home in many respects. We can always see in him something of this home that looks down on its children from its great green hills. The cold lines of the streets of the metropolis and the melancholy of the Brandenburg pine-forests cannot be traced in him. In later years Berlin assumed more and more in his thoughts the shape of an antipodal city. His works are full of the sharpest strictures on Berlin science. It was at an earlier date the city of Ehrenberg and Reichert, whom he did not love; later it was associated with Du Bois-Reymond and Virchow, who gradually became his bitterest opponents. But he detested it generally as the home of Privy Councillors, of science in the Procrustean bed of official supervision. When he compared what he himself had done at Jena with the slenderest possible appliances, and what, in his judgment, had been done by the heads of the Berlin schools in their princely institutes, he would humorously—though it has been taken very seriously—lay down the "natural law" that the magnitude of the scientific achievement is in inverse proportion to the size of the scientific institute. The official people at Berlin did not fail to make a biting retort to these Radical strictures—that in 1881, when he wanted to go to Ceylon, he was formally refused assistance by the Berlin Academy from the travelling-fee (then at liberty) attached to the Humboldt foundation. He made the journey without their assistance, and had the splendid revenge of giving us, in the description of this very voyage, the most brilliant account of the tropics that has appeared in Germany since the time of Humboldt. It was a finer contribution to the general ideal of the Humboldt foundation than the timid payment of a hundred pounds could have secured. However, we are anticipating. Before that time he was to spend a short but happy period at Berlin in the fifties, in the best days of his youth—a Berlin of a different scientific character from the present city, being at once less pretentious and more profound, whichever the reader chooses to dwell on.

Certain traits could be recognised unmistakably in the boy. He had a great love of nature, of light, colour, and beauty, of flowers and trees and butterflies, of the sun and the blue heavens. There was also a strong sense of independence and individuality. This did not imply that he was lacking in gentler feeling. It is said that he would do anything that he was asked but nothing that it was sought to compel him to do. The little fair, blue-eyed lad would sit quietly if they gave him a daisy to pull to pieces. First he would, as if he were a student analysing it, detach the white leaves from the central yellow ground. Then he would carefully replace them, piece by piece, round the yellow centre, clap his little hands and cry out, "Now it's all right again." It is a very pretty trait that tradition has preserved. In the play of the child we seem to see the chief lines of the man's character like two branches of a tree; the analytic work of the scientist and the reconstructive tendency of the artist who restores the dissected world to harmony.

His excellent training in those early years fostered his feeling for nature and his sense of independence with wise adaptation to the personal character of the boy. The mother gladly cultivated his love of nature. On the deeper development of his character a decisive influence was exercised, with every regard for freedom, by a friend of the family, the physician Basedow. His ideal was education without compulsion, by means of a sort of constant artificial selection and cultivation of the good that grew up spontaneously in the soul of the child. The father, a great worker, was content to give a word of praise occasionally; to urge him to go to the root of things always, and never to coquet idly with his own soul. If the young dreamer stood at the window and looked up at the clouds, his father would pat him on the shoulder and say, "Every minute has its value in this world. Play or work—but do something." It was, in a sense, the voice of the restless nineteenth century itself that spoke. The whole life of the youth and the man was to be an eternal proof that he had heard the message. He has pressed unwearyingly forward, as few other men have done. There was ever something in him of the mountaineer, hurrying on and watching every hour that he may reach the summit. The day of rest may come afterwards, down below in the valley. In truth, it never came. It is well known that the man wrote some of his most difficult, most widely read, and most controverted works subsequently in a few months, encroaching upon his night's rest until his health was endangered. In a remote Cingalese village in Ceylon, where the enervating tropical climate forces even the strongest to indulge in the afternoon siesta, he tells himself that, in view of the great expense of the journey, each day is worth a five-pound note. He refuses to sleep long hours or take the siesta, rises at five in the morning, and uses the hottest hours of the day, from twelve to four, for "anatomical and microscopic work, observing and drawing, and for packing up the material collected." He met to the full the claim of the nineteenth century, for all the inner poetic tendency of his character. Such a character he must have had to become a philosopher, as he has done; but it lay, as it were, in deeper recesses of his being. To the eye of the observer he seemed to be ever rushing on with a watch in his hand until old age. When we think of the enormous number of problems and the vast range of interests that brought him into the front rank in the nineteenth century, we may say that he advanced at a pace that would have given concern to the aged adviser of his youth in his small world.

In the long run we may say of all education as of the physician in the old saying, "The best doctor is the one we don't need, because we are not ill." Haeckel was sent to the school at Merseburg. This instruction came to a close in his eighteenth year. He thought of some of his old teachers with affection forty years afterwards. On the whole his later opinion of the usual schooling was as severe as that of many of his contemporaries. In his *General Morphology* (1866), his most profound work, he speaks of the "very defective, perverse, and often really mischievous instruction, by which we are filled with absurd errors, instead of natural truths, in our most impressionable years." Sixteen years afterwards (in a speech delivered at Eisenach) he hopes that the triumphant science of evolution "will put an end to one of the greatest evils in our present system of education—that overloading of the memory with dead material that destroys the finest powers, and prevents the normal development of either mind or body." "This overloading," he says, "is due to the old and ineradicable error that the excellence of education is to be judged by the quantity of positive facts committed to memory, instead of by the quality of the real knowledge imparted. Hence it is especially advisable to make a more careful selection of the matter of instruction both in the higher and the elementary schools, and not to give precedence to the faculties that burden the memory with masses of dead facts, but to those that build up the judgment with the living play of the idea of evolution. Let our tortured children learn only half what they do, but learn it better, and the next generation will be twice as sound as the present one in body and soul. The reform of education, which, we trust, will be brought about by introducing the idea of evolution, must apply to the mathematical and scientific, as well as the philological and historical sections, because there is the same fault in them all, that far too much material is injected, and far too little attention is paid to its digestion." Seventeen years later again, in the *Riddle of the Universe*, the elementary schools are severely handled. Science is still the Cinderella of the code. Our teachers regard it as their chief duty to impart " the dead knowledge that has come down from the schools of the Middle Ages. They give the first place to their grammatical gymnastics, and waste time in imparting a 'thorough knowledge' of the classical tongues and foreign history." There is no question of cosmology, anthropology, or biology; instead of these " the memory is loaded with a mass of philological and historical facts that are quite useless either from the theoretical or the practical point of view." In these expressions, which recur constantly throughout the whole of a thoughtful life, we can clearly see a very intense general experience of youth, and this is a more valuable document than any individualised complaint against this or that bad teacher in particular.

However, Haeckel (who, in point of fact, took everything seriously and would have all in the clearest order) made a very thorough appropriation of his Latin and Greek. When the new Darwinian zoology and botany needed several hundred new Latin-Greek technical terms in after-years, he showed himself to be an inventor of the first rank in this department. No other scientist has made anything like the same adroit use of the classic vocabulary for the purposes of the new system and created a new terminology for the entirely new science. His creations were certainly ingenious, and not without grace at times; in other cases, as was almost inevitable, they were less pleasing. And to this we must add thousands of names of new species which he had to coin, as the discoverer of radiolaria, medusæ, sponges, &c. In the radiolaria alone he has formed and published the names of more than 3,500 new species. I fancy that even the oldest pastor of the most fertile congregation has never conducted so many christenings. In each case it was necessary to impose two names, the generic and specific. We may well expect to find a few that will not last, but the reader is amazed at the philological creative power of this busy godfather and the inexhaustibility of his vocabulary; they show far more than the usual training in humanities.

His real predilection was pronounced enough in those early years. It was what the classical pedagogue would regard as child's play and waste of time —zoology and botany. A large double window in his parents' house was fitted up as a conservatory, and plants were gathered very zealously. His love of botany was so great that any one would have

EARLY YOUTH

pronounced him a botanist in the making. But fate determined that he was to be a zoologist. In his eleventh year the boy, while paying a visit to his uncle Bleek (a professor of theology!) at Bonn, spent a whole day searching the remotest corners of the Siebengebirg for the *Erica cinerea*, which he had heard could not be found in any other part of Germany. At the Merseburg school he had two excellent teachers, Gandtner and Karl Gude, who fostered his inclination, and changed it from a mere collector's eagerness into the finer enjoyment of the scientific mind. The young student wrote a contribution to Garcke's *Flora Hallensis*. The professional decision gives many a troubled hour.

It is significant to find that as the novice tended his herbarium it dawned on him that there was a weak point somewhere in the rigid classification given in the manuals of botany. The books said that there were so many fixed species, each invariably recognisable by certain characters. But when the youth tried to diagnose his plant-treasures in practice by these rules, there seemed to be always a few contraband species smuggled in, like the spectres in the Wahlpurgis night to which the sage vainly expostulates, "Begone: we have explained you away." Often the individual specimens would not agree with the lore of the books. There were discrepancies; sometimes they cut across one type, sometimes another, and at times they shamelessly stretched across the gap between one rubric and another. What did it mean? Were there really *no* fixed species? Was "species" only an idea, and was the reality of the plant-world in a state of flux like the sea? Teachers and books insisted that the "species" is, in its absolute nature, the basis of all botanical science, the great and sacred foundation that the Moses of botany and zoology, Linné, had laid down for ever. How could it be so?

The mature worker would look back on this dilemma of his youth with a smile of satisfaction thirty years afterwards. He would know then what sort of a nut it was that he was trying to crack in his early speculations. It was nothing less than the magnificent problem that presented itself to Darwin, the crucial question of the fixity or variability of species. "The problem of the constancy or transmutation of species," he wrote, "arrested me with a lively interest when, twenty years ago, as a boy of twelve years, I made a resolute but fruitless effort to determine and distinguish the 'good and bad species' of blackberries, willows, roses, and thistles. I look back now with fond satisfaction on the concern and painful scepticism that stirred my youthful spirits as I wavered and hesitated (in the manner of most 'good classifiers,' as we called them) whether to admit only 'good' specimens into my herbarium and reject the 'bad,' or to embrace the latter and form a complete chain of transitional forms between the 'good species' that would make an end of all their 'goodness.' I got out of the difficulty at the time by a compromise that I can recommend to all classifiers. I made two collections. One, arranged on official lines, offered to the sympathetic observer all the species, in 'typical' specimens, as radically distinct forms, each decked with its pretty label; the other was a private collection, only shown to one trusted friend, and contained only the rejected kinds that Goethe so happily called 'the characterless or disorderly races, which we hardly dare ascribe to a species, as they lose themselves in infinite varieties,' such as rubus, salix, verbascum, hieracium, rosa, cirsium, &c. In this a large number of specimens, arranged in a long series, illustrated the direct transition from one good species to another. They were the officially forbidden fruit of knowledge in which I took a secret boyish delight in my leisure hours."

These little scruples, however, did not interfere with what he felt to be the chief interest of botany. The collecting of plants harmonises well with a general love of nature and a passion for wandering over hill and valley. Long walks had already become a feature of his life. The scientific interest made it superfluous to have a companion. Botany went with him everywhere as his lady-love, and remained ever faithful to him. "I have preferred to travel alone most of my life," he used to say to me; "I never feel *ennui* when I am alone. My love of and interest in nature are much better entertainment than conversation." One of the features in this interest at all times, even in later years, was botanical research. The material for it is found everywhere. Darwin, a great traveller with an unusually strong appreciation of good scenery, has said that the traveller who would combine the pursuit of knowledge with æsthetic satisfaction must be above all a botanist (in the closing retrospect of his *Naturalist's Voyage Round the World*, one of the finest passages in the work). Whenever Haeckel spoke in later years of his adopted Jena, he never failed to explain, amongst the other excellent qualities of the little university town, that so many fine orchids grew in its woods. When he left Jena to make the long voyage to Ceylon, his last look was at the drops of dew that sparkled like pearls " in the dark blue calices of the gentians, with their tender lashes, that so richly decked the grass-covered sides of the railway cutting." The *Letters from India*, that described his voyage, owes a good deal of its peculiar charm to his skill in botanical description. I know no other work that approaches it in conveying so effective an idea of the luxuriant vegetation of the tropics.

In those early years there was one particular point of close union between botany and the sense of beauty. It was only two years before Haeckel's birth that Goethe, the man who had put into inimitable verse new and pregnant truths of botany, passed to his rest at Weimar.

It is no longer a special distinction of any prominent personality of the nineteenth century to have been influenced by Goethe. It is a kind of natural necessity from which one cannot escape. All that is great in the century can be traced back to Goethe. He flows beneath it, like a dark stream through the bowels of a mountain. Here and there the flanks open and the stream becomes visible; not a restless bubbling spring, but a broad mirror. There is, however, a closer following of Goethe. There are a few strong spirits that have been consciously inspired by him from the first in all their thoughts; have throughout life felt themselves to be the apostles of the "gospel of Goethe"; and in every new creation of their own have held that they did but reflect or expand his ideas, did but carry on his principles to these further conclusions. Haeckel is, in his whole work, one of this smaller band; his whole personality is, in fact, one of its most conspicuous manifestations in the second half of the century.

In Goethe we find the basic ideas of his philosophy. Goethe took from him his God, and gave him a new one: took from him the external, transcendental God of the Churches, and gave him the God that is in all things, in the eternal development of the world, in body and soul alike, the God that embraces all reality and being, beside whom there is no distinct "world," no distinct "sinful man," no special beginning or end of things. When Haeckel found himself, at the highest point of his own path, by the side of Darwin, he was the first to see and to insist that Darwin was but a stage in the logical development of Goethe's ideas.

Fate decided that Haeckel should be even externally in some sense an heir of the Goethe epoch. Jena, the university that Goethe had regarded with such affection, and at which Schiller had toiled with his heart's blood in "sad, splendid years," owes its fame in the last third of the century to Haeckel. It is not an excess of adulation, but a simple truth, to say that among the general public and abroad the reputation of Jena passes directly from Goethe, Schiller, and Fichte to Haeckel. His name stands for an epoch in the life of Jena, like theirs; all that lies between is forgotten and unknown. In the district itself it is as if the old epochs and the new came into direct touch.

I shall never forget the hour when this thought came upon me in all its force. It was on a snowless December day, when the dying fire of autumn still lingered on the trees and bushes where the blackbirds sang in front of the observatory. The table and seat of sandstone stood out bleakly. A tablet indicated, in phrases of Goethe's, that Schiller had dwelt there. It was there that the Wallenstein was born. There the two often sat in conversation—the conversation of two of the greatest minds of the time, each in his way a master spirit. To-day the little dome of the observatory looks down on the spot; it is not a luxurious building, but it is a stage in the onward journey, a symbol of the nineteenth century as it leaps into the twentieth. A little farther off rises the modern structure of the Zoological Institute. In Goethe's day no one dreamed that such a building would ever be seen. It was opened by Haeckel in 1884. The zoological collection it houses was chiefly brought

JENA.

From "Jena in Wort und Bild". (Frommann'sche Hofbuchhandlung, Jena).

To face p. 42.

together under his direction. Amongst its treasures are, besides Haeckel's corals and the like, the outcome of the travels of Semon and Kükenthal in Australia and New Guinea—lands whose very outline could barely be traced in the mist when Schiller was a professor at Jena. At the entrance there are two stuffed orangs, our distant cousins. One wall of the lecture-hall is covered with huge charts depicting the genealogical tree of life, as it is drawn up by Haeckel. With what eyes Schiller would have devoured them! Yet classic traits are not wanting. From Haeckel's fine study in the Institute the eye falls on the Hausberg, " the mountain-top from which the red rays stream." It is the room in which the deep-sea radiolaria of the *Challenger* Expedition were studied, a zoological campaign in depths of the ocean that were stranger to Schiller's days than the surface of the moon is to us. Behind this Goethe-Schiller seat at the observatory there is a natural depression full of willows that reminds us of the time when all was country here. But just beyond it is a modern street—" Ernst Haeckel Street," as it was named, in honour of him, on the occasion of his sixtieth birthday. Close to it is the villa where he has lived for many years with his devoted family, full of wonderful reminiscences (oil-paintings and water-colours from his own hand) of his many travels. In Schiller's day a voyage to Ceylon would have been a life's work. To-day it is an episode in an infinitely richer and broader life. On the stone seat now we see the proud and handsome figure of the man himself, recalling pleasantly the masters who have stood here before him, the wide hat covering the white hair that is belied by the rosy cheeks; a straight and strong figure, yet revealing in the finer lines of the face the sensitive, æsthetic temper that does not look on scientific investigation as a brutal power of the dissecting knife, but remembers he is the heir of Goethe, even in the Zoological Institute yonder. Over my mind came the feeling of a strange rebirth of things. I felt that life is an eternally new and mystic resurrection, immeasurably more wonderful and profound than all the crude ideas of resurrection that have yet prevailed. A mind such as we love to picture to ourselves in our ideal of the future historian must seek the eternal and constant features in all change, even in two epochs that are so distinct and in the men who have lived in them. It is our incorrigible schoolmaster disposition that divides things. In the real world there must be one straight line of development. To-day the highest is sought in the melody of immortal verse : to-morrow a Zoological Institute rises on the spot where the poet had stood.

It is said that the boy did not come under the influence of Goethe without some difficulty. His mother did not like Goethe; she preferred Schiller. Goethe was too great for every true soul to follow him in his arduous path. Weimar itself had more than once been disposed to desert him. How much more the general public in its conventional fetters! How many fell away from him when he published the *Roman Elegies*, and again when he brought out the *Elective Affinities*. In Haeckel's youth people remembered Börne's narrow and hostile strictures. Goethe began to penetrate into the German family as a classic in spite of the general feeling. But the German family was still far below him. He had gradually to lift it up from its Philistine level. At times it rebelled against him, as every stubborn level does against a peak. It was his aunt Bertha that first put Goethe's works into the boy's hands. He received them as a delightful piece of moral contraband.

Gottfried Keller has finely described, about the same period, in his *Green Henry*, the effect of such a revelation on a sensitive young man. A bookseller brings to the house the whole of Goethe's works, fifty small volumes with red covers and gilded titles. The young Swiss Heinrich, Keller's picture of himself, reads the volumes unceasingly for thirty days, when they are taken away because his mother cannot pay for them. But the thirty days have been a dream to the boy. He seems to see new and more brilliant stars in the heavens as he looks up. When the books are removed, it is as if a choir of bright angels have left the room. "I went out into the open air. The old town on the hill, the rocks and woods and river and sea and the lines of the mountains lay in the gentle light of the March sun, and as my eye fell on them I felt a pure and lasting joy that I had never known before. It was a generous love of all that lives, a love that respects the right and realises the import of each thing, and feels the connectedness and depth of the world. This love is higher than the artificial affection of the individual with selfish aim that ever leads to pettiness and caprice; it is higher even than the enjoyment and detachment that come of special and romantic affections; it alone can give us an unchanging and lasting glow. Everything now came before me in new and beautiful and remarkable forms I began to see and to love, not only the outer form, but the inner content, the nature, and the history of things." The poet compresses his experience into one episode. In real life it comes slowly, step by step. In fine, a third element was born in the young botanist and lover of beauty—Goethe's view of life behind all else: that which Goethe himself called "objective." The mystic might call it a return to God: but it was Goethe's God.

Three other books influenced Haeckel in his school-days, besides the works of Goethe. The first was Humboldt's *Aspects of Nature*. This is another work that has had an effect on all the sensitive spirits of the nineteenth century. It is most unjustly depreciated by the young, *blasé* generation of our time, which dislikes the older style. In the first two volumes of the *Cosmos* we see the play of a great mind wherever we look for it.

Then came Darwin's *Naturalist's Voyage round the World*. The ardent youth had as yet on suspicion what the name would one day mean to him. Darwin was then regarded as a completed work on which final judgment had been rendered. He was appreciated as a traveller, a student of the geology of South America, and especially as the gifted investigator of the wonderful coral reefs of the Indian Ocean. His name stood thus in all the manuals, close even to that of Humboldt. Probably the young reader thought he had died long before. At all events, no one had a presentiment that this quiet naturalist and student of corals was about to light a torch that would flame over the world. The chief advantage that Haeckel drew from the two works was an ardent desire to see the tropics, with their virgin forests and blue coral seas. It has come to so many after reading these works, and persisted in their lives as the vivid image of a dream, like that which drove Goethe to Italy—the dream of a home of the soul that must one day be sought.

The third book was Schleiden's *The Plant and its Life*. Matthias Jacob Schleiden was then in the best of his power, and had an influence that amounted to fascination on many of the younger men. Behind him lay a terrible struggle. He had begun his career as a lawyer, and had been so unfortunate that he even attempted his life. With his interest in botany a new life began, and he worked with the energy of one raised from the dead. He was certainly an original thinker. His name is known to us to-day especially as the founder of the cell-theory. This is the greatest distinction that he has earned. But at that time he had a much more general importance as a leader in the struggle to introduce a certain method of scientific research. A somewhat obscure epoch was coming to a close, a more or less superficial natural philosophy having sought to replace sound investigation. The struggle had ended with the decisive victory of the simple discovery of facts. There was everywhere a vague feeling that the progress of science was best secured by a bald enumeration and registration of bones, of the joints in the limbs of insects, or of pollen-filaments, rather than by the romantic and spirited leaps of natural philosophy over all the real problems into the heavens above. The question now arose whether this narrow method really exhausted the nature of things; whether scientific specialism, with its laurels of victory, would not prove in the end an equally dangerous enemy. What was "better" for the time being might be very far from really "good." It was here that Schleiden stepped in. He fought against the prevailing specialism, at first in his own particular province of botany. He did not, indeed, take up the cause of the exploded pyrotechnics of the older natural philosophy, but pleaded for more general critical-philosophical methods. These must be preserved in any circumstances. The great botanist, he said, is not the man who can determine ten thousand species of plants according to the received models, but the man of clear logic and wide deductions from his lore. Botany must be conceived as a

EARLY YOUTH

distinct branch of general thought; otherwise it is worthless, and its herbarium may rot unnoticed in the corner and its discoveries be the outcome of blind hazard. Schleiden himself had no perception of the great idea that Darwin was to bring into his province afterwards—the idea of the variability of species and of evolution, which brought to a critical stage the question whether the botanist was to be merely a subordinate museum-secretary or a creative thinker, a prophet of nature to whom plants would be part of a general philosophy, a part of God in the ideal sense of evolution. Yet Schleiden's simple warning cry made a deep impression on many of the young men especially. There was a note of aspiration in it, an assurance that they were waiting for a sun that *must* rise somewhere. He was a master of language. There was the stuff of the poet in him. His works strayed out far beyond the range of his own province. Haeckel himself did the same work in later years. It is no wonder that Schleiden had a magical influence over him. In this case, indeed, it seemed as if the attraction was to determine his own career.

Schleiden taught botany at Jena University. Haeckel was still in the higher forms of his school at Merseburg, and remained there when his father resigned his position in the State service, and eventually removed to Berlin. At this time the ardent botanist decided to adopt the science of plants as his life-study when his final examination was over. Schleiden would teach him how to combine philosophy with botany. Then he would try to roam over the world as a practical botanist and visit the far-off zones where Mother Earth poured out her cornucopia of forms so generously.

While still in the higher form at school he made a preliminary visit to Jena. Everything seemed so pleasant and charming. He made the journey on foot. These long walks have always been his pride—to start out like a travelling scholar, with hardly anything in his pocket, to live on bread and water, and sleep in the hay at night; but to enjoy to the full all the incomparable delights that the great magician, nature, provides for the faithful novice—scenery, beautiful orchids, thoughts of God, Goethe, and the world. It was in 1849 that he visited Jena. He has described it himself: " After I had reverently admired the Goethe-room in the castle of Dornburg, I wandered, on a hot July day, over the shady meadows to Jena, singing lustily with my gay comrades. As I entered the venerable old market-place I found a troop of lively students in front of the Burgkeller, with coloured caps and long pipes, singing, and drinking the famous Lichtenhain beer from wooden tankards. It made a great impression on me, and as I took a tankard with them I made up my mind that I would some day be one of them."

CHAPTER II

AT THE UNIVERSITY

IT was botany itself that thwarted all these designs. The examination had passed off happily. Rooms were taken at Jena, at the Easter of 1852, for the advanced study under Schleiden. Then the indefatigable collector had an adventure on a cold March day. He spent hours in the wet meadows by the river Saale, searching for a rare plant, the squill (*Scilla bifolia*). He met with the fate of the angler in the story, who fell into the water in his haste to secure his big pike. He landed the fish, but not himself. The plant was found, but Haeckel's zeal was punished with a severe rheumatism. He had to go home to his parents at Berlin to be tended. At Berlin he begins his studies, and the event to some extent decides his career. It would now be many years before he would see Jena again; and through his efforts it would become one of the leading schools, not of botany, but of zoology—a school of *philosophical* zoology, however, in the sense of Schleiden.

Berlin had secured a botanist of the first rank a year before, Alexander Braun. He, too, was a thoughtful botanist, who would in his way agree very well with Schleiden. He was convinced that botany did not wholly consist in the determination of new plant-forms and the almost fruitless effort to set up a system on which all particular diagnoses would be rigidly played as on a piano. He believed that there must be a more profound conception of it, which would take "form," as such, as one of its problems, and would aim, not at the formation of as large a collection as possible, but at the construction of a science for which Goethe had long ago found a name—morphology, or the science of forms. It happened that Braun was a friendly visitor at the house of Haeckel's parents at Berlin. The now convalescent freshman became devoted to him, body and soul; they became close friends, not merely master and pupil. Berlin at that time afforded many an opportunity for practical botanising. Rare marsh-plants then flourished in the bed of the Spree, which has since been cleared. The Botanical Garden was full of good things. Haeckel used to tell with pride, long afterwards, with what readiness he flung himself into the work, practical as well as theoretical, on these excursions with Professor Braun. "On one of our botanical expeditions we wanted to get a floating chara from a pond. Braun took off his boots in his usual way in order to wade to the spot. But I was before him. I quickly undressed, forgot my naughty rheumatism, and swam to the spot, to bring him a quantity of the plant he wanted. That was my first piece of heroism, perhaps my greatest."

But in all this pleasant botanising there was no serious outlook on his future profession. Haeckel's father, with his official way of looking at things, could not reconcile himself to scientific research as an avocation. It is an old belief that the way to all preoccupation with the science of living things lies through medicine. One may question that to-day. It was the rock on which Darwin nearly came to grief. A man may be a very gifted botanist, yet be quite unfitted for the medical profession. One must have a real vocation to become a physician, more than for any other calling, or else it is a hopeless blunder. The talents are divided in much the same way as between the historian and the soldier. It is true that the two may be united, but it is equally true that very good historians have made very poor soldiers. What the medical man learns in his studies is, of course, always valuable. But it offers no test of personal talent for scientific research, nor should it be supposed that a capacity of this kind would be able, by mere formal study, to acquire the true qualities of a physician. We must learn to appreciate the physician's calling too much ever to look on it as an incidental occupation. It always reminds me of the amiable notion of the Philistine, that a man with a turn for poetry must first take up some solid profession, and then, once he is "in the saddle," pour out verses in his leisure hours. Poetry can never be a mistress: it demands marriage or nothing. Otherwise—well, we have instances enough.

Haeckel himself afterwards said that he only acceded to his father's wish, that he should study medicine, with a botanical mental reservation. He thought of going through the discipline conscientiously until he became a physician, and then secure a place as ship's doctor, and travel over the world and see the tropics. Things turned out very differently. He never became a medical man such as his father had wished, but he passed over the profession into zoology. Botany remained the lost and never-forgotten love of his youth. When we look back on his whole career we can see that he was, on the whole, fortunate. Zoology afforded a richer, more abundant, and more varied material at that time. It proved to be more "philosophical." He went after his father's asses and found a kingdom. But to him personally it seemed to be an unmistakable renunciation—the first in an active career that was to see many resignations.

. . . . .

"He goes farthest who does not know where he is going."

Haeckel once applied this motto to himself and his star, in a humorous after-dinner speech. With this kind of safe predestination he reached Würtzburg in the autumn of 1852 as a medical student. Medicine had in those days received an entirely new theoretical basis from Würtzburg—a basis that was calculated to attract a young inquirer, who brought much more of the general Faust-spirit to his work than aspiration to the profession and the doctor's cap, or the practical side.

Let us recall for a moment how medicine had gradually reached the position of an independent science. Medicine was the outcome of a remote mythical epoch. It was content with the effect of certain venerable traditional medicaments on the living body, but knew little or nothing of the inner structure of the body on which it tried its drugs. The dissection and examination of even a corpse was regarded as a deadly sin, and was visited with secular punishment. Scientific medicine did not exist until this prohibition was removed; its first and most necessary foundation was anatomy, the science of the bodily structure and its organs. The art of "cutting up" bodies had seemed too revolting. Moreover, no sooner had the science of anatomy been founded than the range of the human eye itself was considerably enlarged. The microscope was invented. A new world came to light in the dissection of the body. Beyond their external appearance it revealed the internal composition of the various organs. The eye sees a shred of skin, a piece of intestine, or a section of the liver. The microscope fastens on a tiny particle of this portion of the body, and reveals in it a deeper layer of unsuspected structures. It is well known in the history of microscopic discovery that the more powerful lenses and the improved methods of research were only gradually introduced, and enabled students to found a new and much profounder anatomy. As soon as this science appeared it was given the special name of "histology," or the science of the tissues (*hista*). Its particular achievement is the discovery that in man, the animal, and the plant, all the parts of the body prove, when sufficiently magnified, to be composed of small living elements, which are known as cells. The discovery of the cell was made in the latter part of the third decade of the nineteenth century. These cells join together in homogeneous groups in order to accomplish one or other function in the body, and thus form its "tissues." Their intricate structure is unravelled by the histologist, microscope in hand. It is evident that in this way a new basis was provided for anatomy, and therefore also for medicine. In the fifties Würtzburg was the leading school of histology, or the science of these tissues composed of cells. Albert Kölliker, professor of anatomy there since 1847, published his splendid *Manual of Histology* at the very time when Haeckel was studying under him. Franz Leydig, a tutor there since 1849, was working in the same direction. The third member of the group, made professor in 1849, was Rudolf Virchow, a young teacher then in his best years. It was Virchow who did most to bring practical medicine into line with histology. As the vital processes in the human body seemed to him, with his strict histological outlook, to be traced back always to the tissue-building cells, he concluded that disease also, or the pathological condition of the body, and therefore the proper field of the medical man, was a process in these cells. Man seemed to him to be a " cell-state " : the tissues were the various active social strata in this state : and disease was, in its ultimate source, a conflict in the state between the citizens, the tissue-forming cells, that normally divide the work amongst them for the common good. Pathology must be cellular pathology. The science was already being taught by Virchow at Würtzburg, and the dry bones of it were covered with flesh for his hearers. But his ideas were not published until a few years afterwards (1858).

In the first three terms Haeckel studied chiefly under Kölliker and Leydig. They taught him animal and human embryology, as it was then conceived. Embryology was the science of the development of the individual animal or man, the description of the series of changes that the chick passes through in the egg or the human embryo in the womb. This science, also, had been profoundly affected by the invention of the microscope. Firstly, the spermatozoa, the active, microscopically small particles in the animal and human sperm, had been discovered. Then, in the twenties, Karl Ernst von Baer had discovered the human ovum. The relation of these things to the cell-theory was clear. It was indubitable that each of these male spermatozoa and each them. There is a large aquarium at hand. You sit down to your microscope, and work. The material is "fresh to hand" every day. There are now many of these stations at well-exposed spots on the coast in various countries—sea-observatories, as it were, in which the student examines his marine objects much as the astronomer observes his planets and comets and double stars at night. To-day, when a young man is taking up zoology, and he is asked what university he is going to, he may say that he is going down to the coast, to Naples, to do practical work. When the long vacation comes, swarms of professors go from the inland towns to one or other seaside place, as far as the purse will take them. All this is a new thing under the sun. The zoologist of the olden days sat in his study at home. He caught and studied whatever was found in his own district. The rest came by post—skins, skeletons, amphibians and fishes in spirit, dried insects, hard shells of crustacea, mussels and snails of all sorts; but only the shells always, the hard, dry parts of starfishes, sea-urchins, corals, &c. Animals of the rarest character were thrown away because they could not very well be preserved in spirit and sent from the North Sea or the Mediterranean to Professor Dry-as-dust. In this state of things the advance in microscopic work brought no advantage. But at last it dawned on students that the sea is the cradle of the animal world. Whole stems of animals flourished there, and there only. Every wave was full of innumerable microscopic creatures, of the most instructive forms. Amongst them were found the young embryonic forms of familiar animals. At last the cry, "To the sea," was raised. The older professor of zoology had suffered from a kind of hydrophobia. It was not possible to teach very much at Berlin about the anatomy, histology, and embryology of the sea-urchin from a few dried flinty shells. At Würtzburg, animals were subtly discussed by men who had never made a journey to see them, while they were trampled under foot every day by the visitors bathing in Heligoland. They must move. It was not necessary to go round the world: a holiday journey to the North Sea or the Mediterranean would suffice. Every cultured man had always considered that he must make at least one pilgrimage to classic lands before his education was complete. It was only a question of changing material. They were not to confine themselves to examining ruined temples and aqueducts, but to take their microscopes down to the coast, draw a bucketful of sea-water, and examine its living contents—the living medusa and sea-urchin, and the living world of the swarming infusoria. But it was like the rending of the great curtain of the temple. Zoology seemed to expand ten-fold, a hundred-fold, in a moment. A room in an obscure inn by the sea, a microscope, and a couple of glasses of salt-water with sediment every morning—and the finest studies at Paris and London were as ploughed land, without a single blade, in face of this revelation. It was a Noah's ark in the space of a pinch of snuff.

One day the young medical student heard, in the middle of his histology and zoology, that Kölliker had come back from Messina. He had been studying lower marine life there. In 1853, two young men were together in the Gutenberg forest near Würtzburg. One of them, Karl Gegenbaur, had been abroad with Kölliker. With his impressions still fresh, he tells Haeckel about his zoological adventures in the land of the Cyclops.

Gegenbaur, eight years older than Haeckel, was by birth and education a typical Würtzburger. He, too, had studied medicine, and had practised at the hospital. But he had already advanced beyond that. His stay at Messina had been devoted entirely to zoological purposes. A year later he would be teaching anatomy at Würtzburg, and a year later still he would be called to Jena. From that time he began to be known as a master of comparative anatomy—especially after 1859, when his *Elements* of the science was published, a classic in its way that still exercises some influence.

There is nothing romantic in his career, nor could we seek any element of the kind in a man of Gegenbaur's character. But his young and undecided companion seemed to catch sight of a new ideal as he spoke. He would complete his medical studies, and then shake himself free of surgery and hospital. He would take his microscope down South, where the snowy summit of Etna towered above the orange-trees, and study the beautiful marine animals by the azure sea and the white houses, in the orange-laden air, and drink in ideas at the magic fount of these wonderful animal forms, and live out the lusty, golden years of youth on the finest coast in Europe. From that moment Haeckel felt a restless inspiration. He had no idea what it was that he was going to investigate at Messina; and he certainly did not know when and how he was to get there. But he continued his medical studies with a vague hope that it was only preliminary work; that some day he would do what his friend Gegenbaur had done.

They were very good friends, these two. They were drawn together by the strong magnetism of two true natures that understood each other to the golden core, though in other respects they were as different as possible. Gegenbaur was no enthusiast. His ideal was "to keep cool to the very heart." But he was at one with Haeckel in a feeling for a broad outlook in scientific research. He never shrank from large connections or vast deductions, as long as they were led up to by a sober and patient logic. This logical character he afterwards recognised in Darwin's idea of evolution, and so the friends once more found themselves in agreement, and for a long time they were a pair of real Darwinian Dioscuri. This feeling for moderation and at the same time for far-reaching logic was combined in Gegenbaur with a certain steady and unerring independence of character. He made little noise, but he never swerved from his aim. What he accomplished with all these qualities, in many other provinces besides Darwinism, cannot be told here. It may be read in the history of zoology. He had, as far as such a thing was possible, a restful influence of the most useful character on Haeckel. If we imagine what Darwinism would have become in the nineteenth century in the hands of such men as Gegenbaur, without Haeckel, we can appreciate the difference in temperament between the two men. With Gegenbaur evolution was always a splendid new technical instrument that no layman must touch for fear of spoiling it. With Haeckel it became a devouring wave, that will one day, perhaps, give its name to the century. In other natures these differences might have led to open conflict. But Haeckel and Gegenbaur show us that, like so many of our supposed "differences," they can at least live together in perfect accord in the freshest years of life, each bearing fruit in its kind.

. . . .

When we find Haeckel intimate in this way with Gegenbaur, his senior by eight years, we realise how close he was at that time to the whole of the Würtzburg circle. The two generations were not yet sharply divided, as they subsequently were. Most of them fought either with or against him at a later date, but they belonged, at all events, to the same stratum. But the split between the two

AT THE UNIVERSITY

generations was felt when one pronounced the name of Johannes Müller, of Berlin—the physiologist (not the historian).

All who then taught histology, embryology, comparative anatomy, or cellular pathology at Würtzburg had sat at his feet, either spiritually or in person. Johannes Müller, born at the beginning of the century, was appointed Professor of Anatomy and Physiology at Berlin the year before Haeckel was born. That indicates the distance between them. It was in Müller's incredibly primitive laboratory that, as Haeckel tells, the theory of the animal cell was established by his assistant, Theodor Schwann, after Schleiden had proved the vegetal cell. Müller himself had founded histology in his own way. He was the real parent of the idea that the zoologist ought to go and work by the sea. We have a model of this kind of work and at the same time a superb work for embryological matters in Müller's epoch-making *Studies of the Larvæ and Metamorphoses of the Echinoderms*. He had brought comparative anatomy beyond the stage of Cuvier, to a point where Gegenbaur could begin. From his school came Rudolf Virchow, who applied the cell-theory to medicine, and Emil du Bois-Reymond, who opened out a new path in physiology by his studies of animal electricity. Müller had done pioneer work with remarkable vigour in all the various branches of research, diverging afterwards to an enormous extent, that pursue these methods. The many-headed (young and half-young) generation, in which Haeckel was growing, saw the whole previous generation embodied in the single name of Müller. He seemed to be a kind of scientific Winkelried, except that the fifty spears he bore on his breast were so many lines of progress emanating from him alone.

Johannes Müller had the great and splendid gift of never lying on the shoulders of his pupils with an Alpine weight of authority. It was a secret of his personality that we admire but can hardly express in words to-day. Everybody learned from him what a great individuality is. He exerted a kind of moral suggestion in teaching men to be free, great, enlightened, and true. His pupils have worked at the development of his ideas with absolute freedom. No part of them was to be regarded as sacred, and, as a matter of fact, in the chief questions no part has remained.

One approaches the inner life of a man like Müller with a certain timidity, and asks how he became what he was. There can be no question that the fundamental trait of his character was a peculiarly deep religious feeling. At heart he was a mystic. The whole magic of his personal influence sprang from these depths. By profession he was a physiologist, an exact scientist. Never did he swerve a hair's breadth from the iron laws of research. But beneath it all was a suppressed glow of fervour. Every one who understood him, every one who was a true pupil of his, learned it by a kind of hypnotism. Externally he was all for laborious investigation, whether in dissecting a star-fish for you or classifying fishes—though he would have a full sense of your ardent longing for an inner trust in life and a philosophy of life. Both elements might change considerably in the pupil: the method of investigation without—the ideal of the comprehensive vision within. But what never left any man who had followed Müller was the warning cry that these things, within and without, should go together; that, in the larger sense, it is not possible to count the joints in the stalk of an encrinite without feeling a thrill in the deepest depth of the mind and the heart.

It is so common a spectacle in history for disciples to condemn their masters with cold smiles that we forget how pitiful it is. No pupil of Johannes Müller has ever felt that he had done with him, and might quit him with ingratitude. He had pupils, it is true, who did not lack belief in themselves, and who became famous enough to give them a sense of power; men who have eventually come to conclusions diametrically opposed to those that Müller had taught them. Yet they respect him. Living witnesses still tell of the glance that bored into you, and could not be evaded. But there must have been a greater power in the man than this piercing glance. It was a glance that survived the grave, and laid on one a duty; a glance that shot up in the darkness of memory if the duty was not fulfilled—the duty of going to the foundation of things. Whether you are examining the larva of an echinoderm or the light of a distant star, God is there. Whether you explain glass containing sea-water. "I shall never," says Haeckel, "forget the astonishment with which I gazed for the first time on the swarm of transparent marine animals that Müller emptied out of his fine net into the glass vessel; the beautiful medley of graceful medusæ and iridescent ctenophores, arrow-like sagittæ and serpent-shaped tomopteris, the masses of copepods and schizopods, and the marine larvæ of worms and echinoderms." Müller called these very fine and generally transparent creatures, of whose existence no one hitherto had had any idea, "pelagic sweepings" (from *pelagos*, the sea). More recently the word "pancton" (swimming matter) has been substituted for his phrase. As we now send whole expeditions over the seas to study "pancton," the word has found its way into ordinary literature. The regular anglers who were then in Heligoland must have looked on this subtle work with a butterfly net as a sort of pleasant joke born from the professional brain. The young student must have made an impression on them with his vigour, though he had not yet turned himself into a marine mammal, living half in the water for days together. They called him a "sea-devil." What pleased the master most in him was the talent he already showed of quickly sketching the tiny, perishable creature from the surface of the sea while it was fresh. Haeckel had been passionately fond of drawing from his early years. Now the old bent agreed with the new zeal for zoology. "You will be able to do a great deal," Müller said to him. "And when once you are

FISHING IN HELIGOLAND IN 1865.

Anton Dohrn (Naples). Richard Greef (Marburg). Ernst Haeckel (Jena).
Max Salverda (Utrecht). Pietro Marchi (Florence).

To face p. 70.

fairly interested in this fairy-land of the sea, you will find it difficult to get away from it." The dream of Messina, that Gegenbaur had conjured up, seemed to draw nearer.

These lively days at Heligoland provided Haeckel with the material for his first little zoological essay. It dealt with the development of the ova of certain fishes (*On the Ova of the Scomberesoces*, published in Müller's *Archiv* for 1855). Müller lent him ova from the Berlin collection to complete his study. It is the same volume of the *Archiv* in which, in Reichert's introduction, the great controversy breaks out over Virchow's pregnant assertion that each human being is a state composed of millions of individual cells.

Haeckel remained with Müller at Berlin for the whole winter, and was drawn more and more into the province of comparative anatomy, or, to speak more correctly, zoology. The official Professor of Zoology at Berlin at the time was really the aged Lichtenstein, who had occupied the chair since 1811. Haeckel has humorously described himself in later years as self-taught in his own subject, saying that he had attended many most excellent colleges, but never visited an official school of zoology. The only opportunity to do so at the time was under Lichtenstein, but that professor bored him so much that he could not attend his lectures. Lichtenstein was a venerable representative of the old type of zoologist; his ideal was to give a careful external description of the species on the strength of specimens chosen from a well-stocked museum. A whole world lay between these surviving followers of Linné and the splendid school of Johannes Müller.

However that may be, the fact was that under these alluring attractions Haeckel's studies were drifting from the medical profession to an "impecunious art." But as medical work had been chosen, if only as a temporary occupation, Haeckel had to tear himself away from the great magnet, at the Easter of 1855, by removing to a different place. He chose, as the least intolerable compromise, to return to Würtzburg. At all events we find him spending three terms there. I have already said that Rudolf Virchow was one of the distinguished Würtzburgers at the time who sought most keenly the solution of the new problems of biology on the medical side. Hence Virchow had to help him to find the bridge between the work he really loved and the work he was obliged to do. As a fact, Virchow directed the whole of his studies on this side in the three terms.

Virchow was not so fascinating as Johannes Müller, even in his best years. But it was something to be initiated into medical science by such a man. A later generation has, unfortunately, grown accustomed to see mental antipodes in Virchow and Haeckel. In 1877 they had a controversy with regard to the freedom of science that echoed through the whole world of thought. Yet seventeen years afterwards Haeckel himself (who was first attacked by Virchow), looking back on the days he spent at Würtzburg, had nothing but grateful recognition to say of Virchow. "I learned," he says in 1894, "in the three terms I spent under Virchow the art of the finest analytic observation and the most rigorous control of what I observed. I was his assistant for some time, and my notes were especially praised by him. But what I chiefly admired in him at Würtzburg was his wide outlook, the breadth and philosophic character of his scientific ideas."

The theory that Virchow put before his pupils was pure Monism, or a unified conception of the world without any distinction of physical and metaphysical. Life was defined, not as a mystic eccentricity in an orderly nature, but plainly as a higher form of the great cosmic mechanism. Man, the object of medical science, was said to be merely a higher vertebrate, subject to the same laws as the rest.

We can see very well that this was quite natural. If there was any man likely to put forward such views it was Virchow. He had passed through Müller's school, but was now one of the younger group who, even during Müller's life, were gradually adopting certain very profound views on life and man, without any particular resistance on the master's part. The chief characteristic of nearly the whole of this group was the lack of the volcanic stratum below of deep and personal religious feeling; in Müller this had been throughout life an enchained Titan among the rocks of his logical sense of realities, yet it had given a gentle glow and movement to the floor of his mind. Rudolf Virchow was the coolest, boldest, and clearest-minded of the group. He went to the opposite extreme. If Müller was standing on a volcano, which he only repressed by the giant force of his will—a nature that was above all master of itself—Virchow, on the contrary, was standing on a glacier, and he had never taken the trouble to conceal it. I should not venture to count him amongst the instinctively Monistic minds, in the sense of Goethe, to whom the unity of God and nature, the inorganic and the organic, the animal and the man, comes as an ardent and irresistible feeling. But it would have been strange if, in those years and in the middle of the whole scientific current of his time, his own organ, his icy logic, had not led him to the same conclusion; that it is a simpler method of research to believe in natural law alone, to regard the living merely as a complex play of the same forces that we have in physics and chemistry, and to consider man, with the bodily frame of an ape-like mammal, to be really such an animal. I believe, indeed, that Virchow never abandoned this simple solution in his own mind at any part of his career. The controversy he afterwards engaged in ran on different lines. It seems to me that at an early stage of his development he became convinced that there must be limits to scientific inquiry, not on logical, but on diplomatic grounds; because it is not an absolute agency, but only a relatively small force amongst many more powerful institutions, the

AT THE UNIVERSITY

Church, the State, and so on. Hence it would have to respect limitations that were not drawn from its own nature; in given cases it would have to keep silent in order not to jeopardise its existence as a whole. It is my firm belief that this diplomatic attitude as such would lead to the destruction of all pursuit of the truth. It carefully excludes the possibility of any further martyrdoms, but at the cost of science's own power to illumine the world. In my opinion the free investigation of the truth is an *absolute* right. Churches, States, social orders, moral precepts, and all that is connected with them, have to adjust themselves to this investigation, and not the reverse.

However, the point is that under Virchow—more particularly under Virchow, in fact—Haeckel would be educated into the general attitude with regard to God, nature, life, and man, to which he has since devoted his whole energy. In spite of Goethe—and who would be likely to take Goethe as his guide in his twenty-first year?—the ardent young student was as yet by no means firmly seated in the saddle. He grubbed, and sought, and rejected. In his *Riddle of the Universe* he tells us that he "defended the Christian belief in his twenty-first year in lively discussions" with his free-thinking comrades, . . ./ "although the study of human anatomy and physiology, and the comparison of man's frame with that of the other animals, had already greatly enfeebled my faith. I did not entirely abandon it, after bitter struggles, until my medical studies were completed, and I began to practise. I then came to understand Faust's saying, 'The whole sorrow of humanity oppresses me.' I found no more of the infinite benevolence of a loving father in the hard school of life than I could see of 'wise providence' in the struggle for existence."

When the three terms of medical training were over, he received another impulse to his own particular interest in science. Kölliker invited him in August, 1856, to spend the two months' holiday with him on the Riviera. It was the first Mediterranean school of zoology, though as yet only a kind of "payment on account." On the journey he made the acquaintance of the zoological museum at Turin and its well-travelled director, Filippo de Filippi, and he saw the grandeur of the Maritime Alps on the Col di Tenda. The master, Kölliker, Heinrich Müller, Karl Kupffer (afterwards professor at Munich), and he established themselves at Nice, and fished for all sorts of creatures with the Müller net at Villefranche. Fortunately, Müller himself happened to be visiting the Riviera at the same time, and they received a direct stimulus from him. The first result of this journey in the summer and autumn was that Haeckel secured his degree with a zoological-anatomical work, instead of with a strictly medical treatise. As he had done from Heligoland two years before, he now brought home from the Mediterranean the material for a short technical theme. He again spent the winter at Berlin to put it together. It was an histological study of the tissues of crabs, and therefore lay in the province of the articulates, an animal group, it is curious to note, which he has not entered into more fully in the course of his long and varied work as special investigator. At Nice he made a thorough study of the nerve-tubes of the spiny lobster and other available marine crustacea, and discovered several remarkable new structural features in them. At Berlin he entered upon a minute microscopic study of the common craw-fish. His dissertation for the doctorate embodied the main results of his research. It was entitled *De telis quibusdam Astaci fluviatilis*, and was printed in March, 1857. It appeared the same year in an enlarged form in Müller's *Archiv*, with the title *The Tissues of the Craw-fish*. On March 7th he received his medical degree, Ehrenberg, the great authority on the infusoria, presiding. In the customary way the young doctor had to announce and defend several theses. One of them is rather amusing in view of later events.

He most vigorously contested the possibility of "spontaneous generation." The meaning of the phrase is that somewhere or at some time a living thing, animal or plant, has arisen, not in the form of a seed or germ or sprout from a parent living thing, but as a direct development out of dead, inorganic matter. Haeckel had not made a personal study of the subject. What he said in his thesis was merely a faithful repetition of Müller's opinion. At that time it was believed that science had empirically disproved spontaneous generation. An old popular belief held that fleas and lice were born every day from non-living dirt and dust, but that had been refuted long before. No egg, no animal: every living thing develops from an egg. This had been laid down as a fixed rule. When the microscope revealed an endless number of tiny creatures in every drop of stagnant water, in the air and the dust and the soil, it was a question whether the rule was not wrong. Surely these simplest of all living things, apparently, were born by spontaneous generation? However, the question was believed to have been settled in two ways. Schwann, the co-discoverer of the cell-theory, had made certain experiments which seem to prove directly that even these tiny beings, the infusoria and bacteria, were never formed in a vessel containing water and dead matter, if it had been carefully assured beforehand that the minute living germs of these animals that floated in the air could not penetrate into the vessel. At the same time Ehrenberg and others stoutly denied that the infusoria were the "simplest" organisms, or that they could conceivably be born in that way. They declared that the infusoria were "perfect organisms" in spite of their smallness. The belief that these tiny creatures consisted of "one cell," and so formed, as it were, the ultimate elements of the plant and animal worlds on the lines of the cell-theory, was seriously menaced, and apparently on the way to be destroyed. Finally, the tapeworm and similar parasites had been declared to evolve by a kind of spontaneous generation from the contents of the intestines. But this also was proved to be untrue. Thus there was ample material for a solid dogma: there was no such thing as spontaneous generation. The dogma, moreover, harmonised with the prevailing belief in a special vital force and a radical distinction between the living and the dead, which was still shared in a subtle form by even a man like Müller. The dogma was formulated. Spontaneous generation was struck out of the scientific vocabulary as unscientific and a popular superstition. The young doctor, duly initiated into these ideas of the time, could not resist the temptation to give his own kick to the fallen theory. Yet how strangely things have changed since then! Two years afterwards Haeckel ceased to believe in a special vital force; he was now absolutely convinced that there were unicellular beings; his whole theory of life seemed to demand spontaneous generation as a postulate, and he even doubted the force of the experiments of Schwann and others. Haeckel himself became the keenest apostle of the theory of spontaneous generation. Whenever it is mentioned to-day, we think of the weight of his name which he has cast in the scale in its favour. So the leaves change even in the forest of science: yesterday green, to-day red and falling, to-morrow green once more. On the same branch as the dogmas we find the correctives growing, that will at length split them open and cast them as empty husks to the ground.

The history of Haeckel's medical doctorate can be written in a few plain and touching lines. After receiving his degree he was sent by his prudent father, to keep him away from crabs and other monsters of the deep, to Vienna for a term, to do hospital work under Oppolzer, Skoda, Hebra, and Siegmund. All that we find recorded of this term is that his old love of botany revived in earnest. Immense quantities of dwarf Alpine plants were collected. When the traveller passed by the spot twenty-four years afterwards on a quiet autumn Sunday, on his way to take ship at Trieste for the tropical forests and giant trees of Ceylon, the memory of Schneeberg and the Rose-Alp came upon him like a dream. However, the hospital work, together with a short span of cramming in the winter at Berlin, must have had some effect, as he passed the State-examination in medicine. In March, 1858, he was a "practising physician." He had in his hand the crown of prudent ambition —and he felt like a poor captive. There was one source of consolation—Johannes Müller. While one was near him there was a possibility of more real work. He discussed with him the plan of the study of the development of the gregarinæ (parasitic protozoa), which he wanted to conduct in Müller's laboratory in the summer of 1858. Then he was stricken, like so many others, with the thunderbolt of the news of Müller's sudden death, on April 28th of the same year. What must he do now? He began to practise. It is said on his own authority that he fixed the hours of consultation from five to six in the morning! The result was that during a whole year of this philanthropic occupation he had only three patients, not one of whom died under his earnest attention.

"This success was enough for my dear father," says Haeckel. We can well believe it.

The kindly old man consented to one more year of quite extravagant study, in which all was to come right. It was to be a year of travel, in Italy. He was to devote himself to the study of marine animals, not merely for pleasure, but earnestly enough for him to find a basis for his life in the result. This he succeeded in doing. Like the children of fortune, who at the very moment when they cannot see a step before them make a move that the Philistine regards as the safest and last refuge, Haeckel becomes engaged that very year to his cousin, Anna Sethe. After that, in January, 1859, he goes down to the coast. He makes for the blue Mediterranean, which he already knows will prove anything but an "unprofitable sea" for him. He will conjure up treasures of science from its crystal depths with his Müller-net; then on to fortune, position, marriage, and the future. The fates have added a world-wide repute, if they have denied many a comfort.

CHAPTER III

THE RADIOLARIA

IN the January of 1859 Haeckel, then in his twenty-fifth year, came to Italy with the determination "to do it thoroughly." By the autumn the body of the peninsula had been covered down to Naples, Capri, and Ischia. The winter, until April, 1860, was spent at Messina.

There are plenty of very strenuous students, later Privy Councillors as well as archæologists and zoologists, who find a year in Italy a very simple matter. They arrive, make the due round of sights, and then at once disappear into some library or institute, burying themselves like moles in some special work or other, just as they would do at home. The only time you can see them is over their Munich beer in the evening; and if there are a number of them together they smoke their cigars and sing a German student's song, as they would do at home. These good folk have very different dispositions behind their goggles, but they have never been lit up by the fire of Goethe. They are quite content to write home like the churlish Herder; Italy is pretty enough in Goethe's writings, but one ought not to go there oneself. The modern scholar of this type may add that the cigars are bad and beer dear. Very different was Haeckel's verdict. "In Sicily I was nearly thrown out of my line and made a landscape-painter." The æsthetic man in him was the first to lift up his arms with vigour under this new, free, inspiring sun. His words are no idle phrase. The moment he tried it Haeckel discovered that he had a genuis for landscape-painting. Even in regard to this gift we see the truth of what I have already said in other connections; the sternest materialists and scientific revolutionaries of the nineteenth century were men of considerable artistic power. There was the solid Vogt, a painter and poet; Moleschott, the soul-comrade of Hermann Hettner; Strauss, who wrote some poems of great and lasting beauty; Feuerbach, and others. Even Büchner, the boldest and most advanced of them all, has written poetry under a pseudonym.* Darwin took only two books with him in the little cabin of his ship, Lyell's *Geology* and *Paradise Lost*. There is a complete gallery of fine water-colours in Haeckel's house to-day that have been brought from three quarters of the globe. His son Walter has inherited the artistic gift, and become a painter. It might be said that a good landscape-painter would hardly recompense us for the loss of the philosopher

* Büchner's brother tells how, when Ludwig furtively brought to him the manuscript of *Force and Matter*, he at once guessed it was a romance or an epic that so much secret work had been expended on. [Trans.]

and scientist that Haeckel became in the nineteenth century. The simple steel pen, the inspired pencil of the thinker, did more for humanity in his hand than could have been done by the most splendid colour-symphonies of the most inspired landscape-painter. I have often thought this as I looked over, in the evening at Haeckel's house, the then unpublished treasures of his artistic faculty. A work like his *History of Creation* has counted for a stratum in the thought of humanity. What are even the masterpieces of a Hildebrandt in comparison with it! Yet there was undoubtedly the note of genius in these drawings; some of them showed more than Hildebrandt's cleverness (we know to-day that Hildebrandt's highly coloured pictures did not even approximate to the real natural light of southern scenes) and glow of colour. It seemed to me that here again the man had dreams of a lost love: a dream of the gay, wandering *pittore*, who asks nothing but a sunset in violet, carmine, and gold, instead of being the sober unriddler of the world's problems. Since that time the house of Fr. Eugen Köhler, to which we owe the fine new edition of Naumann's classic work on birds, with its coloured plates, has undertaken to publish Haeckel's water-colours, as "Travel Pictures," in a splendid and monumental work.

During the year in Italy all these gifts were employed together. Italy was exactly the land for Haeckel's temperament, with its mixture of lofty classic elements and natural beauty and simple, naïve unpretentiousness. For the first time he felt that he was a cosmopolitan student. He had never been a devotee of the student's beer-feasts. He had no need of alcoholic stimulant. Gegenbaur of Würtzburg, the insatiable smoker, once said to him in joke, "If you would only smoke, we might make something out of you." It was done, in any case. His personal inclinations were in his favour: an illimitable love of travel, good spirits that rose in proportion to the absurdity of his accommodation, and a simple delight in everything human that enabled him to talk and travel with the humblest as if they were his equals. He spent a night with a young worker in a haystack, and when he was asked what he was, he pointed to his paint-box and brush: "House-painter." "I thought so when I saw you," said the youth, and he asked Haeckel to start a workshop together with him. Italy was the ideal land for a visitor of that type. There was no part of the world from which he was so pleased to receive recognition in his years of fame as Italy; and he received it in abundance, for the appreciation was mutual.

I will add a page here that was supplied for the present work by a friendly hand, a man who is as well known to thousands as Haeckel himself—Hermann Allmers, "the poet of the fens, chief of Frisia, and splendid fellow," as Haeckel has called him. He died in the spring of 1902 at an advanced age. He met Haeckel in Italy, and tells the story in his verse and prose. Forty years after their meeting he wrote me that Haeckel was "the finest man he ever met."

"TO ERNST HAECKEL.

Dost thou remember the magic night,
A night I never cease to see,
That brought us both to Ischia?
How smooth the boat sailed gently in,
How silent was the great broad bay
Unutterably noble and sublime,
In all its star-lit loveliness,
As sky and sea met in embrace.
With fairy-light the waters gleamed
As helm ploughed gently through the wave,
And overhead a deep red glow
Vesuvius from its larva poured.

We were yet strangers at the time,
One hour alone had each the other seen,
Yet something urged us both to speak—
To speak, anon, from heart's great deeps.
To speak of all we held of worth,
All that had led us to the spot,
All the fair gifts of happy fate,
And the untoward accidents of life;
Of distant home, of fatherland,
Of the full days of beauty's quest.
Hand clasped in hand we told our joy:
Need I recall it from the mist?

In fine of thy dear love thou told'st
And sacred silence fell on thee.
On moved the barque with leisured pace
Across the deeper silence of the bay.

Behind us vanished Posilippo
And Baja's gulf and Cape Miseno.
As Procida passed slowly by
The gentle dawn stole o'er the night,

And Epomeo's head was lit,
With the first rays of new-born sun,
And Ischia, nobler than our dreams,
Uprose before our wondering eyes.
Above, mantled in its own loveliness,
Calling us sweetly from the bay
Up to its gentle, vine-clothed heights,
Sat radiant Casamicciola.

How thou and I the glad days spent
Thou knowest well. And now?
Now all is ruin and decay,
A ghastly tomb. We'll let it rest.
Think rather of the linkèd lives
We spent, and the whole joy of earth,
That never more will gladden us
While sun and stars gleam overhead.
What was it opened then our hearts?
What was it forged the golden chain?
It was—thou know'st it well, comrade—
The sailing on that magic night."

" Yes, dear reader, whenever I let these verses and their splendid truth vibrate again in my soul —and how often and how gladly I do it!—I have to say, Such days thou shalt never know again— such happy entrance into another's heart. And what a heart it was that bared itself to me with all it hid and would soon reveal! We were in a café at Naples, a copy of the *Allgemeine Zeitung* lying between him and me. It was in the best part of the spring of 1859. We both reached for it, and told our names, and the friendship was begun. 'You must excuse me,' Haeckel said, 'I have to go to Ischia to-night by the market-boat.' 'To Ischia? That's good: I am going there myself.

'I am very glad, because I heard I was to be alone. It starts at nine o'clock.' That was all that had passed between us before the crossing. What I have described in the above verses only began when we, the only Germans on board, made ourselves comfortable on the open deck. Before the journey was over we were intimate friends, and have remained friends in joy and sorrow to this moment, though the mental differences between us are enormous. However, Casamicciola brought us together in a wonderful way. We had common quarters, and always went out together for walks or botanising; we were never separated when we painted or drew, as Haeckel did with real passion. On the third morning, when we found some rare thermal plants in an almost broiling meadow and discovered nearly at the same spot the ruins of an ancient Roman bath, the remarkable coincidence affected us so much that we embraced each other joyously and dedicated the rest of our flask to them. We both felt that we could not do otherwise. So we pleasantly enjoyed the magnificent scene that lay at our feet from the height of Epomeo. We stripped off nearly the whole of our clothes, and dipped, in almost primitive nakedness, in the warm muddy streams that shot up out of the dark depths under a growth of tendrils and ferns. We shouted out, 'How fine it is in these warm and beautifully shaded brooks! How delightful it must be in the ravines of Atlas! We must go there.' We spent more than a whole day in the most marvellous ravines of Atlas, though neither of us had

THE RADIOLARIA

the least idea of them. But we determined to make the journey there, and sketched it out in detail, to be undertaken as soon as we left Italy. He contracted a perfect fever for travelling. We were four weeks in Pagano's excellent inn at Capri with a few artists, and he completely lost himself with delight. He became intimate with the young artists; being hitherto surrounded by men of scientific interests, he had avoided them. The intermediary between Haeckel and them was myself. I liked no one better than genial artists. Now Haeckel was seized with a passion for painting landscapes day after day. He was especially interested in the most fantastically shaped rocks. On the other hand, he neglected his marine animals, and did not return to them entirely until he got to Messina, where he devoted himself to the radiolaria, which were destined to play so important a part in his work. Darwin, who was soon to dominate his whole thought, had little significance for him at that time, as the struggle for life had not yet been discovered. We rarely spoke of it, but talked constantly of Johannes Müller. He was Haeckel's ideal, as long as I kept in touch with him. He also spoke often and generously of his university friends, Dr. W. D. Focke, who was his special botanical comrade, Dr. Dreyer and Dr. Strube, who were his chief friends at the university at Würtzburg. The ordinary life and pleasures of the student, and their heavy beer-drinking, were a torture to him; he avoided them as much as possible. Very often I could not understand how it was that I brought him to the highest pitch of gaiety, whereas on all his earlier travels, especially when botany was still his favourite science, he would, after the common meal, withdraw quietly with his books and plants to the solitude of his own room. Yet he could be the gayest of all. In fact, his hearty and wonderful laugh, in all notes up to the very highest, rings over and over again in the memory of any man who has once heard it; it is the frank laughter of a glad human heart. And whoever has seen the deep earnestness with which the great scientist threw himself into the study of the most arduous problems would be astounded to hear it."

. . . . .

The Strait of Messina is the pearl of Italy. In my opinion it is finer than Naples. The huge volcano and the deep blue strip of water, that seems to be confined between the white coasts like some fabulous giant-stream, give a feeling of sublimity beside which the Bay of Naples seems but an idyll in the memory. The colours are more vivid; you think you would catch hold of the blue bodily if you put your hand in the water. It is a land of ancient myths. The Cyclops hammer their work in Etna. Scylla and Charybdis lurk in the Strait. Once, in the days of Homer, when the sun of civilisation still lay on a corner of Asia, a dim Münchhausen-world was lived here, such as we find to-day in the heart of Africa or New Guinea. But times changed. Zoologists came and fished with Müller-nets for tiny transparent sea-creatures in the gentle periodic currents, that may once have given rise to the legend of Scylla and Charybdis. There is no place more favourable for the purpose than the harbour of Messina. The basin is open only at one spot, towards the north. The westerly wind is cut off from the town by the mountains, and can do no harm. Even the detested southern wind, the sirocco, that lashes the Strait till it is white with foam, cannot enter. There is only the north wind that drives the water into the basin. The waves it brings in are full of millions of sea-animals, which accumulate in the *cul-de-sac* of the harbour. In fact, if the sirocco has previously been blowing in the Strait and gathered great swarms of animals from the southern parts at the mouth of the harbour, and then the north wind drives them all inside, the whole of the water seems to be alive with them. If you dip a glass in it, you do not get water, but a sort of "animal stew," the living things making up more of the bulk than the fluid—little crystalline creatures, medusæ, salpæ, crustacea, vermalia, and others of many kinds.

It was at this classic spot that Haeckel would lay the foundation of his fame as a zoologist, by the study of a group of minute creatures that appealed equally to the æsthetic sense by the mysterious beauty of their forms. There can be little doubt that we can see in this, not only a fortunate accident, but also the play of some hidden affinity. In such a spot the artist in Haeckel could compromise with the zoologist. His æsthetic nature had revelled in landscape, peasantry, and song. Now the Müller-net and the microscope revealed a new world of hidden beauty that none had appreciated before him. In devoting himself to it he was still half engrossed in his quest of beauty; but the other half of him was rapidly attaining a mastery of serious zoology.

It is a common belief that æsthetic appreciation ceases as soon as we sit down to the microscope. There is the magnificent blue Strait of Messina. Your eye, embracing its whole length, drinks in its beauty in deep draughts. What will your microscope make of it? Its field can only take in a single drop of water, and this does not grow more blue when you thus analyse it. Let science go further afield: this is the land of beauty. All those doctrines of histology, embryology, and so on, built on the microscope, are thought to be poles removed from æsthetic enjoyment. They dissolve everything—man's soft, white skin, the perfumed leaf of the rose, the bright wing of the butterfly—into "cells.' It is mere ignorance to talk in this way. Nature's beauty is by no means so thin a covering that the microscope must at once pierce through it. Rather does it reveal to us in incalculable wealth a whole firmament of new stars, a new world of beauties, if we choose the right way to see them. Haeckel did choose the right way.

At his very first dips into the harbour of

THE RADIOLARIA

Messina, in October, 1859, he got certain curious lumps and strips of jelly. The local fishermen called them *ovi di mare* (sea-eggs). It was, in fact, natural enough to regard these inert creatures as strings of mollusc-eggs, when their real nature was unknown. But our young student already knew what they were. They were social *radiolaria*.

The word "radiolarium," from *radius* (a ray), means a raying or radiating animal. It is difficult for the inexpert to imagine the structure of one of these creatures. He must first put entirely on one side all the features that he usually associates with an "animal." The radiolarian lives, moves, has sensations, breathes, eats, and reproduces, but in a totally different way from that we are accustomed to see. Its body consists essentially of a particle of homogeneous living matter. There is merely a firmer nucleus in the centre of it, and the soft gelatinous matter is thickened at the surface to form a kind of capsule. Otherwise there is no trace of any real "organ." The little blob of jelly eats—but it has no stomach; it eats with its whole body, its soft, jelly-like substance closing entirely over particles of food and absorbing them. It breathes (with the animal type of respiration)—but it has neither lungs nor gills; the whole body takes in oxygen and gives off carbonic acid. It swims about—yet it has neither legs nor fins; the pulpy mass of its body flows, when it is necessary, into a crown of streamers or loose processes, that keep the body neatly balanced; when they are no longer required, they sink back into the gelatinous mass. We study the "histology" of these curious social-living creatures under a powerful microscope. As I have explained, the tissues and organs of the higher animals break up under the microscope into a most ingeniously constructed network of tiny living gelatinous corpuscles with a nucleus in the centre—the cells. But our radiolarian has no more got tissues composed of cells than it has stomach or lungs or any other organ. It is merely a single cell with a nucleus and a jelly-like body. Yet in this case the single cell is a whole individual, a complete animal, that lives, moves, eats, breathes, and so on. The radiolarian is, in comparison with the splendid cell-tapestry of the higher animals, a poor little atom of life. It must be put deep down in the animal series. What a vast distance! Above is man, built of myriads of cells woven into the most ingenious tissues and the most perfect organs for each function of life; below we have the radiolarian, in which a single cell must discharge all the vital functions, because its whole body is merely one cell. But there is another wonder. This tiny particle of living slime, floating in the blue waves at Messina, hardly more visible than a drop of spittle, has a most remarkable quality. It is able to assimilate a kind of matter that the chemist calls silicious (flinty) matter—the stuff that forms, when it is crystallised in chemical

A Radiolarian.
(*Lychnaspis miranda.*)

THE RADIOLARIA

purity, the well-known rock-crystal. This flint matter (and sometimes a similar substance) is then exuded again by the radiolarian—no one knows quite how—from its gelatinous body, and built into so beautiful a form that even a child will clap its hands and cry, "How lovely!" when it sees it through the microscope. We may put it that the radiolarian forms a coat of mail for itself from this siliceous matter: we may at the same time call it a float or buoy. The hard flinty structure serves to keep it balanced when it is swimming, just as when a loose piece of jelly attaches itself to a cork disk. Thus a round trellis-work shell is formed about the animal, and through the apertures it thrusts gelatinous processes that act as oars, and can be put forth or drawn in at will; outside this shell, again, may be all sorts of structures, such as zigzag shaped rods, radiating stars, bundles of streamers, and so on. It is a most wonderful sight. It is as if each class of these beings had its private taste, and, in virtue of a kind of tradition, built a different type of flinty skeleton from all the others. Here begins the peculiar artistic wizardry of these tiny and lowly creatures, that lifts them at once high up in the scale of animated natural objects with a great display of beauty. We find every possible variation of ornament within the limits of the particular type: an infinite number of crystalline and superb variations on the theme of trellis-work, stars, radiating shields, crosses, and halberds. They give an impression at once of human art-work, for there is nothing else in the whole of nature with which we may compare them. The radiolarian, therefore, is an animal of the utmost simplicity of bodily frame that, by some force or other, creates the highest and most varied beauty that we find anywhere in nature living or dead, below the level of human art.

Haeckel's good genius brought him to these radiolaria. Until the winter of 1859-1860 he knew very little about them. When a radiolarian dies its soft body naturally melts away and perishes. But the art-work of its life, the star or shield of flinty matter, remains; it either sinks to the bottom or is washed ashore, where numbers of them may accumulate. If a pinch of mud or sand from the shore is put under the microscope the observer will see lovely artistic fragments, and ask what is the meaning of the miracle. Ehrenberg, the venerable Berlin microscopist, was the first to have the experience. He was not in the habit of going to the sea himself, but had specimens sent to him, and found in them shells of the radiolaria. Though they were so small, their artistic quality seemed to him to be so great that he assumed they were built by very advanced animals of the starfish or sea-urchin type. That there were unicellular protozoa with a simple gelatinous body and no higher organs he stoutly denied, and he had the support of his leading contemporaries everywhere. But his colleague, Johannes Müller, who fished in the sea himself, came across living specimens in the Mediterranean in the first half of the fifties. It appeared that they were really very lowly animals at least. Müller christened them the radiolaria, classified the fifty species that he discovered, and at his death left the subject well prepared for the first student who should go more fully into it. His final work on them did not appear until after his death, in 1858, the sunset-glow of his brilliant scientific career. Perhaps he would have gone more deeply into the mysteries he had encountered but for a curious accident. Just as he discovered the subject, two years before his death, he had a terrible experience. The ship in which he was returning from a holiday in Norway was wrecked. A favourite pupil of his was drowned, and he himself narrowly escaped by swimming to land. After that he could not be induced to enter a boat during his last trips to the sea, and so the thorough study of these most graceful inhabitants of the Mediterranean was abandoned. But when Haeckel fished at Villefranche with Kölliker of Würtzburg, and Müller was at Nice, he was urged by the master, as a kind of testamentary injunction, that " something might be done" with the radiolaria. And when he fished up a pretty crown of socially-united radiolaria on first rowing over the Messina harbour, he thought it would be a grateful offering to the memory of the dead hero of his zoological dreams to continue the study of the radiolaria. At once he seemed to enter the treasure-house of a fairy tale. When the campaign was ended in the Messina harbour in April, 1860, he had discovered no quickly decided on. It dealt, of course, with his new field: the limit and the system of the animal group to which the radiolaria belonged, the rhizopods. He was immediately appointed private teacher at Jena, and found himself in the lovely valley of the Saale, beneath the mountain about whose summit the red rays lingered. He had been drawn from Berlin to Messina to find a home—a home for ever—in the increasing stress.

In the following year, 1862, the official position of Extraordinary Professor of Zoology was created, and this brought him close, even externally, to Gegenbaur. Everything was, it is true, in a very primitive condition at first. In August he married Anna Sethe—a sunny dream of fresh young happiness. In the same year he published his *Monograph on the Radiolaria*, a huge folio volume with thirty-five remarkably good copperplates, such as our more rational but slighter technical methods no longer dare produce. Wagenschieber, of Berlin, the last of the fine scientific copper etchers, had been in constant personal touch with Haeckel, and reproduced his original drawings in masterly style. With this work Haeckel was fully established in his position as a professional zoologist. It is still one of the finest monographs that was issued in the nineteenth century; from the literary point of view, also, it was one of the purest and most lucid works of its kind, full of great and earnest thoughts, and without any bitterness—a work, perhaps, that Haeckel has not since equalled. The most influential and official scientists of the time had to respect this work : possibly with the sole exception of the aged Ehrenberg, to whom it dealt a deadly blow in this department, without, of course, undervaluing his great antecedent services. He never even studied it sufficiently to be able to quote the title of it correctly.

Nevertheless, a flame broke out at one spot in this monograph. In a very short time Haeckel's whole figure would stand out in the red reflection of its glow—a figure really great, solitary, suddenly deserted by all the bewigged and powdered professors—Haeckel himself, as the world has come to know him.

CHAPTER IV

DARWIN

WE still celebrate, at a distance of centuries, the return of the birthday of great men. In reality it is a mistake. We ought to celebrate the hour when not merely life, but *the idea of their life*, quickened them. That is the really important birth that calls for commemoration. Luther's real birthday was when he nailed his theses to the church door. Then was born the Luther that belongs to the world. Over the world-cradle of Columbus shines, not the trivial and evanescent planet given in his horoscope, but the little red flickering star of Guanahani, the light that he saw from the shore on the night before he landed on an island of the New World.

Life is a voyage of discovery to the man who passes through it. He looks out with his child-eyes and discovers the world—at the bottom, discovers only himself. But one day a greater veil is torn from before his self. Genius, the greater I, stirs within him like the butterfly in its narrow pupa-case. For the world at large that is the hour when the *great* man is born who will leave his mark on it.

Haeckel's biography only begins on a certain day, if we look at it rightly and broadly. Until that day he is merely a young man, an outgrowth from a rich old civilisation: a young man who has felt in him a struggle between artistic and scientific tendencies, like so many: who has vacillated between the choice of a "paying profession" and research for its own sake, and has decided for the former, like so many: who has chosen zoology, and begun to work hard on professional lines at his science: and who has been told prophetically that he will one day do something, though along a line where much has been done already. In the whole of this development we have as yet no indication of the real tenor of his life.

It comes first with the name of Darwin. The arabesque of a very different life begins to blend with that of his own.

In the February of the year in which Haeckel was born (1834), twenty-eight years before the point we have arrived at, Charles Darwin was on a scientific expedition to South America. There is a romantic element in the earlier story of this journey. The naked Fuegians had stolen a boat from an English Government ship that was engaged in making geographical measurements, towards the close of the twenties, on the wild coast of Tierra del Fuego. FitzRoy, the captain, arrested a few of the natives, brought them on board as hostages, and in the end took them with him to England. They were to be instructed in morality and Christianity and then taken back to their people, in order to introduce these elements of civilisation, for the advantage of shipwrecked sailors or distressed travellers who might fall in with them. We feel a breath of the spirit of Rousseau in it. As a fact nothing came of the device. The good Fuegians were clothed and improved by civilised folk for a year or two, returned home, immediately abandoned their trousers and their Christianity, and remained naked savages. But the bringing home of these hostages led, in the early thirties, to a new expedition of FitzRoy to Tierra del Fuego. The Government directed him to draw up further charts, and he looked about for a man of science to accompany him.

The man proved to be Charles Darwin, then in his twenty-second year.

The son of a prosperous provincial physician, he had begun to study medicine without much success, and was transferred to theology, only to find after three years of study that he was as little fitted to become a country clergyman as a country doctor. He had an unconquerable love of scientific investigation. He collected all kinds of things, and desired to travel, without any very clear idea of his destiny. A chance introduction came to the young man as a godsend, and he joined FitzRoy's expedition to South America. Once more, it was this journey that made him "Darwin," the mighty intellectual force in the nineteenth century.

Darwin found an idea in South America. You have to examine it very closely to appreciate it clearly. Let us recapitulate very briefly the hundred years of zoology and botany that had gone before.

In the eighteenth century Linné drew up, for the first time, a great catalogue of plant and animal species. Each species had a solid Latin name, and was provided with its particular label, by which every representative of the species could be recognised at once. Then the species were bracketed together in larger groups, and a general system was formed. It was an immense scientific advance, and is still generally appreciated as such. But we have to make one reserve. It is not man that separates things; nature, or rather God who created nature, has already distinguished them. In this respect zoology and botany are of God. The various species of plants and animals are something firmly established by God. Take the polar bear, the hippopotamus, the giraffe, or a particular species of palm, or vine, or rose. There they are, and all that man has to do is to learn their specific characters in order to determine and name them.

Behind all this we really have the ancient idea of the Mosaic story of creation. God made the animals and plants, species by species, put them in their places, and said to man, "Name them as you think fit, classify them, putting the like together and separating the unlike." So God spake to Adam when he stood before him, naked as a Fuegian. Linné comes on the scene some six thousand years afterwards to set about this naming and arranging in earnest. But that does not make much difference. There are the species created by God. They have ceaselessly reproduced themselves since the days of Paradise according to the command to increase and multiply, each one in its own kind, so that the polar bear has only begotten polar bears, the giraffe giraffes, the hippopotamus hippopotami. Thus, in spite of death, the primitive Paradise is still there, and Linné, the official professor at Upsala, with his venerable wig and embroidered coat, can take up the work of the naked Adam with a good conscience, and finish what the patriarch had not been able to do.

Linné died in 1778 (about the time when Goethe was beginning the *Iphigenia* and *Wilhelm Meister*) in the full fame of all these achievements and all his hypotheses from the giraffe to God. Fifty years elapsed between this and Darwin's voyage; but in those fifty years the following process is accomplished:—

An increasing number of bones and other relics of animal species, that exist no longer, were dug out of the earth. In South America the skeleton was found of a giant-sloth, the megatherium, the remains of a kind of animal, larger than the elephant, that no traveller could find living in the country. The famous mammoth-corpse came to light in the ice of Siberia; an entirely strange elephant with curved tusks and a red woolly coat. Ichthyosauri were found in the rocks in England, and so on. All these " extinct " species had to be named and arranged in the system. A special scientific indication was put on them, which means " extinct." But this was not enough for thought—which cannot be " entirely dispensed with," as some one well said, even in exact science.

Where did these extinct species come from ? What is their relation to the Creator ? Were they created long ago in Paradise with the others, and afterwards conveyed in the ark, only to disappear in the course of time ? And what was the cause of their disappearance ? Must we conclude that part of what Adam saw was not available for Linné and his pupils ? These four remains, a few bones here and there, do not tell us much about them.

Therefore, species may perish : many of them have perished.

There was something new in this, something that obscured the clear lines of earlier science. However, a way of escape was found. It was claimed that these grotesque monsters—ichthyosauri, megatheria, mammoths, &c.—represent an earlier creation, with which Adam had nothing to do. Cuvier developed the theory in his grandiose way in 1812. Before the creation of the animal and plant species that Adam found in Paradise there was a long series of periods in the history of the earth, each of which had its own animal and plant population. It was in one of these periods that the forests grew which we find fossilised in our coal. In another the ichthyosauri, gigantic lizards, filled the ocean. In a third the hideous megatherium dragged along its huge frame, and so on. It is true that there is nothing in the Bible about these ancient and extinct periods; but the Mosaic verses move quickly—they press on to come to man. The repeated creations of the animal and plant worlds are summed up in a single one. We must read something between the lines.

Apart from that, everything is clear. Hence the ancient species were made fixed, solid, and unchangeable by God just like the later species that Adam found in Paradise, and that still exist. Without the will of God they could no more have died out than the actual ones; and there were no human beings there to destroy them. But the divine action intervened. At the end of each of these old-world periods a terrible spectacle was witnessed. The heavens poured out their punishing floods; the seas were heated to steam by fiery masses of rock that were summoned by the divine power from the bowels of the earth. In the course of a single day the carboniferous forests were swallowed up; the megatheria disappeared, legs uppermost, like flies in butter, in the sand dunes of the terrible floods.

The might of the creative act was equalled by the might of the destruction. The science of these vast new creations and divine revolutions before Adam's birth was called geology. It lived in peace with Linné's theory of fixed species. Its parent,

Cuvier, was so great a genius that it seemed quite impossible that he had made a mistake. Before twenty years were out he was, in the opinion of a contemporary and equally able geologist, declared to be certainly wrong on one point.

Lyell wrote a magnificent work in which he proved, from the point of view of scientific geology, that the whole story of these terrible revolutions was a fiction. There are no such sharp sections in the early history of the earth. Everything goes to show that throughout the whole period of the earth's development the same natural laws have been at work as we find to-day. It is true that the relative positions of sea and land, hill and valley, forest and desert, have often changed; but very, very slowly, in the course of millions of years. A single drop of water, constantly falling, will hollow out a stone. In these millions of years the water has swept away rocks here, and formed new land by the accumulation of sand there. In these millions of years the sand has been compressed into the gigantic masses that tower above us to-day as sandstone mountains; they are formed of sand that was originally laid like mud, layer by layer, on the floor of the ocean.

It was all very plausible; it seemed to picture an eternal flow of things in which there was no room for God. The changes in the earth's surface were easily brought about without catastrophes, in the course of incalculable ages. God was excluded from geological discussions of the formation of hill and dale. And when it was fully realised, it brought the question of species to the front once more.

It was impossible to retreat simply to Linné's position. Lyell by no means denied Cuvier's various periods in the earth's development as such. He believed, moreover, that the plant and animal populations were different in these epochs. When the forests flourished which have formed the mass of our coal-measures there were no ichthyosauri; when the ichthyosauri came there were no longer any carboniferous forests; with the ichthyosauri there were no megatheria, and the last ichthyosaurus was extinct before the megatheria arrived. All that Lyell rejected was the great divine catastrophes. But when these were abandoned, it was no longer possible to attribute the "end" of the extinct species to a divine act. We were faced with the slow and natural conversion of terrestrial things in the course of endless ages.

Species must have been liable to be destroyed by purely natural causes. The catastrophes were abandoned, yet species *had* been destroyed. And when that was granted—it was the devil's little finger—a further conclusion was inevitable. If species have died out slowly and naturally in the history of the earth, and new species have made their appearance at the same time, may not these new species have *arisen* slowly and naturally? Suppose these simple and purely natural causes, that had brought about the extinction of certain species, had been for others the very starting-point of development? In one word: if the extinction

as not due to a mighty divine interference, was it
ot conceivable that the origin also may not have
eeded such?

One more deduction, and the demon of knowledge had hold of the entire hand. May not this natural extinction and natural new-birth have been directly connected in many cases? As a fact, some of the species had been wholly extirpated. But others had provided the living material of the new arrivals; they had been *transformed* into these apparently new species. That was the decisive deduction. It did away with the need of any sudden creation. It merely made a claim that was appalling to the Linnéan principles: namely, that species may change. In the course of time and at a favourable spot one species may be transformed into another.

Another fairly obvious deduction could be made. Who brought about the transformation? Lyell proved that, without any catastrophes, terrestrial things are constantly changing—the water and the land, the mountains and the valleys, and even the climate. In this gradual change the environments of living things were at length altered to such an extent that they were bound to cause a change in the organisms. However, different species reacted in different ways. Some gradually died out. Others adapted themselves to the new conditions; just as, in human affairs, one race breaks down under changed conditions while another rises to a higher and richer and new stage on that very account. No creation! Merely transformations of species, development of new forms from older ones by adaptation to new, naturally modified conditions. Even zoology and botany were without the finger of God from the earliest days.

Of course there was no trace of these latter deductions in Lyell. But they pressed themselves with an irresistible and decisive force on the mind of one of his first readers, Darwin.

He took Lyell's book with him to South America. Step by step the logic of it forced him to admit that this was what must have taken place somewhere. First the idea of "extinct species" became a concrete picture to him there, a sort of diabolic vision. The whole substratum of the pampas is one colossal tomb of strange monsters. The bones lie bare at every outcrop. Megatheria, or giant-sloths, as large as elephants, and with thigh-bones three times as thick as that of the elephant, able to break off branches in the primitive forests with their paws: armadilloes as big as rhinoceroses, with coats as hard as stone and curved like barrels; gigantic llamas, the macrouchenias, compared with which the modern specimens are Liliputians; mastodons and wild horses, of which America was entirely free even in the days of Columbus, and lion-like carnivores with terrible sabre-teeth. There they all are to-day—extinct, lost, buried in the deserted cemetery of the pampas-loam.

When the young Darwin stood by these groves, like Hamlet, he did not know how closely this ghost-world came to our own day. At that time the armour of the gigantic armadillo, the glyptodon, that had formed shelters over the heads of the human dwellers in the pampas, like Esquimaux huts, had not yet been discovered. The cave of Ultima Esperanza in Patagonia had not been searched, and no one had seen the red-haired coat of the sloth as large as an ox, the grypotherium (a relative of the real megatherium), cut by some prehistoric human hand, amongst a heap, several yards deep, of the animal's manure—in such peculiar circumstances as to prompt the suggestion that the giant-sloths had been kept tame in the cavern, as in a cyclopean stable, by prehistoric Indians. Darwin thought the remains were very old, though this by no means lessened the inspiration.

As our geological Hamlet speculated over these bones of extinct monsters, the ideas of Linné and Cuvier struggled fiercely in his mind with the new, heretical ideas inspired by Lyell. How was it that these ancient, extinct animal forms of America resembled in every detail and in the most marked characteristics certain living American animals? Before him were the relics of past sloths, armadilloes, and giant-llamas. In the actual America, also, there were sloths, armadilloes, and llamas, though with some difference. And nowhere else on earth, either in past or present time, were there sloths, armadilloes, and llamas. Cuvier had replied, God had pleased to create those ancient megatheria, glyptodons, and macrouchenias of America. Then, one day, he sent his destructive catastrophe, and swept them all away, as a sponge goes over the table. Then, in the empty land, he created afresh the sloths, armadilloes, and llamas of to-day. But why had God made the new animals so like the old that the modern zoologist has to class the megatherium in the same narrow group as the actual sloth, the ancient glyptodon with the modern armadillo, and so on?

Darwin, who had studied theology, was unshaken with regard to God himself. However, something occurred that occurs so often and with such good result in the history of thought. It appeared to him that the notion of a direct creation is by no means the simplest way of explaining things, but the most puzzling and complicated. Darwin believed in Lyell. There had been no destructive catastrophe at all to sweep away the megatherium and its companions. They had disappeared gradually, by natural means. Was it not much more rational to suppose that the actual sloths and armadilloes came into being gradually, by natural means? Part of the old animal population had not perished, but been transformed into the actual species. There was a bond of relationship between the past and the present. One or other grotesque and perhaps helpless giant form may have completely disappeared in the course of time. But the golden thread of life was never entirely broken. Other and more fortunate species had preserved the type of the sloth, the armadillo, and the llama; they had developed naturally into the living animals of America. God might remain at the groundwork of things. He had launched matter into space, and impressed natural laws on it. But these sufficed for the further work. They created America. They developed the mammal into the sloth and the armadillo in the days of the megatherium and the glyptodon. They maintained these types in the country, in a straight line of development; the progressive principle of life bringing about the extinction of certain forms, and transforming others by a more fitting adaptation to their environment.

Darwin always looked back on this first conflict of his ideas in presence of the dead shells and bones of the ancient pampas animals as an hour of awakening. It was the birth of his humanity in the higher sense. It is of interest to us because it coincides exactly with the date of Haeckel's birth in the ordinary sense.

In Darwin's fine account of his voyage, which is mostly arranged in the form of a diary, we find a passage written on the east coast of Patagonia on January 9, 1834, and the next on April 13th. In the meantime the ship had made a short zigzag course, which is spoken of in another connection. But the interval between the two dates is taken up with a passage on these gigantic animals, the reasons for their extinction and the striking fact of their bodily resemblance to the living animals of South America. "This remarkable resemblance," we read, " between the dead and the living animals of one and the same continent will yet, I doubt not, throw more light on the appearance of organic beings on the earth than any other class of facts." This is clearly a summary of Darwin's deepest thoughts at the time. Haeckel was born on February 16th of the same year, 1834. Thus the bodily birth of one of the two men whom we conceive to-day as Dioscuri coincides with the spiritual rebirth of the other. But it would be nearly thirty years before they would meet in spirit never to part again. At the very beginning of their acquaintance Darwin wrote a letter to Haeckel (October 8, 1864) in which he speaks of the earliest suggestions of his theory. The Hamlet-hour comes back vividly to his memory. "I shall never forget my astonishment when I dug out a gigantic piece of armour, like that of a living armadillo. As I reflected on these facts and compared others of a like nature, it seemed to me probable that closely related species may have descended from a common ancestor."

However we take it, Darwin then saw for the first time that his difficulty about the mutability of species was from the first, in his own mind, a difficulty about God. He began his doubts with the ancient armadillo; he ended with God.

On the return journey from South America, which amounted to a circumnavigation of the globe, the struggle was renewed at the Galapagos islands. Volcanic forces had raised these islands from the bed of the ocean in comparatively recent times. They were, therefore, bound to be a virgin province at the time. Now, however, the walls of the crater were clothed with vegetation, birds flew after insects, and gigantic turtles and lizards lived on the shores. Whence did these plants and animals come? Darwin examines them. They have an unusual appearance, and seem to point to America. Yet not a single species is now wholly American; each has its peculiarities. An historical controversy arises over the islands, and men range themselves in parties once more. Empty islands emerge from the blue waters. How are they to be populated? There are two possibilities. One is that God has created the animals and plants—Galapagos animals and plants. But in that case why has he created them entirely on the American model, while diverging from it in small details? The second possibility is that the animals and plants were brought by the current or the wind from the neighbouring American coast; they are American plants and animals. After landing on the islands, they adapted themselves to their new surroundings, and were altered. Hence both the resemblance and the difference. The theory assumes, of course, that species are mutable. If that is so, we can explain everything—without God.

But the greatest and tensest struggle began when Darwin returned home. He approached the most audacious, but most striking fact, for his purpose. Up to this the question had been whether new species were produced by God or by natural necessity. Now a third element was introduced, man himself. He also alters species, as a breeder of pigeons, rabbits, sheep. He has done it with success for ages—only the Linnés and Cuviers had not noticed the fact. How does he accomplish it?

A breeder desires to give his sheep finer wool. He examines the wool of a thousand sheep. The difference between them is so slight that it is of no practical consequence. But the farmer selects the male sheep out of the thousand that has the best quality of wool, and the corresponding female. He crosses the two. Their young have wool of a slightly improved quality, and he picks out the best amongst them once more for crossing. He continues this through several generations. At last, with his continuous selection and crossing, the quality of the wool increases so much that any one can recognise it at once, and it has a distinct cultural value. In this way improved races of animals and large numbers of fine flowers have been produced by breeders: by artificial selection of the fittest to reproduce in each generation. This was done by man—not by God, not by nature in remote times, but under our very eyes, by man.

Now for an analogous process without man. Let our sheep live wild in any country. No human breeder has any interest in them: God does not seem to interfere with them. They live on and on, for thousands of years, generation after generation. Here again, in the wild state, we find the same slight variations in the quality of the wool. One sheep has a thicker coat than another. For thousands of years the fact is without significance. Then occurs a slow change of the environment. The climate becomes colder. Perhaps an ice-age sets in, such as our earth seems to have passed through many times. There are two alternatives. A very hard winter may set in at once and all the sheep perish, because their woolly coat is too thin in all cases. That would mean the extinction of a whole species. But the severe cold may come on gradually. The winters are more trying. So many sheep perish in the first winters; but so many others survive. Which will survive? Naturally, those that happened to have the thicker coats. Those alone live on to the spring, and reproduce. The following year the coat is thicker all round, as the lambs all came from relatively thick-coated parents. The winter decimates them again, and the thickest coated survive once more, and so on. The pressure of external conditions, the "struggle for life," selects just as man does. Only the best adapted individuals survive and reproduce.

The whole earth is a vast field of splendid adaptations. The tree-frogs are green because only green frogs are preserved; all the others are destroyed. The arctic hare is white on the snow, the desert-fox yellow. For a thousand reasons in the course of the earth's development these backgrounds—white, yellow, green; snow, desert, forest, &c.—have themselves been constantly changing under the action of Lyell's changes in the crust of the earth. Hence constantly fresh adaptations, with a certain percentage of complete extinctions. In these ceaseless new adaptations we see a picture of an eternal progressive development. Always a finer selection: always better material: natural things always selecting and being selected. Man is superfluous in this world-old, eternal process. And God, too, is superfluous.

That was Darwin's last and decisive thought. Divine action was excluded from the whole province of animal and plant species. It does not matter whether or no the shrewd idea of natural selection solves the whole problem. Why speak of "whole," when all problems are really unfathomable? He left open the question of the origin of the first slight variations, the first increase in the fineness or thickness of the sheep's wool, for instance. He left open the question of the inner nature of the process—and a good deal more. But these things did not affect the great issue.

What Darwin did was to show for the first time how we might conceive the natural evolution of species; to suggest that the miracle of the purposive adaptation of organisms to their environment could be explained by purely natural causes without introducing teleological and supernatural agencies to bring the disharmony into harmony. The older mind and logic had seen the action of God everywhere; the new thought and logic were gradually restricting his sphere. Darwin took away a whole province from the teleologist when he merely set up the idea of selection. He towered above himself in that moment. Natural philosophy wrested zoology and botany from the hands of Linné and Cuvier. It destroyed the old idea of a design in the interest of natural law and the general unity of nature. "Allah need create no more." We cannot emphasise it too much: it was the conceivability that settled the question. Darwin had shown that "it might have been so," and this possibility stood for the first time in zoology and botany opposed, with all the weight of logic, to the other theory, which was no more understood, but was supplied by imagination to fill a gap—the idea of a special creation of each animal species, the idea that the green tree-frog, had been created amongst the foliage just as he was. The feebler fancy gave way to the better. In this concession lay whole sciences that would have to be entirely transformed on the strength of Darwin's achievement.

Narrow-minded folk have tried to make light of the mere "possibility," creating a distinction between truth and logical theory. As if all truth were not solely in the human mind! What an age can conceive is true to that age. There is nothing higher in the bounds of time and the development in which we are involved. All truth and science began for humanity in the form of possibilities. Copernicus's theory was only a possibility when it first came. All that we call human culture has come of the putting together of thousands upon thousands of these possibilities, like so many stones. It is no use raising up against it the figment of "absolute truth." The main point was that Darwin raised the conceivability of a natural origin of species by the modification of older forms, which were driven ceaselessly to new adaptations under the stress of the struggle for life, to such a pitch that the older possibility of a creation of each species and its deliberate adaptation by supernatural action sank lower and lower. It was a pure conflict of ideas; the greater overcame the smaller—*now* smaller.

Darwin's work, the *Origin of Species*, was published on November 24, 1859, after twenty-five years of study. He kept the theory of selection to himself for more than twenty years. The whole of the young generation from the beginning of the thirties, to which Haeckel belonged, grew up without any suspicion of it. Apart from the constant ill-health that hindered his work, Darwin was tortured with anxiety lest he should be treated as an imaginative *dilettante* with his heretical ideas. In the scientific circles of the middle of the century one was apt to be disdainfully put down as a windy "natural philosopher" if one spoke of "the evolution of animal and plant species" and the like. The word had become the scarecrow of the exact, professional scientific workers; much as when commercial men exclaim, "Dear me, the man's a poet." Hence Darwin wanted to provide a most solid foundation of research for his work, and then to smuggle it into the house like a goblin in a jar.

He took his task so seriously that, as Lyell afterwards wrote to him, he might have worked on until his hundredth year without ever being ready in the sense he wished. Chance had to intervene, and bring forward one of the younger men, who almost robbed him of the title of discoverer. Wallace arrived independently at the idea of selection, and he was within a hair's breadth of being the first to publish it. The aged scholar at Down had to come forward. Then the great book was published, and Wallace disappeared in its shadow.

In Darwin's opinion it was only a preliminary extract, and he added many supplementary volumes as time went on. As a fact it was so severely elaborated that even the thoughtful layman, possibly with a sympathy for the idea, was almost, if not wholly, unable to digest the proofs. It had to be "translated" for the majority of Darwin's educated countrymen. On the other hand, this mass of facts was partly strange and new to the professional biologists. What did so many of the museum-zoologists know, for instance, of the results and problems of the practical breeder? "That belongs to the province of my colleague who teaches agriculture, not to mine." His proofs were taken indiscriminately from zoology, botany, and geology. But at that time it was woe to the man that mixed up the various branches of research. The professor of zoology could not control the botanical material, and *vice versâ*. There was, in addition, the general dislike of the natural-philosophical nucleus. It was impossible to suppose that this very individual book, transgressing every rule, should at once meet with wide encouragement, or even ordinary appreciation.

In England Darwin's repute as a traveller and geologist, and the personal respect felt for him, had some effect. Then came a small circle of friends, Hooker, Huxley, even, to some extent, the aged Lyell, who had seen the manuscript before publication, and had at once started a more or less brisk propaganda. In the first six months three editions of the work were sold, so that it was read by a few thousand men. As a rule there was at that time less dread of "natural philosophy" in England than elsewhere. But pious minds were alarmed at the "struggle against God" that was based on the exact data of zoology, botany, and geology.

Darwin had made that the salient point, as a glance at the work shows, since he closes with a reference to the Deity. He said it was a "grand" view of the Creator to suppose that he had created only the first forms of life on the earth, and then left it to natural laws to develop these germs into the various species of animals and plants. It was prudent to restrict the theistic conflict. God was merely excluded from the origin of species. Natural selection did not apply to the further problem of the origin of the primitive life-forms and of life itself. Theism could retain them. There was something soothing psychologically in the phrase, which was often attacked subsequently, and did not represent Darwin's later views. It was characteristic of Darwin's gentle disposition.

He did not start out from the position that God

does not exist, and that we must, at all costs, seek natural causes for the origin of things. He had not abandoned the idea of the clerical profession because he had lost belief in God, but because he had more attraction for catching butterflies and shooting birds. Still a firm theist, he had been convinced, as a candid geologist, by Lyell's demonstration that God had had nothing to do with the moulding of hill and valley or the distribution of land and water. As a candid zoologist and botanist he had then convinced himself that the analogous changes in the animal and plant worlds had needed no divine intervention.

As yet, however, he saw no reason to draw more radical conclusions. He sought, as far as honour permitted, a certain peace of thought by asking whether this indirect action of the personal Ruler over such vast provinces did not enhance the idea of him instead of detracting from it.

Goethe would have been prepared, on his principles, to recognise the step taken in the direction of natural law as a victory for our increasing knowledge of and reverence for the Deity. For him a natural law was the will of God; if natural selection created species, he would have seen merely the will of God in selection. But Darwin had not yet advanced so far, and still less could this be expected in his pious readers.

However, we find a curious confession a few paragraphs before the theistic conclusion of the book. It runs: "Light will be thrown on the origin and history of humanity." Light, that is to say, from the theory of the transformation of species by natural selection. The words contained the promise of a new twilight of the gods. In the innocent days, when the Creator stood in person behind each species of animal and plant, Linné had seen no great innovation in his defining man as a definite species, the highest species of mammal. God had created the polar bear and the hippopotamus, *Genesis* said, as well as man. That man had transgressed the command in Paradise, fallen into sin, needed salvation, and so on, was another matter altogether. With Darwin the innovation was incalculably important.

On his theory the various species of animals had been developed from each other, without a new creative act. If man was an animal species in this sense, he also must have originated from other animals; and that would be bitter. The phrase shows that Darwin already saw clearly, and had abandoned his belief in a special creation of man. But this point was bound to make more bad blood than all the rest put together. God, now restricted to the direct production of the first living things, had lost man as well as the animals. Moreover, whatever interpretation was put upon the Mosaic narrative, the very source of theistic belief, the Bible, was called into question. How had we come to know of this story of divine creations? By the Bible, the vehicle of revelation. But this Bible was the work of man, and man was now well within the bounds of nature, from which

God had been excluded. How could he learn anything from revelation? The biblical writers had clearly only made conjectures. Some of them—with regard to Adam, for instance—were certainly incorrect. There was nothing in the Bible about evolution by means of selection. Indeed, was not the whole picture of a creating Deity an error? These thoughts were bound to press upon the religious mind with all their logical force. When they did so, the very foundations of theology became insecure, to a far more serious extent than Darwin's moderate conclusion suggested. When the book fell on this contentious ground, it was bound, even if it were only read in the last two pages, to provoke vast waves of hostility against its heretical zoology and botany, especially in England.

.   .   .   .   .

Haeckel was in Italy when the work—the work of *his* life, too, as the sequel shows—was published. We have seen where he was: in sight of the blue sea, penetrating for the first time into a special section of zoology, the radiolaria, and making it his own. He was far from theorising, for the first years of reality were upon him. He returned to Berlin at the beginning of May, 1860, bringing his study of the radiolaria, and resolved to publish it in comprehensive form. Here he learned for the first time that a "mad" work by Darwin had appeared, that denied the venerable Linnéan dogma of the immutability of species.

German official science was now invaded from

two sides at once. Haeckel had returned like a new man from the freshness of Italy; and Darwin's work, translated by Bronn, was bringing some slight extract of the English student's thoughts, like a draught of old golden wine. They were bound to meet this time.

The aged Bronn, a German naturalist of distinction and merit, had found the *Origin of Species* interesting enough, at least, to deserve the trouble of translation. But his interest in it was very restricted. He was one of the thoughtful students of the days following Cuvier, and was not of the kind to pin his faith to one man. The appearance of the plant and animal species in the various terrestrial periods, so sharply separated by Cuvier himself, showed unmistakably an ascent from lower to higher forms. The fish is placed lower in the system than the mammal. At a certain period there were fishes living, but no mammals as yet. At another period the only plants on the earth were of the decidedly lower group of the cryptogams (ferns, shore-grasses, club-mosses), and these were succeeded by pines and palm-ferns, and finally by the true palms and foliage-trees. Cuvier's theory of creation had to take account of this. Agassiz, who held firmly to the fresh creation of species in each new epoch, conceived the Creator as an artist who improved in his work in the course of time. Each new achievement was better than the preceding. It was rather a curious idea of the Creator!

Others, who did not venture to use the idea of

PHOTOGRAPH OF MARBLE BUST BY G. HEROLD.

To face p. 128.

Deity quite so naïvely as Agassiz in zoology and botany, conceived a "law of development" within life itself. It was a time when belief in a "vital force" was universal. Living things had their peculiar force, which was not found in lifeless things. The life-principle might be at work in the law of development. It would raise living things higher and higher in the succeeding geological epochs. It was a vague theory, though it purported to cover not only the fact but the machinery of development. In the course of ages it brought about the appearance of new species. Those who held this idea of an immanent law of evolution rejected the older notion of a personal Deity, putting in an appearance suddenly at the beginning of the secondary period and creating the ichthyosauri "out of nothing." They looked upon Cuvier's catastrophes, to which Agassiz still clung, with a touch of Lyell's scepticism. The "law of evolution" had been the *deus ex machina* of the long procession of life-forms. One day a fish ceased to give birth to little fishes in the manner of its parents. The "law of evolution" was at work in its ova, and suddenly little ichthyosauri were developed from them. Thus, again, a lizard was believed to have engendered young mammals one day. One student would hold that the transition was quite abrupt in this sense. Another would think it more gradual, and approach the idea of a slow transformation of a fish into a lizard, and a lizard into a mammal, or a tree-fern into a palm-fern, and this into a true palm. At the bottom they were all agreed that the whole inner law of evolution had nothing whatever in common with the other laws of nature and was not subordinate to them. They did not hold an evolution in harmony with the great mechanism of natural laws. Their principle got astride of natural laws at certain points, like a little man, and turned them in this or that direction.

Very little philosophic reflection was needed to show that they had merely replaced the Creator with a word. The older Dualism remained. On one side was the raw material of the world with the ordinary natural laws; on the other side a lord and master, the law of evolution, playing with the laws as it pleased, and moulding the material into new life-forms in an advancing series. It is true that they no longer pictured to themselves a venerable being with a white beard creating the ichthyosauri, but the finger of God remained in the law of evolution, attenuated into a special and spectral form. The God that acted from without was banished, but the "impulse from within," reduced to a mere skeleton in substance, was put upon the throne.

The advocates of the law of evolution had assuredly done much in preparing the way for Darwin, as they had insisted that certain advances in detail were undeniable and built up theories from the chaotic material provided by special research—especially seeing that some of the ablest naturalists of the time were amongst them, who determined to retain speculation in zoology and botany. But,

on the other hand, it cannot be questioned that
the confused nature of their fundamental idea,
which, in fact, was not far removed from the theological notion of the vital force, gave the rigid and
"exact" academic workers an apparent right to
reject *all* speculation on the possibility of an evolution of species as an unscientific dream. The aged
Bronn was in 1860 one of the most prudent and
sober of the advocates of the inner principle of
evolution. He candidly acknowledged that Darwin
had struck a severe blow at the great idea of his
life, on one side at least. Darwin's work not
merely dismissed God to the wings as a personality,
but even left no room for the finger of God, for his
spiritual writing on the walls of the living world.
It found evidence of natural laws alone. From
them came, if not life itself, at all events selection, adaptation, and evolution by virtue of this
increasing adaptation—the higher advance that
converted the fish into a lizard and the lizard into
a mammal. The fine old worker, with an age of
indefatigable labour behind him, though he had
not got beyond the idea of a "law of evolution,"
looked on Darwin with a mixture of fear and
admiration as he cut into the very heart of these
problems. He added amiable notes to the work
to the effect that one would like to go so far, but
the distance was intimidating. In fact, he omitted
altogether from his translation the very important
phrase that "light would be thrown on the origin
of man." It would be a terrible affair, he thought,
if the discussion were at once turned on this.

Man himself owing his origin neither to God nor the finger of God, but to natural selection in the ordinary course of natural laws! It was not to be thought of. Hence the phrase was struck out, as quite too extravagant, in his otherwise admirable work.

Bronn had himself become something of a revolutionary amongst his colleagues by the translation. The rigidly "exact" workers crossed themselves before the Germanised work. Most of the "evolutionists" in the older sense had by no means the *bonhomie* to speak even of a "possibility" like the patriarch Bronn. From the first Darwin was — Haeckel was the first to experience it — branded with the anathemas of the two opposite schools of science in Germany. On the one hand the rigorous and exact workers declared that his teaching was pure metaphysics, because it sought to prove evolution and contemplated vast ideal connections. On the other hand the Dualist metaphysicians denounced him as an empiric of the worst character, who sought to replace the great ideal elements in the world by a few miserable natural necessities. It is significant to find that Schopenhauer, the brilliant thinker, regarded the *Origin of Species* as one of the empirical soapsud or barber books produced by exact investigation, which he thoroughly despised from his metaphysical point of view. And there were already (there are more to-day) whole schools of zoology and botany that looked upon Darwin's theoretical explanations as unscientific " mysticism," " metaphysics," and " philosophy in the worst sense of the word."

Haeckel read the dangerous book at Berlin in May, 1860. "It profoundly moved me," he writes to me, "at the first reading. But as *all* the Berlin magnates (with the single exception of Alexander Braun) were against it, I could make no headway in my defence of it. I did not breathe freely until I visited Gegenbaur at Jena (June, 1860); my long conversations with him finally confirmed my conviction of the truth of Darwinism or transformism."

It was, therefore, in the critical days immediately before or during the negotiations with Gegenbaur which led to his setting up as a private teacher at Jena. The names of Darwin and Jena unite chronologically in Haeckel's life—two great names that were to bear him into the very depths of his career, and that have their roots in the same hour.

We may ask what it was in the book that "profoundly moved" the young student of the radiolaria. The name of Braun only partly explains the matter, as Braun was an evolutionist of the same type as Bronn. He was amiably disposed to meet it, but did not openly enter on the new path. We must go deeper. We then understand it clearly enough, if we recollect Haeckel's bent in the last few years.

He had no longer any scruples with regard to religion. The God of tradition had been entirely replaced in him by Goethe's God, who did not stand outside of, but was one with, nature. "There is nothing within, nothing without: for what is within is without." There was not a kernel, God, and a shell, Nature. "Nature has neither kernel nor shell: it is both together."

The years spent in southern Italy had certainly helped to bring out as strongly as possible the contrast between Goethe's conception and the conventional idea of God as an extramundane Creator. No surroundings are more apt to do this than the Romance peoples of the Mediterranean. In the northern, Protestant countries the ecclesiastical tradition of Deity has always a spiritual element, a kind of vague resolution into moral laws, that in some measure approach natural law, though one made by man. There is no trace of this in Naples and Sicily. The supernatural there is the saint, the madonna; they penetrate unceasingly into the natural reality, in every little detail of life and conduct. The antithesis of the poor cosmic machinery and the ever-present heavenly help and supersession of it is raised to a supreme height in the popular belief. Miracles are not relegated to earlier days and ancient books. They are expected, affirmed, and believed every day. The saint fills the net of the fisherman as he chases the edible cuttle-fishes by torchlight. The saint makes the storm that threatens the boat—makes it suddenly out of nothing. The madonna can arrest in a second the glowing stream of lava that rolls towards the village from Vesuvius, and if hundreds of them unite in ardent prayer and the making of vows, she will be appeased and do it. Every hair on a man's head is twofold; there is the natural hair and a hair that can at any moment be changed, transformed, annihilated, or created afresh from nothing, by divine power. The man who has lived in this atmosphere of practical Dualism for years must be saturated to his innermost being with a feeling of the absolute contradiction between this conception of God and nature and Goethe's philosophy. If he is to follow Goethe, this ancient extramundane, ever-interfering Deity must be given up without the least attempt at compromise.

Thus Haeckel's position was incomparably more radical than Darwin's from the very first. He no longer believed in a Creator, either in whole or part.

He asked himself, therefore, how he could now explain certain things in nature. He had learned from the great Johannes Müller that species were unchangeable, and it was impossible to conceive the spontaneous generation of the living from the dead. The essence, the predominant element of the living thing was the mysterious, purposive "vital force." The first of these three ideas of the master's to be surrendered entirely by him was the vital force. Even in Müller's lifetime, and in his own laboratory, so to say, his pupil, Du Bois-Reymond, made the first great breach in the doctrine with his famous study of animal electricity, a really pioneer piece of work, especially as regards method, at that time. It was now more than ever probable that there was no more a special vital force besides the simple natural forces than there was a God distinct from nature. The animal or the plant was a wonderful outcome of the same laws that had built the crystal or the globe. The sharp distinction between living and dead matter fell into the waste-basket, where so many other Dualistic tags lay, cut off by the shears of science.

But if one of Müller's theses was abandoned, another was retained as a real blessing with all the more tenacity by his pupils—the thesis that even the scientific investigator shall always "think"— nay, even "philosophise." Müller called it "using one's imagination," in his desire to emphasise it. Now it was certainly a fair philosophic deduction from Du Bois-Reymond's discoveries that one ought no longer to be so rigid as regards the possibility of spontaneous generation. If the same natural forces are at work in the organic and the inorganic, the living and the dead, it is no longer inconceivable theoretically that life and inorganic matter only differ in degree, not in kind. The distinction might become so slender—either now, or at least in past times—that an apparent "spontaneous generation" might really take place.

Here again, it is plain, Haeckel had a greater freedom than Darwin. Working gradually from above, Darwin desisted when he came to spontaneous generation, and left room for God. Haeckel came into an open field, believing that there was no eternal Deity and that spontaneous generation itself was by no means a forbidding conception. The problem for him was merely, how he could work upward through the plants and animals of all geological periods until he reached man. He was bound to seek to dispense even here with the historical vital force, and explain everything by the great natural laws of the cosmos.

It was in this frame of mind that he received Darwin's book. Can it be in the least surprising that it "profoundly moved" him. It opened out to him the whole way, just as he desired it. Müller's third thesis, the immutability of species, broke down. But what did it matter? It was now possible for the first time to construct a philosophical zoology and botany in Müller's sense, without any vital force and without God.

At the same time this rapid and impulsive acceptance of Darwin's theory was not merely a decisive moment in Haeckel's intellectual development; it was bound to be, even externally, a most important step in his career. The theistic controversy was forced on his attention. It passed out of the province of his inmost life, that had hitherto only been discussed in conversation with intimate friends, into the professional work of his most serious and public occupation—into zoology, into the radiolaria at which he had been working for years.

We must realise clearly what it must have meant at that time for a young zoologist, who wanted to do rigorous professional work and had quickly decided to settle at Jena in order to begin his career as an official teacher, to become "a Darwinian" in conviction and open confession. It might cost him both his official position and his scientific future; and this at the very moment when he had just secured them, or was in a better position to secure them. We have here for the first time the open manifestation of a principle in Haeckel's life that he had hitherto only used inwardly, in application to himself. The truth must be told, whatever it cost. Shoot me dead, morally, materially, or bodily, as you will: but you will have to shoot the law first.

Darwin's ominous book had been available in Bronn's translation for two years. The German professional zoologists, botanists, and geologists almost all regarded it as absolute nonsense. Agassiz, Giebel, Keferstein, and so many others, laughed until they were red in the face, like a riotous first-night public that has made up its mind as to the absurdity of the play from the first act, and torment the author as the cat torments a mouse. Then Haeckel gave to the world his long-prepared *Monograph on the Radiolaria* (1862), the work with which he endeavours to establish—in fact, must establish—his position as an exact investigator, even amongst the academic scholars of the opposite camp. All goes very smoothly for many pages of the work. A few traces of heresy may be detected about page 100. The passage deals with the relation of organ to individual, in connection with the social species of radiolaria that live in communities. It is a subject that Haeckel took up with great vigour later on, as we shall see. Here it affords him an opportunity to say a word about the general fusion of things in the world of life, in opposition to our rigid divisions in classification. Organ and individual pass into each other without any fixed limit. That, he says, is only a repetition of the relation of the plant to the animal. We cannot establish any fixed limitations between them. What we set up as such are only man's abstractions. In nature itself we never find these subjective abstract ideas of limitation "incorporated purely, but always fading away in gradual transitions; here, again, the scale of organisation rises gradually from the simplest to the most complex, in a continuous development." However, these are words that might have been written by Schleiden or Unger or Bronn before Darwin's time.

Yet there is something in the work that would have been a jet of ice-cold water to the Agassizs and Giebels. This brilliant new "Extraordinary Professor of Zoology and Director of the Zoological Museum at Jena University," as it says on the title-page, accepts Darwin in a certain unambiguous passage late in the text.

It is necessary to bring to light once more this passage, buried in a work that is not easily accessible, an expensive technical work separated from us by four decades now. It is worth doing so, not only on account of the courage it displayed at the time, but also as a document relating to the great controversy of the nineteenth century. It is found on pages 231 and 232, partly in the text, but for the most part in a note. Immediately after giving the table of classification Haeckel goes on to say: " I cannot leave this general account of the relationship of the various families of the radiolaria without drawing special attention to the numerous transitional forms that most intimately connect the different groups and make it difficult to separate them in classification, to some extent." It is interesting to note that in spite of our very defective knowledge of the radiolaria it is nevertheless possible to arrange "a fairly continuous chain of related forms." He would like to draw particular attention to this, because " the great theories that Charles Darwin has lately put forward, in his *Origin of Species in the Plant and Animal World by Natural Selection, or The Preservation of the Improved Races in the Struggle for Life*, and which have opened out a new epoch for systematic biology, have given such importance to the question of the affinities of organisms and to proofs of continuous concatenation that even the smallest contribution towards the further solution of these problems must be welcome." He then endeavours in the text, without any more theoretical observations, practically to construct a "genealogical tree of the radiolaria," the first of a large number of such trees in the future. He takes as the primitive radiolarian a simple trellis-worked globule with centrifugal radiating needles, embodied in the *Heliosphæra*. "At the same time," he says, characteristically, "this does not imply in the least that all the radiolaria must have descended from this primitive form; I merely show that, as a matter of fact, all these very varied forms may be derived from such a common fundamental type." In other words, once more, it is *conceivable*—a golden word even long afterwards. The first "genealogical tree," a "table of the related families, sub-families, and genera of the radiolaria," arranged in order from the higher forms down, and connected with lines and brackets, comes next. The text deals thoroughly with the possibility of descent. This closes the first and general part of the monograph. But there is a long note at this point in the text, where Darwin's title is cited, that gives us his first appreciation of Darwin in detail. It begins: "I cannot refrain from expressing here the great admiration with which Darwin's able theory of the origin of species has inspired me. Especially as this epoch-making work has for the most part been unfavourably received by our German professors of science, and seems in some cases to have been entirely misunderstood. Darwin himself desires his theory to be submitted to every possible test, and 'looks confidently to the young workers who will be prepared to examine both sides of the question impartially. Whoever leans to the view that species are changeable will do a service to science by a conscientious statement of his conviction;

only in that way can we get rid of the mountain of prejudice that at present covers the subject.' I share this view entirely," Haeckel continues, " and on that account feel that I must express here my belief in the mutability of species and the real genealogical relation of all organisms. Although I hesitate to accept Darwin's views and hypotheses to the full and to endorse the whole of his argument, I cannot but admire the earnest, scientific attempt made in his work to explain all the phenomena of organic nature on broad and consistent principles and to substitute an intelligible natural law for unintelligible miracles. There may be more error than truth in Darwin's theory in its present form, as the first attempt to deal with the subject. Undeniably important as are the principles of natural selection, the struggle for life, the relation of organisms to each other, the divergence of characters, and all the other principles employed by Darwin in support of his theory, it is, nevertheless, quite possible that there are just as many and important principles still quite unknown to us that have an equal or even greater influence on the phenomena of organic nature. This is the first great attempt to construct a scientific, physiological theory of the development of organic life and to prove that the physiological laws and the chemical and physical forces that rule in nature to-day must also have been at work in the world of yesterday." Haeckel then refers to Bronn, the translator of the book. With Bronn he calls Darwin's theory the fertilised egg from which the truth will gradually develop; the pupa from which the long-sought natural law will emerge. And he concludes: "The chief defect of the Darwinian theory is that it throws no light on the origin of the primitive organism—probably a simple cell—from which all the others have descended. When Darwin assumes a special creative act for this first species, he is not consistent and, I think, not quite sincere. However, apart from these and other defects, Darwin's theory has the undying merit of bringing sense and reason into the whole subject of the relations of living things. When we remember how every great reform, every important advance, meets with a resistance in proportion to the depth of the prejudices and dogmas it assails, we shall not be surprised that Darwin's able theory has as yet met with little but hostility instead of its well-merited appreciation and test." There is yet no question of man and his origin. But what he says is very bold for the time; and before a year is out we shall find him drawing the most dangerous conclusion of all. And it is found, not in a late page and note in a stout technical volume, but in the pitiless glare of the sunlight, in the most prominent position that could then be given to it in German scientific culture.

CHAPTER V

THE SCIENTIFIC CONGRESS OF 1863

IN the second decade of the nineteenth century, Oken had inspired the formation of large public gatherings of German naturalists and physicians. Oken was one of the advanced thinkers who felt that all technical science was in the end only preparatory to the great work of educating the people. In his opinion the naturalist, even if he spent his whole life in investigating the filaments of plants or the limbs of insects, was a pioneer of culture. In any case these gatherings were a very good practical move at the time. In a time of terrible reaction on all sides a feeling came at last even to the recluse of science that, besides the technical value of his work, it ought to do something towards lifting his fellows out of the rut they were falling into. They felt that if all ideals were going to be lost, the ultimate aim of special research would perish with them. Oken took up a position of democratic opposition. He was soon joined by Alexander von Humboldt, who, with the same feeling at heart, gave the work a certain polish of scientific and impartial dignity. There are features of his work that amuse us to-day, but those were evil days, and every particle of goodwill had to be appreciated. However, there was a serious difficulty.

The bolder elements met in congresses, and encouraged each other in the pursuit of their ideal. But it at once became clear in their public discussions that some of their purely scientific discoveries were dangerous and heretical in such a period of reaction. This or that had hitherto been buried innocently in scientific monographs, quite unknown to the crowd, and the author might be a royal councillor, receive decorations, and almost be an elder of the Church. Suddenly, by means of these assemblies, the sinfulness of all this lore about snails or insects or vertebrates was brought to light and put before the profane public, and there was much anger. The whole of scientific research was full of secret plots, heresies, and bombs—against God.

There was a most appalling illustration of this in the Scientific Congress, held in September, 1863. Nothing is more amusing to-day than to run through the yellow and almost unknown papers of the Congress. They are illuminating to some extent. An idea that belongs to humanity is openly brought into the debate for the first time. Ages lie behind this hour. We must grant all that savours of human comedy, of triviality even, in such an assembly, but after all we must see in it the swell and clash of great waves. Haeckel spoke for the first time on Darwin's theory, at a spot from which the waves were bound to spread through the whole scientific culture of the land. Virchow, afterwards his bitter opponent, supported him. All the deepest questions and consequences of Darwinism were mooted with the first vibrant accents. It was a great and unforgettable hour.

The first speaker at the Congress on the Sunday evening, September 19, 1863, was Haeckel. We must remember the charm that attached to his person even outwardly, the direct charm that did not need any allusion to his growing repute in zoology. It was the charm that had been felt by the simple folk of uncultured Italy, who had never heard even the name of the science. Darwin was never a handsome man from the æsthetic point of view. When he wanted to sail with Fitz-Roy, it was a very near question whether the splenetic captain would not reject him because he did not like his nose. His forehead had so striking a curve that Lombroso, the expert, could put him down as having "the idiot-physiognomy" in his *Genius and Insanity*. At the time when he wrote the *Origin of Species* he had not the patriarchal beard that is inseparable from his image in our minds; he was bald, and his chin clean shaved. The prematurely bent form of the invalid could never have had much effect in such a place, no matter what respect was felt for him. Haeckel, young and handsome, was an embodiment of the *mens sana in corpore sano*. He rose above the grey heads of science, as the type of the young, fresh, brilliant generation. It was an opponent at this Congress, who sharply attacked the new ideas, that spoke of the "colleague in the freshness of youth" who had brought forward the subject. He brought with him the highest thing that a new idea can associate with: the breath of a new generation, of a youth that greets all new ideas with a smiling courage. Behind this was the thought of Darwin himself, a wave that swept away all dams.

The speech was as clear as crystal, and is still useful as an introduction to the Darwinian question. He at once strikes the greatest and the dominant note. Darwin means a new philosophy. All organisms descend from a few primitive forms, possibly from one; and man is one of these organisms. What Darwin had merely hinted in his concluding passage, what the aged Bronn had excluded altogether from his translation as too dangerous, was now set forth emphatically in the very beginning of his speech. "As regards man himself, if we are consistent we must recognise his immediate ancestors in ape-like mammals; earlier still in kangaroo-like marsupials; beyond these, in the secondary period, in lizard-like reptiles; and finally, at a yet earlier stage, the primary period, in lowly organised fishes."

There is something monumental in this passage, as in the previous confession of Darwinism in the *Monograph on the Radiolaria*. Others may have come to similar conclusions at the time on reading Darwin's work. Here we have the profession made at the psychological moment, a trumpet-blast that sent its thrilling alarm from the threshold of a new age, for friend or foe to hear. The speech gives a slightly exaggerated account of the struggle that already existed. All was in confusion. Science was breaking up into two camps. On the one side evolution and progress, on the other the creation and immutability of species. Already there are distinguished leaders of science in favour of evolution. It is time to discuss the matter in full publicity—and the thing is done.

There was, let me say parenthetically, on the Continent at least no question at that time of this clear division, or even of a serious agitation. It was partly this speech, together with Haeckel's next work, that was to bring it about. To the highest authorities the subject seemed to be below the level of discussion. We must recall a passage that the Professor of Zoology at Göttingen, Keferstein, had written a year before in the *Göttinger Gelehrte Anzeiger*. "It gives great satisfaction to the earnest scientific worker," we read, "to see a man like Agassiz, with an authority based on the finest zoological works, reject unreservedly a theory [Darwin's] that would discredit the whole work of classifiers for a century, and to see that the views built up by several generations and the general consent of humanity hold a stronger position than the views of a single individual, however eloquently they may be stated." There is no idea in this of two regular camps of scientists. Humanity is adduced as the one party; against it stands the anarchist, trying to blow up the work of centuries, Darwin. But that gave no concern to the young orator; he saw a whole decade of success in the first attack.

He rolled off geology. Cuvier's theory of catastrophes, Linné's belief in the immutability of species—all a purely theological cosmogony. The "philosophical theory of evolution" rises behind it like a Mene Tekel Pharshim.

All living things, including those of past geological epochs, form one great *genealogical tree*. The word, the new leading word for zoology and botany, comes out with a flash. What is the system that has been awaited so long? It is the genealogical tree of life on our planet. Its roots lie deep in the remote past. "The thousands of green leaves on the tree that clothe the younger and fresher twigs, and differ in their height and breadth from the trunk, correspond to the living species of animals and plants; these are the more advanced, the further they are removed from the primeval stem. The withered and faded leaves, that we see on the older and dead twigs, represent the many extinct species that dwelt on the earth in earlier geological ages, and come closer to the primeval simple stem-form, the more remote they are from us."

This was the great new idea for science to work upon. Paleontology, the science of past life, found at last a common task with botany and zoology. Haeckel's own programme for decades was unfolded. This phrase, too, was a birth-hour. In all the struggle that has followed as to the "how" of evolution this figure of the tree with the verdant branches as the new field of zoological and botanical work, and the withered branches for the paleontologist, has never been abandoned. A symbol from the living world itself, the branching tree, had at last taken a decisive place in the science and the classification of living things. With splendid clearness the speech then enumerates the Darwinian principles: variation, heredity, the struggle for life, selection, and adaptation. A vast duration is claimed for the geological epochs in the sense of Lyell; and it is pointed out that there is a progressive advance of forms throughout these periods. Special stress is laid on the ever-advancing, ever-uplifting element in evolution. Man is again introduced into the subject. He has "evolved" from the brutality of the animal. Language itself has been naturally "developed." (What a shrewd perspective in such a brief phrase! How the philologists would stare!) So the "law of advance" traverses the whole field of culture. A fiery passage follows: "Reaction in political, social, moral, and scientific life, such as the selfish efforts of priests and despots have brought about at every period of history," cannot permanently hinder this advance. The "advance" is "a law of nature," and "neither the weapons of the tyrant nor the anathemas of the priest can ever suppress it." We hear again the older Sethe thundering his intrepid reply: "You will have to shoot the law first."

At the close he glances briefly at the difficulties the theory presents. We must regard even the first beginnings of life as the outcome of "evolution." Naturally. Darwin's God has no use for this prophet. But how shall we conceive it? Was the thing that first developed from the inorganic "a simple cell, such a being as those that now exist in such numbers as independent beings on the ambiguous frontier of the animal and vegetal worlds?" Or was it a particle of plasm merely, "like certain amœboid organisms that do not seem to have attained yet the organisation of a cell"? Again the simple question contained a whole programme.

Schleiden had first shown in 1838 that the body of any plant can be dissolved into tiny living corpuscles, which he called "cells," because they often had the appearance of a filled honeycomb. A year later Schwann proved, in Johannes Müller's laboratory, that the higher animal also is a product of these cells. The cell was recognised as the living unit that composed the oak and the rose, the elephant and the worm. Man himself, in fine, was but a pyramid of these cells—or, to speak more accurately (as each cell has its own life), an immense community of cells, a cell-state.

Virchow had, as we saw, laid the greatest stress on this last and most important deduction from the cell-theory a short time before. He looked upon every individual man as a mysterious plurality—a plurality of cells. Pathology, the science of disease, must take account of this. Health was the harmonious co-operation of the cell-state; disease was the falling-away of some of the cells to special work that injured or destroyed the whole community. This conception had inaugurated a new epoch in medicine, making it a consciously ministering art in the service of the living human natural organism. The Darwinian had now the task of showing the validity of this conception in his own province. The genealogical tree of the animals and plants must at once be drawn up in the form of a genealogical tree of the cell. The cells had combined to form higher and higher communities, and each higher species of animal or plant was in reality one of these social constructions. But this complexity was only found in the upper branches. The lower we descend, the simpler we find organisms. The lowest forms of life represent cruder, simpler, and more primitive cell-structures. And the final conclusion was that all the cell-communities or states must have been evolved from unattached individuals whose whole body consisted of a single cell. We cannot strictly call these lowest forms of life either animals or plants; they can only be likened to the single cell. Though Haeckel himself did not know it at the time, all his [pretty radiolaria at Messina belonged to this category. The whole swarm of bacilli and bacteria fell into this world of the "unicellulars."

THE SCIENTIFIC CONGRESS OF 1863

Haeckel's words threw a brilliant light on the question. Not only the simplest forms of life are unicellulars; the primitive forms also were. With them began the colossal genealogical tree that branches out through the millions of years of the earth's history. If anything on the earth has arisen by spontaneous generation out of dead matter, at the commencement of all life, it must have been a cell, or a still simpler particle of living plasm more or less resembling one. It is true that the point is put in the form of a question; but the veil has been torn away. Given *one* cell, the whole genealogical tree grows on, in virtue of Darwin's laws, until it reaches its highest point in man.

The conclusion of the speech greets Darwin as the Newton of the organic world, a phrase that has often been repeated since.

. . . . .

Let us turn over a few pages more in the faded record of the sitting. Fourteen years later he would speak again at a scientific congress, and speak on Darwinism. He would then put it forward no longer as a hope but a fulfilment, of which he showed one glittering facet. And no other than Rudolf Virchow, his former teacher, would oppose him and deliver his famous speech on the freedom of science in the modern State and its abuse by Darwin's followers. This was at Munich in 1877. The least of his hearers would remember that Virchow had spoken, like Haeckel, at Stettin fourteen years previously.

But we must understand the thirty-sixth speech if we are to understand the thirty-seventh.

It was the second sitting, on September 22nd. Virchow spoke on "the alleged materialism of modern science." The subject was not provoked by Haeckel, but by Schleiden, the botanist, the parent of the cell-theory. The controversy over materialism had raged furiously for many years. We need only mention Büchner (whose *Force and Matter* appeared in 1855) and Carl Vogt. There was an element of necessity, but a good deal of superficiality in the controversy, as it was then conducted. Friedrich Albert Lange has given us a masterly history of it. At this moment it was particularly instructive to point out the difference between general philosophical skirmishing with words and a really able piece of work that, though it had a technical look, suddenly added a new province to philosophy on which every doubting Thomas could lay his hands. However, Schleiden had not advanced. Curiously enough, he, the first discoverer of the cell, attacked Virchow's theory of man as a cell-state as a typical materialist extravagance.

He had published a heated essay, and Virchow defended himself. He gave such a remarkable and characteristic expression of his inmost feelings that it is worth while disinterring it. It is a very rare thing for a thoughtful man to give a natural philosophical speech that begins with crystalline clearness of logic and then makes a most curious *salto mortale* at the critical point.

ERNST HAECKEL, 1880.
Reproduced from the Natürliche Schöpfungsgeschichte.

To face p. 154.

He opens with a vigorous protest that there can be no quarrel about the materialism of science with the "spiritual" and the "privately-orthodox." Such people must regard all investigation of "this world" as aimless. The only thing of value for them is "the next world"; the best attitude towards *this* life is as crass an ignorance as possible, and so all science is worthless. The words are so sharp that he was interrupted and had to explain that he was not attacking anybody personally. He was only speaking "with the candour of a scientific worker, who is in the habit of calling things by their proper names." (At this point there was some applause.) Hence he is not speaking of materialism, he says, on that account, but because of certain objections from men of science, who said that philosophic speculation led us out of our way. Schleiden had branded the theory of man as a cell-state, the conception of man as, not an absolute, but a federal unity, as materialism. But this conception is not a philosophical theory at all; it is a fact. It is a piece of scientific truth, like the law of gravitation. He recurred to the old and often-quoted definition: the kind of research that brings such facts to light has nothing whatever to do with philosophy. On the other hand, "materialism," in so far as it expresses a general theory of the world, is a philosophy. Hence the simple investigation of facts as such can neither be dubbed materialistic nor said to have a philosophic tinge.

There are many objections to this strict

delimitation of the provinces of the human mind, as Virchow lays it down in the old style. It is true that materialism is a real philosophy, especially in the form current at the time and given to it by Vogt and Büchner. But it is a question whether we see, observe, or investigate at all, if we completely exclude philosophy; whether the philosophic thought can be really pumped out of even the most rigorous and exact "observation of facts," like air in the air-pump; whether there are any such things as purely objective "facts" in this sense in any human brain. And it is also a question whether the facts, however objectively we regard them, do not arrange themselves, when they are numerous, in logical series, which force us to draw conclusions as to the unknown by the very laws of probability; in other words, whether they do not always produce a "philosophy" in the long run. However, these questions are all well within the pure atmosphere of science. It is Virchow's practical conclusions that are interesting; and he goes on to draw them freely.

The man of science gives us no dogmatic philosophy of any kind, but facts. But for these facts and for the research that leads to them he must have an *absolutely free* path. No power can legitimately stand in his way that does not offer him more of what he regards as his palladium—facts. And, curiously enough, when we think of later events, the illustration that Virchow takes in 1863 to enforce this is—the Darwinism that Haeckel had just put before them.

Haeckel and Virchow were friendly colleagues at the time. We have already said that Haeckel was Virchow's assistant at Würtzburg. Not only as a man, but especially as a scientist, Virchow was then (and long afterwards) greatly admired by him. The idea of the cell-state got into his blood; it was one of the bases on which he built up the Darwinian theory. Though he had never recognised this distinction between the mere investigation of facts and philosophic reflection on them, he respected Virchow as a master of methodological education. What was "method" at the bottom but philosophy! Was not the method that expressly excluded "miracles," that sought always the natural law and the causal connection and the continuous series, a "philosophy"? This was the only method taught under Virchow as long as Haeckel worked with him. At the time the divergence of their ideas was not shown more openly. The one called "philosophy" what the other said was "the purely objective method of investigating the truth." The figure of Pilate rises up behind the dilemma with his question: "What is truth?"

However, Virchow takes Darwinism by way of an example of which he approves, a point that seems to be established in the province of pure facts. In the Munich speech of 1877 there are polite references to "Herr Haeckel." "As Herr Haeckel says." "As Herr Haeckel supposes." At Stettin we find Herr Haeckel described as "my friend Haeckel," with whom "I quite agree,"

&c. Haeckel himself, by the way, was still convinced—in his essay *On the Generation of Waves in Living Particles*—two years before the schismatic Council of 1877 that Virchow had had a decisive influence on his own Darwinian career. "If I have contributed anything myself in an elementary way to the building-up of the idea of evolution, I owe it for the most part to the cellular-biological views with which Virchow's teaching penetrated me twenty years ago." "As Herr Haeckel supposes," was the cool repayment of this sincere expression of gratitude. However, that is another matter. Let us return to Stettin. We read, where "my friend Haeckel" comes in, that he has shown how scientific research (the pure investigation of facts without the least tincture of philosophy) has gone on to deal with "the great question of the creation of man." It is merely conceded that there are still certain small outstanding difficulties, as, for instance, at the root of the genealogical tree. According to Darwin it is conceivable that there were four or five primitive forms of life. Haeckel is inclined to restrict them to a single stem-cell. It seems to him (Virchow) that there may have been a number of different beginnings of life. We have here the opening of the controversy as to the monophyletic (from one root only) or polyphyletic (from several roots) development of life, which is still unsettled as far as the commencement of life is concerned, but a very secondary question. It would be well if there had never been any more

THE SCIENTIFIC CONGRESS OF 1863

serious difference between Haeckel and Virchow. The speaker himself thinks it an unimportant matter beside the great question of freedom for scientific inquiry. One thing is as clear to him as it is to Haeckel. The biblical dogma of creation has broken down. It is impossible to take seriously any longer the breathing of the breath of life into a lump of clay, if these Darwinian ideas are sound. Once it is fully proved that man descends from the ape, "no tradition in the world will ever suppress the fact." Scientific inquiry alone can correct itself. And what it holds to be established must be respected beyond its frontiers as well. What does he mean by "beyond its frontiers"? He means, as he makes it clear here, the same as Haeckel himself. "Church and State," he says, must " reconcile themselves to the fact that with the advance of science certain changes are bound to take place in the general ideas and beliefs from which we build up our highest conceptions, and that no impediment must be put in the way of these changes; in fact, the far-seeing Government and the open-minded Church will always assimilate these advancing and developing ideas and make them fruitful." What more do we want?

If this were the conclusion of Virchow's speech, it would be merely a confirmation of Haeckel's—the kind of support that the older worker can give to ardent youth, though on different grounds. But the cloven foot has still to peep out. I believe that, in the pure struggle of ideas, we can determine here, in 1863, precisely the point where Virchow falls—falls into a line that has nothing in common with the ideal struggle of the really free and liberating thought of humanity. We come to the great *salto mortale*, which one must see from 1863 onward in order to understand the Virchow of 1877.

The passage is the more interesting as it refers to one of the chief stages in the development of Haeckel's mind. The conception of man as a cell-state, established by Virchow in so masterly a fashion, involved a very curious conclusion. This conclusion, however we take it, came so close to the roots of every philosophy that it justified Schleiden to some extent when he protested that the whole cell-state theory was a philosophical element.

If the human body is composed of millions of cells; if all the processes and functions, the whole life of the body in Virchow's sense, are merely the sum of the vital processes and functions of these millions of individual cells; is not what we call "the soul" really the product of the millions upon millions of separate souls of these cells? Is not man's soul merely the state-soul, the general spirit of this gigantic complex of tiny cell-souls? The lowest living things we spoke of, which consist of a single cell, showed unmistakable signs of having a psychic life. There was nothing to prevent us from thinking that in the combination of these various cells into communities each of them brought with it its little psychic individuality. And just as the individual bodies of the cells combined externally to form the new individual of the human body, so the cell-souls would enter into a spiritual combination to form the new psychic individuality of the human mind. I say there was nothing to prevent us from thinking this, in the line of deductions from the plain principles of the cell-state theory which Virchow claimed to be a naked "fact." Philosophically, however, an immense number of questions, problems, doubts, and hopes lurked behind it. The whole conception of individuality took on a new aspect. First, in the material sense; the individual human being seemed to be, bodily, only the connecting bracket, as it were, of countless deeper individuals, the cells. But it was more significant on the spiritual side. The individual human soul could be analysed into millions of smaller psychic individualities, the cell-souls, of which it was the sum. The unified ego, the consciousness of self and unity of the psychic clamp, "man," remained as the connection of all the cell-souls. A ray of light was thrown on the deep mystery of the *origin* of individualities, material and spiritual. Haeckel devoted himself afterwards to the question with all his energy. But at the time it was Virchow who, unconsciously enough, started the great wave that welled up from the depths of his theory.

He had marked out his path very clearly in the first part of his speech. Scientific research collects facts. It puts them before us without any reference to philosophy. The less philosophy there is in the investigation of facts the better. But the other side of the matter is that no power in heaven or on earth has anything to say as regards its work on things that it holds to be facts. The only possible logical conclusion from this, with reference to the question of the cell-soul, was for the investigator of facts to say: Even in respect of the psychic life we go our way and look neither to right nor left, whatever conclusions and assumptions the philosopher makes. Virchow acted very differently.

He first grants that this dissolution of man into a federal unity of countless cells *must* somehow affect the " unified soul." We are compelled " to set up a plurality even in the psychic life." He has reached the limit of his radicalism. We expect him to continue: Hence, as in the case of the Mosaic story of creation, of Darwinism, of the cell-theory as a whole, so here we men of science go our way unmoved; even if the whole of the teaching that has hitherto prevailed in philosophy and theology in regard to the soul breaks down, we simply go our way, and do not ask anybody's permission. This he does not do. Take one step further, he says, and we " can easily believe that it is necessary to split up our whole psychic life in this way and ascribe a soul to each individual cell." Haeckel believed a little later that this *was* necessary; that the most rigorous logic compelled us to do it. But, says Virchow suddenly, we must protest most vigorously against this. This deduction from the cell-state theory reaches a point where "science is incompetent," namely, "the facts of consciousness." Taboo! The path of the scientific inquirer is barricaded. What follows rests on no scientific grounds, but is a sort of confession. Up to the present natural science has not been able to say anything as to the real nature, the locality, and the ground of consciousness. "Hence I have always said that it is wrong to refuse to recognise the peculiar character of these facts of consciousness that dominate our whole higher life, and to yield to the personal craving to bring these facts of consciousness into accord with an independent soul, a spiritual force, and let the individual formulate his religious feeling according to his conscience and disposition. That is, I think, the point where science makes its compromise with the Churches, recognising that this is a province that each can survey as he will, either putting his own interpretation on it or accepting the traditional ideas; and it must be sacred to others." The direction of the logic is clear enough. The application of the cell-state theory to psychic life must lead to the problem of consciousness. But we must not follow it, because science has never yet penetrated into this province. It is the province of peaceful compromise with " the Church," and we must respect it.

It seems to me that the explanation is clear. The whole field of conflict that Haeckel found *within* the science of his time is opened out, though Virchow was by no means disposed at that time to take Darwinism as an example of the thing to be avoided, as he did at Munich fourteen years afterwards. The kind of scientific inquiry that Virchow advocated is what was called "exact" at a later period. It kept clear of all philosophical speculation, and repeated over and over again that it was only concerned with facts. It had, however, another card to play—peace with "the Churches."

Philosophy was shunned in order to leave a free field for the Churches to build in. Then the exact scientist took his hat and said, I am afraid I am incompetent, and the philosopher is incompetent, to do anything here; let the Church take the vacant chair, with my compliments. No philosophy: on this we will make war to the knife. This is "a point where science makes its compromise with the Churches." No one can understand Haeckel's career who does not grasp this antithesis. The contrast between Haeckel and Virchow, known to all the world since 1877, is clearly indicated. Virchow's speech in 1877 is obscure. We must go back to 1863 to get behind the veil—the veil that hides Virchow, that is to say, the most prominent representative of the hostility to Haeckel. We cannot understand otherwise how this yawning gulf came about between Haeckel's ideas and a school that professed to follow "exact" research. Haeckel was building up a natural philosophy which, starting from the solid foundation of scientific research and its results, went on to further, and greater, and more far-reaching issues, that could not be seen, but could be reached philosophically by more or less happy deductions from the scientific data. It might or might not have lasting value in points of detail. He was subject to the law of evolution. He worked with analogy, and the things he compared thereto were ever changing. It was all the same to him. In any case the dawning glimmer of the perfect light broadened out and lit up vague outlines even in the cloud-wreathed unknown. The others worked in such a way as to leave beside them provinces of a virgin whiteness, untouched by thought or logic. At times they slipped into these provinces, and celebrated their reconciliation-festival with "the Churches." The layman continued to think that the Churches wielded an absolute authority; that the scientist, abandoning his natural philosophy, came to pay them tribute. This situation has done infinite mischief, more than the wildest and even obviously perverse philosophy ever did. It put the scientist in the position of a tolerated vassal in the world of thought—the world that the Churches had held in chains for ages. Woe to the man who ventured to discuss " consciousness "! Not because science had but the slender proportions of a pioneer in that field, and because there was a danger of it making great mistakes with its natural philosophy. No, but because the white neutral field began here that we had agreed to respect—we "exact" scientists and "the Churches." This was the real reason why Virchow and so many others who advocated the strict investigation of facts had forfeited the right to oppose Haeckel's bolder natural philosophy and its conclusion—will have forfeited the right, at least, in the judgment of a future and more impartial generation. They did not oppose him on the lines of an equal zeal for the truth, but on much lower and reactionary lines. Their concern was not for the absolute triumph of truth, but for a compromise with certain forces in public life whose supremacy was not grounded on logic but on inherited external power. It required a certain amount of diplomatic shrewdness to enter into this compromise, in view of the practical power of those forces. Haeckel never had this "shrewdness." We grant that. But it is certainly a confusion of all standards when the shrewdness of the individual tries to entrench itself behind ostensible claims of scientific method; when research abandons all advance on certain sides on the plea of "exactness" instead of philosophising—and then itself makes use of this exactness for compromising with an ecclesiastical tradition that only differs from real philosophy in its antiquity and rigidity, its disdain of rational argument, and its employment of secular weapons that certain historical events have put in its hand without any merit on its own part.

The darkest cloud that hung menacingly on the horizon of Darwinism came from this quarter. At the moment we are dealing with it did not cause much concern. This early Darwinism thrilled with optimism as with the magic of spring. Haeckel had to speak once more in the course of the Congress. The geologist, Otto Volger, made a polite but energetic protest against the new theory in the final sitting. It was a curious connection of things that brought Volger into such a position.

Volger is the man who saved for Germany the venerable Goethe-house at Frankfort-on-the-Main. The Free German Chapter received it from him as a gift. The action has nothing to do with geology, but it stands in the annals of culture. Thus the shadow of Goethe came to Stettin, to be present at the open birth of German Darwinism— Goethe, who had once stood on the very brink of the evolutionary ideas. And the man who brought him was a geologist who felt moved to attack the ideas of Darwin and Haeckel!

No part of science became in the succeeding decades so fruitful for Darwinistic purposes as geology. It might very well be called a continuous argument for Darwin; from the little slab of Solenhofen Jurassic schist that yielded, in 1861, the first impression of the archeopteryx, the real connecting link between the lizard and the bird, to the incomparable discoveries of Othniel Marsh, Cope, and Ameghino in America, which put whole sections of the genealogical tree of the mammals before us, on to the skull and thighbone of the ape-man (pithecanthropus) of Java, found by Eugen Dubois, which brings so vividly home to us the transition from the gibbon to man. But, as if it had been scared away by the new idea of evolution and its demand for proof, the most and the best of this material was not forthcoming made the starting-point of infinitely new and more complex movements? Or — was the work of these natural laws but a ceaseless poking and thrusting and bubble-blowing without any inner meaning? Was it the play of waves that rise and fall, and rise and fall again, in the ocean, an eternal melting into smoke and nothingness? Was the whole of "evolution" an absolutely meaningless play of innumerable tendencies, not one of which would ever come to anything?

This note also was found in the first melody. Something would have been lacking if it had not been struck. Here again there could be a parting of ways, not only in the crowd, but amongst the thoughtful. The whole struggle of optimism and pessimism might be dragged in. At all events, the problem was bound to be pointed out from the start.

When Volger, not a bad opponent at the bottom, and Haeckel had made their speeches, indicating at once certain lasting antitheses within the subtle philosophy of Darwinism, Virchow closes the debates and the Congress with a most dangerous blessing. In essentials he is once more on the side of Haeckel. He suggests that geology should be allowed to mature a little before final judgment is passed. The strongest evidence for evolution is found in embryology (the science of the embryonic forms and uterine development of living species of animals). The prophecy was fulfilled, if ever prophecy was, and in Haeckel's own most particular field of work. But, in fine—

he returns to his point—the main thing is the "pursuit of truth." And since "the most earnest ecclesiastical teachers" declared that "God is truth," he could not do better than close with a reminder (I quote him *verbatim*) of "the compromise that may be effected between science and the Church." Translated into plain language, that means : My dear children, fight it out as you will, but respect the Church always as the main thing, and you will do well, however much you differ. Thus closed this remarkable Scientific Congress—as quietly as a bomb that smokes noiselessly, like a whiff from a tobacco pipe. But one day it will burst.

CHAPTER VI

THE "GENERAL MORPHOLOGY"

THE speech at the Scientific Congress in 1863 was the first open confession that Haeckel felt bound to make. But the real work for the new ideas began on his return to Jena. Nothing was further from Haeckel's thoughts at that time than the idea of becoming merely the populariser of Darwinism in Germany. He has often been spoken of since in lay circles as such. It is entirely wrong. He had the courage to recognise his debt whenever he contracted one; and certainly Darwin supplied the groundwork of his colour-scheme. But he was much too independent and individual in his nature not to take the axe in his own hand at once and begin to hew away himself.

Darwin had strengthened his book with a large amount of the best material that zoology and botany could supply. But there was something else to be done: a theoretical treatment of a general character with cleverly grouped illustrations from the facts already provided by two sciences, and to reconstruct these sciences from their foundations on the basis of the new theory. At that time Haeckel was doing an incredible amount of work, with body and mind. He had an iron constitution. In the year of the Stettin speech he won a laurel crown at the Leipsic athletic festival for the long jump, with a leap of twenty feet. His physical strength seemed so inexhaustible that his host, Engelmann, put a pair of heavy iron dumb-bells in his bed, in case he should want to take exercise during the night. He had a proportionate strength of mind. Everything seemed to promise very well for the next few years, so that he could devote his whole health and strength to the great task of his life. His teaching did not give him very much trouble in a small university like Jena, that was only just beginning to have a scientific name. The happiness of his home life, with a highly gifted woman who shared all his ideas with the freshness of youth, began to chain the restless wanderer with pleasant bonds to his place. He, of course, expected to have his sea-holiday in the old way for the study of his little marine treasures, but otherwise he remained quietly in the valley of the Saale. The warmth of genial and most stimulating friendships gathered about his life. With his comfortable material position he set to work on his great task under the best auspices.

He would have had at the start material enough to work upon without Darwin. From Müller's time he still had another special class of material, similar to the radiolaria, the medusæ.

The ship cuts through the ocean. It rises like a lofty fortress from the illimitable blue plain, with the white clouds on the far horizon. No land has been in sight for days. Yesterday a poor wind-borne butterfly rested on the deck. To-day it is gone, and all is sea. Then they suddenly appear silently in the blue mirror: mysterious discs, red as the anemones on a Roman meadow in spring, golden as the autumn leaves on a dark pond in the park, then blue, like a lighter blue floating on the general azure. They are the medusæ. At one time the ship sails through a whole swarm of them—thousands, hundreds of thousands, millions, a veritable milky way of coloured stars. On the next day they have all gone. No inhabitant of the ocean seems to be so close to it as this creature. The whole animal is only a shade more substantial than the water. You take it out, and try to catch hold of it. It stings your hand like a nettle: that is its one weapon. But it is already destroyed, melted away, a formless nothing. You put it on a piece of blotting-paper, and it dries up into the spectral outline of a shadow, a tiny "fat-spot," summary of its whole existence.

Yet this soap-bubble of the water is a real animal. Its transparent body is shaped like a bell, and moves through the water by regular contraction and expansion, like the lung in breathing. Where the clapper of the bell should be, we find a stomach, with a mouth for eating, hanging down from the curved upper part. At the edge of the curved surface are many long fibrils that close on the approaching prey and paralyse it by their sting. Then it thrusts it into its mouth and swallows the object into the stomach. The medusa is, of course, a very lowly creature, but it is much more advanced in organisation than the tiny radiolarian. The radiolarian consists of a single cell. The medusa is a cell-state, a community of countless cells with a division of labour amongst them. Some of the cells form the wall of the bell, some the stinging threads, some the devouring and digesting stomach. In this the medusa comes nearer to man than the radiolarian. Some of the cells see to the reproduction of the medusa. Ova and spermatozoa are detached from the cell-community of the medusa's body, blend together, and thus form the germ of a new medusa. In most cases the process is curious enough. From the germ-cell we get at first, not a real medusa, but a polyp that attaches itself to the ground, a little creature that may be remotely compared to the pretty water-lilies that meet the eye in an aquarium. Then the polyp produces something like a plant that grows buds, the real medusæ; it may produce these out of its substance as buds, and they then float away like detached flowers, or (in other species) it may gradually change itself into a chain of medusæ, of which the uppermost is detached first, then the next, and so on.

Since this peculiar method of reproduction

became known, in the thirties or forties, the medusæ were regarded as amongst the most interesting objects in the whole of zoology. They offered an extremely difficult task to the investigator who would care to take up the study of them.

When Haeckel was with Johannes Müller in Heligoland in 1854 he made acquaintance with them for the first time. His artistic eye was caught with their beauty, as it was afterwards with the radiolaria. "Never shall I forget," he says, "the delight with which, as a student of twenty years I gazed on the first *Tiara* and *Irene* [species of medusæ], and the first *Chrysaora* and *Cyanea*, and endeavoured to reproduce their beautiful forms and colours." His predilection for the medusæ never disappeared. At Nice in 1856 he met them again in the Mediterranean. Gegenbaur's *Sketch of a Classification of the Medusæ* provided his studies with a starting-point, just as Müller's writings did afterwards for the radiolaria. At Naples and Messina he completed his mastery of them. When he had done with the radiolaria for the time after publishing the great monograph of 1862, the next task that loomed up on his horizon was the need for a "monograph on the medusæ." It would be a long time, however, before he could complete the work in any fulness. A work of Agassiz that purported to do it, but, in his opinion, only confused the subject—he disliked both the Agassizs, father and son, and the father became one of his bitterest opponents on the

Darwinian question—gave him a negative impulse to the study. He thought it would be best to deal with one family of the medusæ after another in separate monographs, as time permitted. The first of these essays appeared in 1864 and 1865, and dealt with what are known as the "snouted-medusæ" (*geryonidæ*). The first volume of the complete work was not published until fourteen years afterwards. If Haeckel had decided to work as a specialist he would have had material enough here to occupy him fully throughout the whole of the sixties, and even longer. The keen student of the radiolaria would be succeeded by the equally keen student of the medusæ. More folio volumes would have accumulated, with beautiful plates, such as only the technical student of zoology ever takes out of the library. His name, like that of his friend Gegenbaur almost, would never have reached the crowd.

It was the influence of Darwin that prevented this. His attention was turned in another direction, and we begin to realise the full greatness of his power when we remember that he nevertheless continued with unfailing quality to publish such detailed studies as those on the medusæ.

Darwinian ideas were fermenting intensely in his mind at that time. The most audacious practical and theoretical problems arose from the fundamental theory, and forced themselves on him at every moment. A great deal was sketched in outline in the Stettin speech, but the serious scientific work would have to be begun on his return to Jena, in his view. First, he thought, two features of Darwin's system must be given a completely new and original complexion. Firstly, the bottom of the tree, where life begins. Secondly, the crown of all terrestrial evolution : the manner in which man is connected with the tree. It was his philosophic vein that settled both points, the philosophy of unity that sought to replace God by natural development, both below and above, in regard to the primitive cell and in regard to man. But the way in which he set about it was very far removed from all conventional philosophy. The whole rigour of his professional zoology found expression in it. And that was really the novelty of it. The same conclusions might have been drawn by any dozen ordinary philosophers, once they got on the right track. Even they could see that, if two and two are four, one and one are two, and three times three nine. Haeckel went very differently, and much more profoundly, to work.

As an old pupil of Virchow's he applies the cell-theory to Darwinism—in the lower stage. The first living things, the roots of the great tree of life, consisted of a single cell. The logic of the cell-theory itself went as far as this. But is the individual cell the simplest of all living forms? Here there was a long-standing controversy as to definitions. At first the cell was regarded literally as a kind of chamber, like the cell in the honeycomb. Then it was found that the jelly-like, mobile matter within the cell-chamber was the essential element, the vehicle of life. Finally, it

ERNST HAECKEL, 1890.
From a relief-portrait modelled by Kopf, of Rome.

was possible to conceive this slimy substance without any firm membrane, without a chamber. Inside it, however, there was always (it was then thought) a thick and hard substance, the nucleus. If that was the fundamental and only really essential form, the Darwinian primitive and initial type of all terrestrial life must have been a similar drop of living matter with a solid central nucleus, a nucleated individual cell.

How could we pass from this primitive cell to the "inorganic," the "lifeless," the "dead," the ordinary matter of stone, metal, and crystal? Haeckel believed that it was possible to make a step in that direction—not theoretically and philosophically, but practically—by showing that there were still living things on the earth that did not come up to the definition of a true cell, things that had not yet a nucleus in their soft gelatinous body. He discovered a number of tiny creatures that had a homogeneous particle of living matter for body, and showed no trace of a nucleus. The nucleus seemed to be the first beginning of an organ. It was altogether wanting in them.

To these most primitive of all living things he gave the name of *monera,* or the absolutely "simple."

In these investigations it is very difficult to determine whether one of these tiny drops of plasm has a more or less transparent nucleus or not. It has often been affirmed in later years that these monera of Haeckel's did not correspond to their description as living things without a nucleus, or creatures that were below the level of the true cell. It is, at all events, certain that there are to-day large numbers of the unicellular beings known as the bacteria in which no nucleus has yet been discovered by the most sceptical Thomas with the most powerful microscopes and best technical appliances of our time. It is the same with the chromacea (chroococci, oscillaria, nostoc-algæ), very lowly primitive plants whose whole body consists of a globule or granule of living plasm. However, here again the question is no longer of the first importance, now that evolution is entirely and generally accepted. At the time we are discussing the method chosen was all-important. Haeckel drew no conclusions without a solid basis. He believed he could give ocular proof of the existence of beings that were below the level of the cell. It was clear, at all events, that research in this department was only in its beginning, and could pour out wonder after wonder before the world recovered from its first fright over Darwinism.

Then there was the other end of the system—man. Here again it was not merely a question of concluding on philosophic grounds that man *must* have descended from the lower animals. Huxley had dealt in England with the question of man and the ape on the strict lines of zoology. He came to the important conclusion that man differs *less* zoologically from the highest apes, the gorilla and chimpanzee, than they do from the lowest apes. He proved his point by a technical study of skulls

THE "GENERAL MORPHOLOGY" 181

and brains, not from abstract philosophical principles. It could be demonstrated in the museum or zoological institute to any student with some knowledge of anatomy as easily as the existence and position of any particular bone in the skeleton. Haeckel went even further.

He constructed a genealogical tree stretching far below the apes. Next to them came the lemurs. The lemur, the ghostly nocturnal inhabitant of Madagascar, came from the Australian marsupial (kangaroo, &c.). The marsupial came from the duck-bill; the duck-bill from the lizard; the lizard from the salamander; the salamander from the dipneust or mud-fish; this from the sturgeon or the shark, and the shark from the lamprey. Below the lamprey, at the lowest limit of the vertebrate kingdom, was the amphioxus (or lancelet). This must have come from the worm—it was not at all clear how, at that time. And so the series ran on down to the unicellular protozoa, the amœbæ and the monera.

The construction of this tree would have been impossible for one who had not already done gigantic work. The whole of the new system of animals and plants, conceived in the form of a genealogical tree, had first to be sketched in outline. Then the narrower thread that led up to man, the Ariadne-thread of God-Nature, would gradually come to light.

Both ends of the system, the lower one in the monera, the upper one in man, were first thoroughly treated by him in 1865, and in part somewhat later. His exhaustive *Monograph on the Monera* was not published until 1868. Man's genealogical tree was privately circulated at Jena in two essays in October and November 1865. They were published in the Virchow-Holtzendorff collection in 1868 (" The Origin and Genealogical Tree of the Human Race "). But in both cases the substance of the work, as an accumulation of facts, is much older. And this work was, of course, only possible in connection with a number of further conclusions: in regard to spontaneous generation, life and death, the crystal and the cell, the mathematical form of organisms, the nature and limits of individuality, the method of research, the new natural philosophy, God, and so on.

It was an enormous programme, with a Paradisaic freshness. Everything was new and great; and all came from one brain. There was only one man with whom he discussed his ideas as they formed, Carl Gegenbaur, who has undoubtedly had a great, if unconscious, influence on them. Haeckel's grateful recognition of Gegenbaur's help in later years was endless and touching. " Thou it was," he writes to him a little later, " that led me to begin my academic teaching at our beloved Jena six years ago, at the Thuringian university in the heart of Germany, that has, like a beating heart, sent out its living waves of freedom and alertness of mind over Germany for three hundred years. At this nursery of German philosophy and science, under the protection of a free State whose princely rulers ever gave a refuge to free speech and have linked their names for ever with the reform movement, the golden age of German poetry, I was able to work in association with thee. Here we built up our common structure of science in the happiest division of labour, teaching and learning cordially from each other, in the very rooms in which Goethe began his studies of 'the morphology of organisms' a half-century before, and partly with the same scientific means, the germs of comparative and philosophic science that he had scattered. We have shared with each other as brothers the happiness and the sorrow that came in the hard struggle for life, and our scientific efforts have been so intimately blended and so mutually helpful, through our daily working and talking together, that it would have been impossible for either of us to determine the particular share of each in our spiritual communism. I can only say in a general way that the little my restless and impulsive youth could offer thee here and there is out of all proportion to the enormous amount I have received from thee, eight years my senior, a more experienced and mature man."

Goethe stood behind the friends as the quiet *genius loci*, giving his blessing to all who worked in his spirit on the old spot. Nor was the place itself without influence. " Much," Haeckel writes, " may have been even the outcome of the common uplifting enjoyment of nature that was afforded us by the artistic lines of the Jena hills, as they brought before us once more at sunset the magic of the Calabrian mountains by the colour-harmony of their purple and gold banks of cloud and their violet shadows."

"What are the hopes, what are the plans, that man, the creature of a day, builds up?"

The words were written by a poet, in his fatal illness, at the spot where the two strong spirits now worked. In the midst of all his hopes and plans Haeckel was struck by a Niobe-shaft. On February 16th, 1864, just on his thirtieth birthday, his wife, only in her twenty-ninth year, in the full force of mind and of love, succumbed to blood-poisoning.

I turn to the thick volume of Haeckel's *Monograph on the Medusæ*. Part I.: "System of the Medusæ:" with an atlas of forty beautiful plates: published by Gustav Fischer, of Jena, in 1879. Few people except zoologists with a technical interest in it have ever opened this voluminous work—why should they? It is a heavy work, with dry diagnoses. The author seems to be far away from all general questions, if ever he was, in the utter stillness of his study. This pure accumulation of matter for truth's sake does not reach the ear of the world. It lays up material for remote days, before which the individual fades away; it is merely catalogued material of the most technical character. Yet, as I turn over the pages, I seem to see a little image from time to time that is almost like the rose-red or golden-brown medusæ in the sterile, illimitable ocean. In truth neither ocean nor book is sterile; but they are grey

THE "GENERAL MORPHOLOGY" 185

and broad. And just as the swimming medusa gladdens me in the one, so a little personal trait of the author does in the other. It is in the choice of the Latin names. A little crown is woven that unites æsthetics and science. I find splendid names, invented by the Professor, on all sides. But I notice that his heart was in these things. He has discovered new species of medusæ, and must christen them. As he turns over his Latin or Greek lexicon a ray of humanity steals into the most severe scientific soul at such moments. I read that a disco-medusa is called the *Nausicaa phæacum:* "I observed the *Nausicaa phæacum* in April, 1877, at Corfu, on the shore of Phæaca, in the heart of the Nausicaa." A cyaneid is given the fine name of the *Melusina formosa.* It is noted, with great regret, that "so fine and classic a name for a medusa" as *Oceania* must be struck out on scientific grounds. Amongst descriptions of species in a severe scientific tongue that unnerves the timid reader, amongst gonods, styles, perradial bundles of tentacles, and ocellar bulbs, we find, *apropos* of the medusa, *Lizzia Elisabethæ:* "As Forbes dedicated the pretty genus *Lizzia blondina* to a 'blond Elizabeth,' I do the same, and wish to honour, not only St. Elizabeth of Thuringia, but also the 'blond Elizabeth' of Immermann and my own dear daughter Elizabeth."

Then, in the middle of the large volume, we find the following passage on page 189. A medusa is given the name of *Mitrocoma Annæ.* The name was given at Villefranche, near Nice, in April, 1864. This medusa had "a fairy-like appearance" to its discoverer; its tentacles hung down "like a mass of blond hair!" A note to the name tells us that it was given "in memory of my dear, never-to-be-forgotten wife, Anna Sethe. If it is given to me to do something during my earthly pilgrimage for science and humanity, I owe it for the most part to the blessed influence of my gifted wife, who was torn from me by a premature end in 1864." In the *Art-forms in Nature*, Haeckel's work of 1899, we find a medusa *Desmonema Annasethe* similarly — after thirty-five years — apostrophised: "The specific name of this pretty disco-medusa, one of the most beautiful and interesting of all the medusæ, immortalises the memory of Anna Sethe, the gifted and refined wife (born 1835, died 1864) to whom the author of this work owes the happiest years of his life."

If one would fathom the depths of human emotion one must reflect what these words, in such a context, contain; it is the last gentle vibration of a most deep inner experience breaking out into this prosaic, scientific material. A medusa is a trivial, possibly a funny thing, to the layman. The man of science looks deeper into it, and sees a wonderful revelation of nature; the eye of Goethe's God shines on him from it. But when he has devoted years to the most careful study of it, it assumes also a naïve individual interest for him, as the companion of his solitary hours of observation in the heart of nature, far from all the whirl and bustle of the world. Only the deepest and most intimate feelings break out in such moments. And here they have left their monument—in a Latin name that science will go on coldly entering in its catalogues for ages to come. It seems to me that this simple fact tells us more of the character of this true-hearted man, in whom nothing human was lacking, than long narratives could.

. . . . .

When the aged Sethe saw the break-up in 1806 of the State of Prussia, in the invulnerability of which he had believed as a gospel, he sought refuge in the comfort of work. "I succeeded in benumbing my mind: I experienced in myself that hard work is a soothing balsam, co-operating with our tardy healing force." The grandson, wounded in a more terrible way and cut to the very heart, tried the same remedy.

Thirty years afterwards, when crowns were prepared and speeches delivered in honour of Haeckel's sixtieth birthday, when the whole of Jena fêted him as their own, and the veil fell from his marble bust in the Zoological Institute, to which seven hundred of the best known names in German and foreign science had contributed, the hero of it all went back to that dark hour. "I thought at the time that I could not survive the blow, thought my life was closed, and purposed to bring together all the new ideas that Darwin's theory of evolution had evoked in me in a last great work. That was the origin, amid bitter struggles, of the *Generelle Morphologie*. It was written and printed in less than a year. I lived the life of a hermit, gave myself barely three or four hours sleep a day, and worked all day and half the night. My habits were so ascetic that I really wonder I am alive and well before you to-day."

In his hour of collapse Haeckel sat down and wrote "the book of his life." There were only two alternatives for a book written in such circumstances. It would be either very bad or very good. When a young man in his thirties throws himself into a great effort of this kind and writes a work that he conceives as a testament—a work in which he will speak for the last time, but will say everything—it is a desperate test of all that he has done in his three decades of life and is about to give to the world. In this case the test succeeded beyond all expectation.

The *General Morphology of Organisms** was published in 1866, with the sub-title: "General elements of the science of organic forms, mechanically grounded on the theory of descent as reformed by Charles Darwin." It consists of two thick volumes of small print, containing more than 1,200 pages. The preface is dated September 14, 1866. It is now one of the most important works in the whole mental output of the second half of the nineteenth century. In respect of method of scientific research it is a landmark by which we may characterise and appraise the whole half-century. For

* This work of Professor Haeckel's has not been translated into English. [Trans.]

general biological classification it inaugurates a new epoch, as had been done fifty years before by Cuvier, and again fifty years earlier by Linné. What it did for zoology in the narrow sense was thirty years afterwards summed up in one phrase by a writer of acknowledged competence, Richard Hertwig : " Few works have done as much towards raising the intellectual level of zoology." Among Haeckel's own achievements, great and varied as they are, this work occupies the highest place. Setting aside certain special pieces of research, and regarding him mainly as a man of great ideas, we find his whole programme in this work. The *History of Creation*, that has taken his name far and wide over the globe beyond the frontiers of zoology, is only an extract from this work. He put his heart in it. The others are only the improved blood-vessels of his system of ideas, partly duplications, partly simplifications. I do not say this either in blind admiration or in criticism, but as the expression of a plain fact. Posterity will turn to this work when, either in hostility or in sympathy, it wishes to appreciate Haeckel.*

His contemporaries did not accept the work without difficulty. It came out without noise, exerted a tremendous influence in a quiet way, and at last disappeared altogether from the book-shops. It is still attacked, but has never been refuted. At libraries one finds, as I know from experience, that it is always " out," and therefore

* Professor Huxley described the *General Morphology* as " one of the greatest scientific works ever published." [Trans.]

must be read continually. It is found occasionally at second-hand booksellers; an antiquarian price running to five pounds and more is put on it, after forty years' active production on the part of its author. At present you could count on your fingers the German works that have this distinction of being highly priced and out of print. One such is Vischer's *Æsthetics*, and another is the first edition of Gottfried Keller's *Green Henry*. Keller had threatened any one who ever attempted to republish this first edition (afterwards modified but not improved by him) that their hand would not rest quietly in the grave. But the price of the work went up amongst antiquarians. I feel, in speaking of Haeckel's *General Morphology*, that I am describing a book which has become so rare that one must treat it as something new, a codex that is only accessible to a few. It is certainly not known to the general reader.

Let me endeavour in a few words to give a general idea of the chief contents of the work.

All the intellectual forces that had had any influence upon Haeckel now concentrated for a supreme achievement. First of these was Goethe, who supplied the title, "Morphology." In its simplest signification morphology is merely "the science of forms." If I take houses, furniture, statues, fishes, flowers, crystals, &c., and only regard and describe their forms, I am a morphologist in the literal sense of the word. But when Goethe invented the term he sought to give it a more restricted application, writing in the style

THE "GENERAL MORPHOLOGY" 191

of earlier days, but clearly enough, at Jena in 1807. We have, he says, natural objects before us, especially living objects. We try to penetrate the secrets of their nature and their action. We are not merely observers, but philosophers. It is from this point of view that we approach the subject. It appears to us that the best way to proceed is to separate the various parts. Such a procedure seems calculated to take us very far. Chemistry and anatomy are instances of this analytic kind of research, and both are greatly esteemed and successful. But this method has its limitations. "We can easily break up the living thing into its elements, but we cannot put these together again and restore them to life. We cannot do this in the case of many inorganic, to say nothing of organic, bodies." What are we to do? "Hence," Goethe continues, "even scientific men have at all times had an impulse to recognise living things as such, to grasp connectedly their external visible and tangible parts, and take these as indications of the inner life, and thus in a sense to compass the whole in one glance." "Hence we find at the threshold of art and knowledge and science a number of attempts to establish and elaborate a science that we may call *morphology*."

Perhaps Goethe's meaning can be realised best if one takes a great work of art—say, the Venus of Milo—and imagines how these different kinds of knowledge would deal with it. Purely analytic anatomy would dissolve the superb artistic form into a rubbish-heap of bits of marble. Chemistry would still further break up these bits of marble into the chemical elements of which every block of marble is ultimately composed. The "form" would disappear altogether. But in this case the form means—the Venus of Milo. We see at once that we need another branch of science and investigation besides anatomy and chemistry: we need a morphology, or science of the complete form in which the block of marble is moulded into the Venus of Milo. In the case of our work of art, morphology would be identical with æsthetics, or at least with a branch of it. There can be no doubt that the first and most imperative need for the establishment of a special science of morphology arises from artistic and æsthetic feelings. It is not without significance that it was founded by the poet Goethe, and elaborated with such great success in the nineteenth century by the born artist Haeckel. However, that does not prevent the analogy of the Venus of Milo, which happens to be a creation of human art, being applied equally to every individualised form in nature, to every crystal, plant, and animal. Goethe himself immediately transferred his morphology into the province of botany with such vigour that the term is still regarded, in its narrower sense, as a technical botanical expression. It extends, however, to the whole world in so far as its contents come before us in "forms." When Haeckel adopted the term he deliberately restricted it, in harmony with the general definition, by calling his work the "Morphology of Organisms," or the science of the forms of animals and plants.

But there was one danger in the conception of a morphology of animals and plants, namely, the danger of taking it to mean a purely external description: so many thousand species of plants, soberly described, labelled, and numbered, a huge cabinet of stuffed skins, a herbarium of hay. A whole scientific school had really taken it in this sense since Goethe's time; much as if one were to think æsthetics consisted simply in forming an illustrated catalogue of all the art-treasures in the world, a realistic catalogue in which the marble statues from the Parthenon and the Moses of Michael Angelo would simply be given as number so-and-so in class so-and-so.

Haeckel was preserved from this school by his more immediate masters, as well as by Goethe himself; firstly by Johannes Müller, then by the botanist Schleiden, finally by the influence of Gegenbaur. There was at the time enough, and more than enough, of this external museum-morphology. It was far from Haeckel's intention to produce a new compendium, in several volumes, of this kind of science of plants and animals. His morphology was to be "general," to have a broader range, be a programme. As Richard Hertwig said very happily at a later date, he saw his science, not as it then was, but as it *ought* to be, in his opinion.

The science of forms was to be in the fullest sense

a "philosophy of forms." "Zoological philosophy" was the name given by the hapless Lamarck, in France a century ago, to a work that appeared in the year that Darwin was born, and anticipated his most advanced thoughts. Haeckel, also, gave a new "philosophy of zoology and botany." The title embodies the magic formula that gave him courage to take up resolutely once more the proscribed word, that seemed to have been scalded and spoiled for ever in the witches' cauldron of "natural philosophy"; it spoke of the "theory of descent as reformed by Charles Darwin." Two sub-titles divided the work into two sections from the start. The first part was, the critical elements of the mechanical science of the developed forms of organisms (animal and plant): the second part was, the same elements of the mechanical science of the developing forms of organisms.

In these titles we see the decisive advance beyond Johannes Müller. As Goethe had already declared, morphology as such can be formed into a real and profound science. It will then not confine itself pedantically to a registration of forms. It will compare them with each other, and seek the hidden law in the straggling phenomena. It will mark out broad lines that will enable the human mind to grasp its objects in all their fulness. Johannes Müller had only been able to confirm that in the narrower sphere of biology. This was the nerve that gave vitality to zoology and botany, and made them a province of the mind in the higher sense. But the question now was: which laws were detected, and in which category of thought were they to be found? Müller had the theory, but was weak on the practical side. There were the "forms" of animals and plants. What was it that really connected them? What was the reality that corresponded to the philosophic craving of the intelligence? Müller's next school, the generation immediately preceding Haeckel, that of Du Bois-Reymond, Virchow, and many others, had apparently indicated the solution. They had replaced Müller's vague general conception of the laws of morphology and life, which was undermined by older influences, by a single great demand. We want to grasp nature as a unity. At one point in nature we have reached deep and apparently fundamental factors — in physics and chemistry and their plain natural laws or forces. Now let us try, starting from the idea of unity and from the plainest of all philosophical principles, that of proceeding from the known to the unknown, to reduce the forms and phenomena of life to these natural laws of chemistry and physics. Let us find out whether the whole form-world of the animals and plants— in other words, the whole province of morphology in the narrower sense—can be traced to the same natural laws that we have in chemical and physical phenomena. The globe is the object of chemistry and physics. Shall these few green or other-coloured things that lie at the limit of the air, water, and rocks, a small minority in nature, the things we call animals and plants, alone in the whole world be exempt from the action of these laws? It is immaterial that Müller's best pupils, Du Bois in his later years and Virchow at an early date, departed more or less from this consistent position of theirs into philosophic and other sidepaths. The younger generation, to which Haeckel belongs, that only came into direct touch with Müller in his last years, heard no other gospel. What further advance was to be made? In chemistry and physics they had before them the deep stratum that yielded good mechanical laws. The first stage of physiology after Müller, as we find it, for instance, under Du Bois-Reymond, yielded some good indications for the organic. But was the whole of morphology to be remodelled? Was the vast labyrinth of the thousands and thousands of animal and plant forms in the museum to be reduced to mechanical laws, corresponding to those of physics and chemistry, and be explained by them?

Darwin brought salvation. Now that he had appeared, Haeckel felt that he could begin to work. The hour and the man were come.

Darwin made it possible for him to raise morphology to a penetrative science, equal to physics and chemistry, and so to make a step towards the unity of our knowledge of a unified world. Hitherto the morphology of the animals and plants had been in confusion. God, imagined in the form of a higher man, had deliberately created the organic forms, the palm, the moss, the turtle, and the man. He had constructed them on a definite plan, as a man makes machines. Now, it appeared, the deeper stratum was peeping out even here. Laws that had built the heavens and the earth reached, by way of the Darwinian theories of selection and adaptation, to the moss and palm, the turtle and man.

It was Haeckel's peculiar distinction to take up this path as the right one. It was then altogether new; to-day, even in the eyes of an opponent, it has at least the solid and consistent support of a considerable party. In later years, apart from open deserters from the free and uncompromising pursuit of truth like Virchow, a school of zoologists and botanists has been formed that will not recognise in Darwinism a reduction of vital phenomena to the simple chemico-physical laws of the rest of nature. They look upon it partly as inaccurate in its allegations of fact, partly as a nebulous confusion, if not, as I have already said, as a false mysticism or metaphysic. In the opinion of these critics, whose own confused ideas very often leave little to be desired in point of nebulosity, and who frequently try to drive out the devil by means of the devil's grandmother (a matter we cannot go into here), Haeckel had made a great mistake in thinking that Darwinism would solve the Du Bois-Virchow problem of reducing all living things to the laws of lifeless matter. Even these, however, must candidly acknowledge that in doing so he was the victim of his consistent and honourable inquiry. At all events he must logically have seen the correct line at that time as it is recognised to-day by this anti-Darwinian but professedly mechanical school. His individual error can only have been that he was deceived as to the true course of the line, and so clung to Darwinism. However, we have said enough on this point.

Haeckel himself, at the time he was producing his greatest work, saw in Darwin the absolute "open Sesame" to all the doors of philosophic morphology. With this Sesame came an entirely new impulse, namely, to write the natural history of the animal and plant form. It was just the same as when æsthetics perceives a new world, a world that alone is worthy of it, the moment it passes from the making of a mere catalogue of the world's art-treasures to the knowledge of even one single law of artistic creation, in virtue of which one single work of art has been actually built up.

It is impossible to begin with more general considerations than this book does. The method of scientific research generally is explained in order to give an idea of the new Darwinian morphology. With a calmness that must have made most of the contemporary zoologists and botanists shiver, the discredited idea of natural philosophy is restored from the lumber-room. "All true science is philosophy, and all true philosophy is science. And in this sense all true science is natural philosophy."

The various periods in the development of morphology are coolly schematised. These epochs are characterised by the vicissitudes of the struggle between the simple description of forms in the animal and plant worlds and the philosophic exposition of the laws that lie behind these forms. In the eighteenth century, under Linné, there is a period of purely external description and classification. It is succeeded in the first third of the nineteenth century by a triumph of the philosophic treatment of animal and plant forms. This increases with Goethe and Lamarck, and grows into the older (and now generally abused) imaginative natural philosophy. Then there is a general reaction; with Cuvier comes the least philosophical of methods, though at the time it is a real advance. While Linné only gave an external description of forms and catalogued them, Cuvier's epoch penetrated to the inner structure, the inner world of forms, and thus rendered great service. The last and greatest workers of the period, Müller, Schleiden, &c., give the signal for a reaction in the hour of its chief triumph. Haeckel now follows this up as "the element of fact in their ideas." With Darwin he inaugurates the fourth epoch, the triumph of natural philosophy for the second time. But it is now far deeper and clearer; it embodies all the good that preceded, all that Cuvier and his followers have done, without the irresolution of earlier days. Now that we have studied the living form in its innermost structure, as was never done before, in the earliest stages of embryonic development in the ovum and womb, in the past geological periods of the earth's history, we will *think* over this form, think with all the means at our command, reason, synthesis—even *imagination*, when it is necessary to press on to the great final conclusion, a new synthesis of the defective positive data. What does Johannes Müller say? "Imagination is an indispensable servant; it is by means of it we make the combinations that lead to important discoveries. The man of science needs, in harmonious co-operation, the discriminating force of the analytic intelligence and the generalising force of the synthetic imagination." That is spoken from the depths of Haeckel's heart, and he drives it home.

Nothing is more amusing than to find Haeckel's later opponents saying, *apropos* of any particular question, that his statement springs from his "imagination," as if it were something wholly unscientific that the naturalist must shun like the pest; or again, that Haeckel here or there falls a victim to the deadly enemy of all scientific research, natural philosophy. It is pointed out to him as a great discovery which he must approach in a proper penitential spirit—to him who has discussed these matters so unequivocally in his first theoretical work.

As a fact, these methodological chapters in the first volume are as clear as crystal. The titles will seem strange to the man who thinks he can do without any philosophical instruction in zoology and botany, and wants to hear only of cells, tissues, stalks, leaves, bones, scales, and so on, in a general morphology. One chapter has the heading: "Empiricism and Philosophy (Experi-

THE "GENERAL MORPHOLOGY" 201

ence and Knowledge)." Another heading runs: "Analysis and Synthesis." Then there are: "Induction and Deduction," "Dogmatism and Criticism," "Teleology and Causality (Vitalism and Mechanism)," "Dualism and Monism." The last three antithetic headings are united under a general title as "Critique of Scientific Methods that are Mutually Exclusive." Such a title illumines the whole situation like a flash of lightning. Many years afterwards Haeckel himself said of his *General Morphology* that it was a comprehensive and difficult work that had found few readers. At least the whole of this first and most difficult part of the book must be defended against the criticism of its parent. If it is far from adequately appreciated to-day, especially by professional philosophers, that is certainly not due to its style, which is a model of clearness in the eyes of any one with the least philosophical culture. The real evil was that people did not look to it for instruction from the philosophical side. The title, "Morphology of Organisms," had a technical sound. The empty space between professional philosophy and professional zoology is wide enough to-day, but it was far wider thirty-four years ago. Books like Büchner's superficial and popular *Force and Matter*, or Haeckel's own later work, the *History of Creation*, that can only be regarded as a brief and incomplete popular extract in comparison with the *General Morphology*, with all its peculiar literary charm, stole into the philosophy of the time like foxes with burning straw tied to their tails. Professional philosophers have written whole libraries on them. The matter recalls a fundamental defect in academic philosophy: it has little or no sympathy with real scientific work; in fact, it studiously avoids such sympathy in the consciousness of its own weakness. Hence it has, like every other layman with general interests, to wait for attempts to popularise scientific work before it can know what is going on in the serious camp. The man who wants to-day to criticise the mechanical conception of nature should first make himself acquainted with these chapters of the *Morphology*. How many know the mere title of the work? How many even of those who evince great hostility whenever Haeckel's name is mentioned?

The book contains much more than the methodological introduction. This only takes up the first hundred pages, but it contains the whole programme. We start off, therefore, under full sail for a new epoch of thought, for natural philosophy; but we must keep an alert mind. The deeper task, that Darwin only gave the means of accomplishing, was to reduce all living things, animal or vegetal, to the inorganic. The laws of life must be merely certain complications of the simple laws that are encountered directly in chemistry and physics, and rule throughout nature. It must be one of the first aims of a general philosophic morphology to open out a path in this direction.

The living and what is called the "dead" must

be compared. Linné's three rigid kingdoms—animal, plant, and mineral—needed definitions in harmony with the new ideas. Haeckel himself had discovered the "monera," the living particles of plasm that did not seem to have reached the stage of the true cell. Here, clearly, was the lowest level of the living. At the same time we reach the most complex specimen of the inorganic from the morphological point of view—that is to say, the most interesting in its individual form—the crystal. The differences begin to give way. What marvellously similar functions! From the dead mother-water is built up, purely by chemico-physical laws, the beautiful structure of the crystal. From the lowest living particle of plasm without any special organs, as we see in the radiolaria, are formed the beautiful siliceous frames that Haeckel had collected in such quantities at Messina. Is it more than a hair's breadth to pass from one to the other? The deeper we go in the study of living things, the slighter become the differences that separate them from "dead matter." On the other hand, the higher we go in the structure of crystals, the more striking is the resemblance to the living thing. Two chains of thought seem to be started. What we call "dead" is really alive: what we call living is really subject to the same laws as the "dead." The solution is found in complete Monism. Living and dead are not antithetic. Nature is one; though we see it in different stages of development. We call one of them the crystal, another the cell, or the moneron, or the protozoon; another the plant, another the animal. Historically it all hangs together. The same laws hold sway throughout. In framing my arbitrary definitions I can say either that the dead is living, or that the living does not differ essentially from the dead. In the chain of living things man comes from the primitive cell, the moneron. This in its turn has developed from something earlier—"naturally" developed. The very idea of life forces us to seek the predecessors of the monera. Hence we speak of "spontaneous generation," as what was dead according to our ordinary use of language has begun to live. In point of fact it is merely development of a unified whole. There is no gap, no leap, no act that is not natural. The dead and the living never were really antithetic.

The insistent statement that not only does the living approach the inorganic, but the inorganic approaches the living, is quite "Haeckelian." The study of the "life" of crystals is one of the best parts of the book. Later generations will appreciate it. We are much too narrow to-day when we merely reflect that life, even the life of man, can be traced by evolution down to what we call dead matter. We forget that this "matter" is already high, since it potentially contains life, and even man, the crown of life. Many people imagine that the derivation of man from "dead matter" is equal to turning a king into a beggar. They do not reflect that, on the other hand, a beggar is turned into a king. When I say that life

THE "GENERAL MORPHOLOGY" 205

arose one day out of the inorganic, or that a crystal was turned into a cell, my statement really involves the complementary truth that the inorganic potentially contains life in itself. Otherwise we have the old miracle over again of something being produced out of nothing, in spite of our spontaneous generation. Haeckel has always been clear on this point. His later studies of the soul of the atom and the plastidule only carry out the absolutely logical treatment of the question that we find in these chapters of the first volume of the *Morphology*.

Incidentally the question is raised whether the plant or the animal was evolved first. Animal and plant are, of course, not rigidly distinct from each other. They are only the two great branches of the Darwinian evolution of living forms, and are united at the bottom, however much they diverge above. Gegenbaur had represented this years before (1860) in a figure that Haeckel quotes in his *Monograph on the Radiolaria* in 1862. The whole kingdom of living things must be conceived "as a connected series, within which we find two lines diverging from a common centre and representing a gradual differentiation and development of organisation." The terminal points of these lines (the highest plant and the highest animal) are very different from each other, but the difference gradually disappears as we go back towards the common centre, and the lowest stages in each kingdom can hardly be distinguished from each other. For these lowest stages Haeckel now carries out a plan that very quickly forced itself on him.

He forms them into a new kingdom of life. To the animal and plant kingdoms he adds the primitive realm of the beings that showed unequivocal signs of the possession of life, yet were neither animals nor plants. He gives them the name of "Protists." To botany and zoology is now added protistology.

The name "protists" (from *protiston*, the very first) is familiar to every one in biology to-day. If protistology has not yet been securely established as a special branch of science, that is due to the circumstance that a strict limit cannot be determined on either the plant or the animal side, so that the botanist encroaches on the province at one point and the zoologist at another. But when we remember that Haeckel's protists include the well-known bacilli, on which whole libraries are accumulating to-day, it is clear that the province must be definitely marked off at some date in the near future, whether one accepts Darwinism or no.

These important innovations in technical biology show very clearly how sound and fruitful the new "natural philosophy" was. We have to go back to the untenable and utterly impracticable systems of Hegel, Schelling, and Steffen, which were immediately rejected as the trifling of *dilettanti*, or even to much that the admirable Oken did on the scientific side, if we would measure the whole distance between what people understood in the sixties by "natural philosophy" and the real

THE "GENERAL MORPHOLOGY" 207

reformed philosophy that Haeckel gave to the world. This becomes clearer at every step we take in his work.

The first book has determined the method that leads to morphology, the science of forms. The second has ranged the organic forms—protists, plants, and animals—over against the inorganic or " dead " forms, as far as this is possible from the new evolutionary point of view. We feel that the third book will pass on to Darwin, and explain the world of organic forms by the Darwinian laws of evolution. Then the programme would be carried out in its main features.

But Haeckel writes two whole books before he comes to this, and they are, perhaps, the most characteristic in the work. He only " adopted " the theory of evolution in the sense that he applied it far more thoroughly than Darwin to practical problems. In these two books he is entirely himself. They are, at the same time, the most difficult in the work. Even to-day they place him on a lofty and lonely height apart from the great and strenuous controversy over Darwinism. I believe that the time will yet come that will fully appreciate these books. Through them Haeckel will play a part in philosophy of which we have at present no prevision.

There is a word that is inseparable from the word " form "—individuality. Morphology, which does not analyse, but studies the form-unities as a whole in the sense of Goethe's definition, comes from the nature of things to deal with the individual. In our artistic illustration the Venus of Milo, as a form-unity, is an æsthetic individuality. When its form is destroyed, its individuality perishes.

Let us apply this to any one of the higher plants or animals. Take a turtle, for instance. A definite individual embodies the definite form to which I give the name. This form as such is entirely lost if I cut up the turtle until it is unrecognisable. The limit of morphological study seems to be, just as in the case of the Venus of Milo, the integrity of the individual turtle. Yet in the living turtle we find an enormous difference.

If I grind the Venus of Milo into dust, I am at once in a totally different world with this dust. I am amongst the raw material of nature, untouched by æsthetic influence. From this calcareous powder I can, in reality or imagination, pass on to the world of crystals, molecules, and atoms. In that case I shall have done with æsthetic morphology. I come to the morphology of the inorganic, a very different branch. What do we find in the case of the living turtle?

It is true that I can break up the turtle into simple chemical substances. In that case I make the same transition; I abandon organic morphology, and pass, with the same *salto mortale* as in the case of the Venus of Milo, to the lower science of inorganic morphology.

But when I examine the structure of the living individual turtle before me I notice a special feature. Let us suppose that I break up the Venus

THE "GENERAL MORPHOLOGY" 209

of Milo only to a certain degree; or, with less vandalism, I do not break it up, but light up its inner structure to some extent by a sort of Röntgen-ray apparatus. And suppose I found that this one æsthetic individuality is made up of millions of much smaller and æsthetically finer and more unified images. I do not mean of millions of repetitions of the large Venus in miniature, but of real and unmistakable little works of art, each of which, regarded separately and without any injury to its narrower individuality, might be just as excellent a subject for æsthetic examination as the whole Venus.

This is, of course, nonsense as regards the Venus of Milo. There is nothing of the kind in it. I have given the paradoxical supposition merely for the purpose of showing what we really find in the case of the turtle.

When the organic individual turtle is closely studied it breaks up first into so many *simpler* organic individuals, which undoubtedly belong as such to the province of organic morphology. They are the *cells*. The theory of Schleiden, Schwann, and Virchow here comes into direct touch with morphology. Every higher animal or plant has its own individuality; and within this individuality there is a conglomerate, a community, or a state, of individuals of a lower order, that have their own life and their corresponding individual life-form. Man himself, the highest of animals, is a cell-state. So Virchow taught. Each one of us is an individual, and as such an object of morphology.

The cell, each single cell in each of us, is also an individual, and as such is equally an object of morphology. Hence it is the task of the morphology of organisms, not only to describe these higher individualities as such, but also to look on them as glass-houses, as it were, with so many shelves, divisions, and smaller houses within of a lower rank. These internal arrangements have to be described, piece by piece, with the same fidelity.

This will probably suffice to convey a general idea of the subject. Clearly, the great work that ought to form the general part of morphology at this point was the precise determination of all these various layers of individuality that are found in the animals, plants, and protists, and, as we rise upward, enter into more and more complex relations to each other.

The difference between, say, a turtle or a man and the cell which combines in its millions to form them is not the only one. Between them we seemed to find individualised, or almost individualised, links. Think of the idea of an organ. What is my heart? It is made of a number of cell-individuals, like my whole frame. But these cells form a sort of intermediate individuality in me. We may go further. What is a segment of a worm? What is an arm of a star-fish? They have so much independence that they can continue to live, rapidly producing new cells and forming a new worm or star-fish of the higher individual type, if they are cut off. The arrangement is still more difficult in the case of the

THE "GENERAL MORPHOLOGY" 211

plant. Where in their case shall we find the stages of individuality that correspond to the animal-human? The cells are distinct in both cases. The individual plant-cell corresponds to the individual animal-cell. But what is there in the plant that corresponds to *me*, as the animal-human multicellular individual? Does the oak-tree, for instance? Certainly, the oak is an individual. But it seems that it is the single sprout of it that corresponds to what I am. What is the relation of the tree to this sprout?

Here our ideas grow dim and confused. We human individuals unite to form certain higher communities. The word "social" reminds us of the fact: then we have the nation, the race, humanity. At least the earlier of these stages certainly perform various combined functions, and are understood to form, or wish to form, new individuals. We speak of the social organism, the body of the people, the soul of the people, and so on.

We see that still more clearly in the case of the animals about us. Individuals, that correspond to our conception of an individual man, combine and form stocks and colonies, with division of labour. We find this in the medusæ, corals, anemones, tunicates, and vermalians. One of these animal stocks, to which our human social combinations only correspond in a much wider sense, gives us a stage that is represented by the tree in the plant-world. Infinite perspectives open out, and also infinite complications. Infinite problems spring up for morphology to deal with; it must make its way through the labyrinth of these complicated types of individualisation.

The matter is still more intricate if I begin at the bottom of the biological series and proceed upwards. I, man, am an individual of a certain stage in my own collective activity. It is true that I am made up of millions of cell-individuals, but when we look at the whole these are merely elementary units. But take a being from the protist-world that is too lowly to be either animal or plant. In respect of its whole activity it is an individual just as much as I am, and therefore in this regard at the same stage as I. At the same time it consists of a single cell. The distinction in me between unit and whole does not exist in it. Its unit is the whole. It would seem a Sisyphean task to reduce all this to a system.

Yet that is just what Haeckel has done.

With crystalline clearness he separates and reunites and arranges everything, from the primitive organic individual, that is not yet a true cell—the monera he had himself discovered —upward. Organic morphology begins with them as its first object, the first complete individuality, the first "form." All that lies below it is beyond the province of morphology. The last conceivable organic individuality is, perhaps, the atom; and that is not the concern of morphology. We start from the organic. Above the pre-cellular individuals and the true cells the next form-unities are the organs. Above the organs, after a few subtle intermediate stages, are the "persons." Thus a new word is given to what we have hitherto conventionally called an "individual," when we wanted to denote a turtle, a bird, a man, or an higher animal as a whole. To this corresponds in the plant the sprout. The stage above the "person" is the "stock." We might also call it the social individual; in the plant-world it is the tree, in the coral the coral-stock, in the human case the social combination of a number of men for common action.

We are reminded of Virchow's speech, and how "consciousness" was dragged into the debate on the cell-state. What psychological perspectives are opened out by this doctrine of individuality! Each form-unity, each single individuality in the series, with a soul! Souls combining for common action, and forming higher psychic unities! There is no detail in Haeckel's whole life-work in which he speaks more boldly and freely and philosophically than he does here. His lucid treatment raises to a higher stage a philosophic question that has occupied thinkers for ages.

That is the third book. The fourth takes up a different subject. Let us adopt in organic morphology this wonderful theory of individuality, the theory of stages within the form. Then let us turn to consider impartially the vast multitude of living forms. How can we now arrange this infinite confusion by merely looking at it? Artificial classification has attempted it a hundred times, and always without success. On this side there is only one way to proceed—the mathematical.

I study them with strictly mathematical figures. I determine their axes, and the mathematical aspects of their forms. Possibly that will give a practical result; the only kind of artificial system that can be accommodated with the Darwinian theory, and perhaps render it assistance by the sharpness of its lines. Does it answer? Take a crystal, a specimen from inorganic morphology. The description of it is susceptible of a strictly mathematical form. Now take a star-fish, a worm, a human being. We find that even these organic structures have a mysterious relation at bottom to certain mathematical, stereometric forms. We might almost say, to certain forms of human thought. Everything in the organic world is in a state of flux. But through the whole moving stream we can trace the outline of one stable element, something like a mathematical idea. A sort of Platonism of the living forms vaguely takes shape.

Haeckel speaks of lines, axes, circles, radii, and all kinds of rhythmic structures. It does seem that the countless individual forms of living things fit into a scheme of a limited number of mathematical forms. Strictly speaking this is not a real morphology of living things. We only find these clear and rigid forms schematically in the wild profusion of forms of the protists, plants, and animals. They are only a reminiscence of the laws of the purely inorganic, which the eye of the observer just detects as the lowest stratum. Hence Haeckel calls this section the "promorphology" of organisms.

It is true that this section, which essays to compress all living things into a very simple scheme, is the hardest to read in the whole work. A number of strange and difficult words have to be invented for this stereometric scheme to which he would reduce the animal and plant forms. Haeckel himself declared, twenty years afterwards (in the second part of the *Monograph on the Radiolaria*), that this stereometry of organic forms had found little favour in biology " especially on account of the difficult and complicated nomenclature." But he had complete confidence as to the substance of it, even after so great a lapse of time.

In point of fact we have here, it seems to me, a gigantic preparatory work, not so much for the strict purpose of classification, as for a real philosophy of botany and zoology that will be founded some day. This recurrence of sharp stereometric structures, not only in the crystal, but also, if less clearly, in the biological world, will one day prove an important source of knowledge, in a sense that is not even clear in Haeckel himself.

We are already entering upon a period that has a glimpse of the truth that the deepest power of Beethoven's music, or Goethe's poetry, or Raphael's painting, or Michael Angelo's sculpture is a mysterious revelation of the most subtle mathematical relations and effects—produced without conscious perception of these relations, though a human mind is at work in them. In spite of all our "consciousness," the obscure intuitive power at work in these human artistic achievements differs very little from the curious force with which a radiolarian builds up its little house in the deep sea or a caseworm fits on its fine, rhythmic, snail-like coat. In both we have the same profound, crystal-like constructive power that brought forth the wings of the butterfly, the feathers of the bird, the bodily frame of all the animals and plants, that harmonises so well with strict mathematical forms. In Beethoven and Raphael it is not more conscious or unconscious, not clearer or vaguer, not more mystical or more natural, than in the poorest worm or the microscopically small radiolarian. The æsthetics of the twentieth century will take up these ideas.

· · · · ·

It is a great work. How few there are in the whole of the nineteenth century that show the wealth of ideas we find in the first volume alone.* And this is only one volume. We have as yet said nothing of the idea that is of the greatest

* The reader may be interested to know that Haeckel gives a popular summary of his early work on individuality and on the mathematical types of organisms in a more recent work. This has been translated into English with the title *The Wonders of Life*. The two chapters that deal with these questions are omitted from the abridged cheap edition. [Trans.]

Haeckel's Villa at Jena.

consequence in connection with Haeckel's own development. He was a Darwinian from 1862 onwards. After 1866 and the publication of the *General Morphology* we find him dominated in all his work by one single idea from the Darwinian group. He brought this idea so effectively to the front, improved and developed it so assiduously, and applied it in so many ways, that it has come to be regarded as his own most characteristic work. It is inseparable from his name. Whatever the future may be, wherever Haeckel's name is uttered people will add the phrase that was made peculiarly his after 1866, that colours and pervades all his works—technical, popular, polemical, or philosophical—as much as the word "Monism." It is the phrase: the biogenetic law.

Here and there even in the first volume of the *Morphology* a note is struck that the reader cannot clearly understand. It increases in the second volume until it dominates the whole book.

The phrase is known far and wide to-day. This is partly due to Haeckel's own insistence on it, but perhaps still more to the real value of the idea itself. It crops up in a hundred different fields—psychology, ethics, philosophy, even in art and æsthetics. I have been able to trace it even into modern mysticism. For the moment I will only point out that it has been attacked and misstated with real fanaticism, in spite of the splendid and perfectly clear account of it that Haeckel has given.

The proper place to read of it is, as I said, the second volume of the *Morphology*. This volume has to give an account of the evolution of organic forms. What is given rather casually, almost Socratically, in Darwin is now developed into a number of strict laws. This method of expounding more or less hypothetical, new, and insecure ideas in the form of laws has since been frequently attacked. Some have been led by it to take the ideas as so many dogmas, and even to learn the laws by heart as if they were texts in Scripture. Others have then laid the blame of this dogmatic interpretation on Haeckel himself. It is quite true that there was the possibility of a misunderstanding. People do not always think for themselves, and the statement of a proposition in the form of a law may prove a pitfall for them. The blind learning of them by heart is always mischievous. On the other hand, it might be urged that the statement of the ideas in this bald way affords the best opportunity for a thorough and rational criticism of them, precisely because they give such pregnant expression to the writer's meaning. I do not find that order and strict logical definitions have ever done any harm of themselves, whatever it is that is put in order and defined. On the contrary. People must confuse order sometimes with real dogmatism. Of this there is not a word in the whole book, while at an important juncture the reader is actually warned to be on his guard against undue pressure. "In this," we read in the twentieth chapter, "we do not wish to draw up a body of laws of organic morphology, but to give hints and suggestions for drawing them up. A science that is yet only in its cradle, like the morphology of organisms, will have many important changes to undergo before it can venture to claim for its general propositions the rank of absolute and unexceptionable natural laws."

However that may be, it was in this provisional definition of laws that the famous biogenetic law first took shape, and with it a spirit entered into Darwinism in the narrower sense that was never again detached from its master, Haeckel.

Let us once more take a simple illustration from facts. Take a green aquatic frog and a fish, say a pike.

Both of them have a solid vertebral column in their frames, and therefore both must be classed amongst the vertebrates. But within the limits of this group they differ very considerably from each other. The frog has four well-developed legs, its body terminates in a tail, and it breathes by means of lungs, like a bird, a dog, or a human being. The fish has fins, it swims in the water by means of these fins and its long rudder-like tail, and it breathes the air contained in the water by means of gills. When we arrange the vertebrates in a series, with man at their head, it is perfectly clear that the frog stands higher than the fish in regard to its whole structure. It is lower than the lizard, the bird, or the mammal, but at the same time it is a little nearer to these three than the fish is. That was recognised long ago by Linné, who assigned them a corresponding rank. The fishes are the lowest group of the vertebrates; the frogs belong to the group immediately above them. Now let us see how one of these frogs is developed to-day. The frogs are oviparous (egg-laying) animals. The mother frog lays her eggs in the water, and in the ordinary course of nature a new little frog develops from each of these eggs. But the object that develops from them is altogether different from the adult frog.

This object is the familiar tadpole. At first it has no legs, but it has a long oar-like tail, with which it can make its way briskly in the water. It breathes in the water by means of gills just like a fish. It is only when the tadpole grows four legs, loses its tail, closes up the gills at its throat, and begins to breathe by the mouth and lungs instead, that it becomes a real frog. There can be no doubt whatever that the tadpole is very much more like the fish in all the most important particulars than the frog. Between the frog-egg and the frog itself we have a stage of development in each individual case of which we might almost say that the young frog has first to turn into a fish before it can become a frog.

How are we to explain this?

At first people supposed something like the following: All beings in nature are admirably adapted to their environment and their life-conditions. Whatever be the explanation of it, it is a simple fact. Now, the frog lays its eggs in the water. The young ones develop from these eggs, and find themselves in the water. The most practical adaptation for them is to swim about by means of a tail and breathe by means of gills like the fish. They do not reach land until later, and they creep on to it and have an equipment of the opposite character, with legs and lungs.

But this explanation throws no light on the question why the frog lays its eggs in the water. However, there might be some utility or other, some need for protection, for instance, in that. Let us take a few other cases.

There are several species of tree-frogs, and toads, and closely related amphibia like the salamanders, that do not lay their eggs in the water. Some of them bury them in folds of their own external skin, others (such as the Alpine salamander) retain them within the mother's body, as the mammals do. The young animals develop there from the eggs. Even there, however, where there is no question of aquatic life, the young frogs, toads, and salamanders first assume the fish-form. The young frogs and toads have fin-like tails, and all of them have gills. There seems to be some *internal* law of development that forces the frog and its relatives to pass through the fish-stage in their individual evolution even when there is no trace whatever of any external utility.

Now let us examine the matter as Darwinians and believers in evolution.

There are reasons on every hand for believing that the frogs and salamanders, which now stand higher in classification than the fishes, were developed from the fishes in earlier ages in the course of progressive evolution. Once upon a time they were fishes. If that is so, the curious phenomenon we have been considering really means that each young frog resembles its *fish-ancestors*. In each case to-day the frog's egg first produces the earlier or ancestral stage, the fish. It then develops rapidly into a frog. In other words, the individual development recapitulates an important chapter of the earlier history of the whole race of frogs. Putting this in the form of a law, it runs : each new individual must, in its development, pass rapidly through the form of its parents' ancestors before it assumes the parent form itself. If a new individual frog is to be developed, and if the ancestors of the whole frog-stem were fishes, the first thing to develop from the frog's egg will be a fish, and it will only later assume the form of a frog.

That is a simple and pictorial outline of what we mean when we speak of "the biogenetic law." We need, of course, much more than the one frog-fish fact before we can erect it into a law. But we have only to look round us, and we find similar phenomena as common as pebbles.

Let us bear in mind that evolution proceeded from certain amphibia to the lizards, and from these to the birds and mammals. That is a long journey, but we have no alternative. If the amphibia (such as the frog and the salamander) descend from the fishes, all the higher classes up to man himself must also have done so. Hence the law must have transmitted even to ourselves this ancestral form of the gill-breathing fish.

What a mad idea, many will say; that man should at one time be a tadpole like the frog! And yet—there's no help in prayer, as Falstaff said—even the human germ or embryo passes through a stage in the womb at which it shows the outline of gills on the throat just like a fish. It is the same with the dog, the horse, the kangaroo, the duck-mole, the bird, the crocodile, the turtle, the lizard; they all have the same structure. Nor is this an isolated fact. From the fish was evolved the amphibian; from this came the lizard; from the lizard, on Darwinian principles, the bird. The lizard has solid teeth in its mouth; the bird has no teeth in its beak. That is to say, it has none *to-day;* but it had when it was a lizard. Here, then, we have an intermediate stage between the fish and the bird. We must expect that the bird-embryo in the egg will show some trace of it. As a matter of fact it does so. When we examine young parrots in the egg we find that they have teeth in their mouths before the bill is formed. When the fact was first discovered, the real intermediate form between the lizard and the bird was not known. It was afterwards discovered at Solenhofen in a fossil impression from the Jurassic period. This was the archeopteryx, which had feathers like a real bird, and yet had teeth in its mouth like the lizard when it lived on earth. The instance is instructive in two ways. In the first place it shows that we were quite justified in drawing our conclusions as to the past from the bird's embryonic form, even if the true transitional form between the lizard and the bird were never discovered at all. In the second place, we see in the young bird in the egg the reproduction of two consecutive ancestral stages: one in the fish-gills, the other in the lizard-like teeth. Once the law is admitted, there can be nothing strange in this. If *one* ancestral stage, that of the fish, is reproduced in the young animal belonging to a higher group, why not several?—why not all of them? No doubt the ancestral series of the higher forms is of enormous length. What an immense number of stages there must have been before the fish! And then we have still the amphibian, the lizard, and the bird or mammal, up to man.

Why should not the law run: the whole ancestral series must be reproduced in the development of each individual organism? We are now in a position to see the whole bearing of Haeckel's idea, and at the same time to appreciate his careful restrictions of it.

First, let us see a little of the history of the matter. In the first third of the nineteenth century a number of pre-Darwinian ideas of evolution flitted about like ghosts in natural philosophy, as I have already said. The evolutionary ideas of Goethe and Lamarck are well known to-day. Another thinker of great influence was Lorentz Oken, who established the custom of

THE "GENERAL MORPHOLOGY" 225

holding scientific congresses. Oken had been constantly occupied with embryology, the science of the development of the individual organism. He was at all events acquainted with all that was known at the time on the subject. I open an old volume, wretchedly printed on blotting-paper, of Oken's *General Natural History for all Readers* (1833), and turn to a passage in the fourth volume (the first to be issued) on page 470.

We read that the caterpillar of the butterfly resembles the animal form at a stage of development that lies below the insect—the worm. Oken says: "There is no doubt that we have here a striking resemblance, and one that justifies us in thinking that the development in the ovum is merely a repetition of the story of the creation of the animal groups." Oken was quite aware that the chick in the egg had gill-slits like the fish. He bases his idea on that fact. He was very close indeed to the theory that Haeckel has so wonderfully elaborated. However, he was greeted with laughter. His theory was treated as an absurdity from 1833 to 1866. It cannot be denied that he was himself partly to blame for this. Oken made two serious mistakes. On both points Haeckel is perfectly clear and sound. Moreover, the theory of natural evolution that made it possible for us to speak of "ancestors" was still a Cinderella in the days of Oken. No sooner was it rehabilitated than the principle of the old theory of embryonic forms returned once more.

Darwin himself at once appealed to it, but it

was reserved for Haeckel to develop its full importance. He corrected it in two particulars. Oken and his admirers had made an unfortunate mistake. They believed in a genealogical tree of all living things, but they conceived it on the lines of the old classification. Linné had enumerated in succession: mammals, birds, amphibia, fishes, insects, and worms. He put them in one straight line, which is certainly the best arrangement for general purposes. But when Oken came with the idea of natural evolution, he at once took this series as the outline of a genealogical tree. The mammals descended from the birds; the fishes from the insects; and so on. If that were really the case, the highest animals would be expected to reproduce all the animal and plant stages in the course of their embryonic development, on the lines of the theory. The human being would have to be, successively, not only a lizard and a fish, but even a bird, a beetle, a crab, and so on. This was by no means borne out by the facts, and so the theory seemed to be discredited.

Now let us glance at Haeckel's genealogical tables. We find eight of them, artistically drawn, at the end of the second volume. The "genealogical tree" is given in the form of a branching tree, or as a huge forest-like growth of stems some of which only meet in the ultimate roots. There is no trace in Haeckel's designs of the sort of Eiffel-Tower arrangement that the Linnean system involved. At the bottom we find the protists, the most primitive forms of life. From this point two parallel stems diverge, that of the animals and that of the plants; they never touch each other after this point, and so cannot be expected to be reproduced in the embryonic forms. Then the animal stem is split up almost at the root into at least five independent branches, each of which pursues its separate line of development. One culminates in the insects, above the worms and the crustacea. A totally independent stem issues in the vertebrates, and this in turn breaks into many different branches. Beyond the lizards, for instance, we find the development of the mammals and birds, which run on as separate and parallel lines. It was mere nonsense to expect a mammal in its embryonic development to assume the form of a bird, or a crab, or a beetle, or a mussel, or a medusa, even if the biogenetic law were established ten times over.

The second mistake made by Oken was to declare that, whatever it cost, the law must be observed everywhere. He examined the butterfly. It passed through two curious embryonic stages: first the caterpillar, then the pupa. The caterpillar corresponded to the worm; that might be plausibly contended. But the pupa also must stand for something. Between the worm and the insect in classification was the crustacean. It had a hard shell: so had the pupa. Consequently, the pupa is a reproduction of the crustacea-stage. Such were the bold chess-moves of the older theorist.

Haeckel first established that there was such a thing as the biogenetic law. There is a fundamental norm, which is made clear to us in embryology and can at the same time (remember the instance of the lizard-like teeth in the bird-embryo) give us most wonderful suggestions as to the line of ancestral development. But it has certain limitations, as we will now show.

The adaptations in the sense of the Darwinian laws have affected the animal's embryonic life more and more, the higher the tree of life grew. The long recapitulation of the ancestral stages often came into conflict with the young individual's need for protection. The result was that the biogenetic law found itself restricted by the Darwinian laws of adaptation. The too lengthy succession of ancestral portraits was abbreviated and compressed. Whole stages of embryonic or larval development were interpolated that had nothing to do with these ancestral portraits, but were destined for the protection of the fœtus. The butterfly-pupa is really an instructive instance of this description. It does not reproduce a crab-stage, nor has there been any stage in the ancestry of the butterfly when they lived throughout life in pupa-houses. The pupa is simply a later adaptation in the development of the butterfly, a protective stage in which it accomplishes the transition from the caterpillar-form in much the same way as the young bird develops under the protection of the hard egg-shell. Thus only a faint and shadowy trace has been left of the real ancestral forms, though this trace is an extremely instructive one. But we must not expect the impossible from it.

In this way our naked and crude biogenetic law assumes a more finished and scientific form : the embryonic development of the individual is a condensed, abbreviated, and to some extent modified epitome of the evolutionary history of its ancestors. That is more modest, but it is a correct expression of the facts. The essential point of the older idea was not in itself wrong; all that was done was to explain the gaps, and leaps, and contradictions in it.

Now that Oken's share in the theory has been properly appreciated, we may notice another little historical detail. In the period immediately after his time these ideas were ridiculed by men of science, great and small, but they were not exactly "done to death." Agassiz, the most pronounced creationist and dualist of all the nineteenth-century zoologists, expounded them occasionally as a curious instance of the divine action. In fact, he looked upon the whole of zoology as a mystic cabinet of curiosities—the more curious the better. Thus he came to play with this idea and confirm it, but merely took it at first as a fine figure of speech. Agassiz is a tragical form. He survived Darwin, much in the same way that many an elegant *mot-de-salon* on the rights of man survived the French Revolution. Suddenly the whole structure of his ideas seemed to fall about him. Where he had played with roses, he now found torches. He reeled like a smitten man, and cried out against the horrid monsters that brought him pain and bitterness. His anxiety began with Darwin, even as regarded the question of the embryo. But there was another, a man far away in South America, that increased it—Fritz Müller.

Born in 1822, one of the finest pioneers in zoological work, Fritz Müller had wished to become a higher teacher, but had abandoned his plan on account of the oath that had to be taken by every servant of the State. In 1849 he wrote to the Ministry requesting that he might be allowed to dispense with the formula "So help me God, through Jesus Christ." Meeting with a refusal, he went to South America, and began a solitary life as a student in the primitive forest, and sought to accumulate valuable zoological material. Darwin called him "the king of observers." In 1864 he published an essay of ninety-four pages with the title *For Darwin*. He revived and improved the old idea of Oken's, and made fresh contributions to the natural history of the crustacea that were literally stupefying. We may say that the point that he believed he had established, in virtue of the law, in regard to the genealogical tree of the crustacea, was afterwards, with apparent justice, called into question, even by supporters of the law such as Arnold Lang. That, however, did not diminish the extent of his influence at the time. Haeckel has generously acknowledged how strongly he felt that influence himself. Nevertheless all that has been said about Haeckel's priority in fully applying and shaping the law, and in its final formulation, is perfectly correct.

When Haeckel had massed his material he had

first to create the necessary terms for arranging it distinctly. In the language of the old legend, he called the day day, and the night night. To the story of ancestral development, or the evolution of the stem, he gave the name of *phylogeny*, or stem-history (*phylon* = stem). The word circulates very widely to-day. The story of the development of the individual until it reaches maturity was then called *ontogeny* (*on* = being), which coincides generally with embryology (though it may also include the growth of the child). The law then ran: Ontogeny is an abbreviated and frequently disarranged epitome of phylogeny. Special attention was drawn to the qualifications " abbreviated " and " disarranged."

Here again two fresh names were invented. In so far as the embryonic development is a true recapitulation of the stem-history, it is called *palingenesis*, or repetition of the ancestral traits. When the development is altered by new adaptations it is called *cenogenesis*, " foreign " or " disturbing " development.

It has been objected by small-minded critics that Haeckel forces nature to mar its own work. The real meaning is quite clear if we bear in mind the blunder of Oken. In this case " disturbed development " is merely an expression of the fact that the laws we invent are ideal forms, and not always convenient realities. We learn by heart that the earth is a globe, and its orbit is an ellipse. Neither of the two propositions is strictly accurate; no mathematical figure even has objective reality. By the sheer attraction of the water of the ocean to the continents the earth has an irregularity of shape that it is barely possible to express in words. To call the path of the earth round the sun, constantly altering as it does, and still further complicated by the sun's own movement, a real ellipse is the greatest nonsense conceivable.

In this sense every natural law is subject to disturbances, though these in turn are the outcome of natural laws. If we do not cavil over the name, we find that the idea it stands for is of the greatest consequence for any further use of the biogenetic law. Unless it is borne in mind, the law, especially in the hands of the inexpert, falls into hopeless confusion. We read so often that the ancestral history is identical with the embryonic development. The one is a recapitulation of the other. This supposed law is then applied in psychology, æsthetics, and many other directions. If it succeeds, there is jubilation. If it does not succeed (as it does not in a thousand cases), the whole blame is thrown on Haeckel. People discover that "the biogenetic law breaks down here," and they throw over Darwinism altogether.

The second volume of the *Morphology* is the standing palladium against all this nonsense. It marks off the real readers and followers of Haeckel from the superficial talkers who run after him because he is famous, and will leave him unscrupulously for any other celebrity of the hour.

The book must be read. Even in this second volume an incredible amount of matter is compressed. An introduction, consisting of a hundred and sixty pages of small type, gives us an idea of the new system. This is the first scheme of a real "natural classification" of living things. From this we pass to special morphology. But this fearless sketch of the specialised genealogical tree, according to the new ideas, puts general morphology in its true light. We are made to feel that it is not all mere theory. To-morrow—nay, to-day—the whole practice of zoology and botany will have to be remodelled on the new principles. Off with the roof of the ark! The whole museum must be cleared out. We want new divisions, new labels. The old controversy between the Nominalists and the Realists seemed to have come to life once more. How students had played with the word "affinity" as a symbol. The lemurs were "related" to the apes, and to other groups of mammals. The star-fishes were related to the sea-urchins, to the encrinites. The word had, in fact, led to a certain amount of arrangement; the stuffed or dried or preserved specimens in the museum were placed side by side. Suddenly the whole thing became a reality. The things that were "related" to each other had really been connected historically in earlier ages. The lemurs were the progenitors of the apes. Behind them were a series of other mammals. Star-fishes, sea-urchins, and encrinites, formed a definite branch of the great tree, and were historically connected; not symbolically, but in a real extinct common ancestor.

It was a vast work. A single man had at first the whole kingdom in his hands, had to reject the old lines of demarcation and create new ones. There was a certain advantage at the time. Since Cuvier's time an immense quantity of new discoveries had accumulated for the construction of a system of living things. Müller, Siebold, Leuckart, Vogt, and many others, had done a great deal of preparatory work. All this was of great assistance to the man who now came forward with courage and a talent for organisation. Nevertheless it needed real genius, together with almost boundless knowledge, to accomplish the task. We must remember how reactionary (even apart from the question of evolution) was the systematic work of distinguished and assuredly learned zoologists like Giebel at that time; they worked on in a humdrum way as if the more advanced students did not exist. How different it has all become since Haeckel's thorough reform of classification! We are astounded to-day at the skill with which he drew lines in his very first sketch that were so near to the permanent truth. I need only point to the new scheme of the classification of the vertebrates. A good deal of his work was, of course, bound to be defective, because the facts were not yet known; for instance, in fixing the point at which the vertebrates may have evolved from the invertebrates. It was not until a year later that the discovery of the embryonic development of the ascidia by Kowalewsky threw light on this. Again, there was the solution of the problem

THE "GENERAL MORPHOLOGY" 235

of the ultimate root-connection of the great parallel animal stems. In this matter Haeckel himself brought illumination by his gastræa-theory.

On the whole this systematic introduction to the second volume would have sufficed of itself to secure for Haeckel a prominent position in the history of zoology and botany. He himself was chiefly proud of the fact that it was the first natural-philosophical system on the new lines to meet the rigorous demands of academic science, and indeed to revolutionise academic science. This enhances his complete triumph in the last two books of the volume. First man is introduced, with absolute clearness and decisiveness, into the system of evolved natural beings, as crown of the animal world, but subject to the same laws as the animal: a vertebrate, a mammal, whose nearest relatives are the anthropoid apes. Thus at last the "system of nature" was complete. It embodied the unity of nature. It formed the framework of facts for a unified natural philosophy, Monism. The *monon*, the "one," embracing all things, that included nature in itself and itself in nature, became the last scientific definition of what people called "God."

Thus the volume, which had begun the system of nature with the monera, closes with a chapter on the Monistic God—"the God in nature." The conception of God in human fashion is rejected. Man is merely a vertebrate, a mammal, adapted in his whole structure to our little planet. A supreme

Being to whom we ascribe omnipresence could not possibly be confined within the narrow limits of this vertebrate and mammal organisation. When we try to do so we fall into unshapely conceptions that are wholly unworthy of the most exalted of all words, ideas, and beings. It is in this connection that Haeckel uses for the first time the phrase " gaseous vertebrate," that has so often been quoted and attacked since. He means to say that we are driven to such debasing and senseless definitions if we do not recognise in God the essence of the whole system of things ; if we form our idea of him arbitrarily on any particular property of things within the system. We must beware—as he expressly says—of such confused and unworthy comparisons.

"Our philosophy," Haeckel continues, "knows only one God, and this Almighty God dominates the whole of nature without exception. We see his activity in all phenomena without exception. The whole of the inorganic world is subject to him just as much as the organic. If a body falls fifteen feet in the first second in empty space, if three atoms of oxygen unite with one atom of sulphur to form sulphuric acid, if the angle that is formed by the contiguous surfaces of a column of rock-crystal is always 120 degrees, these phenomena are just as truly the direct action of God as the flowering of the plant, the movement of the animal, or the thought of man. We all exist ' by the grace of God,' the stone as well as the water, the radiolarian as well as the pine, the gorilla as well as the

Emperor of China. No other conception of God except this that sees his spirit and force in all natural phenomena is worthy of his all-enfolding greatness; only when we trace all forces and all movements, all the forms and properties of matter, to God, as the sustainer of all things, do we reach the human idea and reverence for him that really corresponds to his infinite greatness. In him we live, and move, and have our being. Thus does natural philosophy become a theology. The cult of nature passes into that service of God of which Goethe says: 'Assuredly there is no nobler reverence for God than that springs up in our heart from conversation with nature.' God is almighty: he is the sole sustainer and cause of all things. In other words, God is the universal law of causality. God is absolutely perfect; he cannot act in any other than a perfectly good manner; he cannot therefore act arbitrarily or freely—God is necessity. God is the sum of all force, and therefore of all matter. Every conception of God that separates him from matter, and opposes to him a sum of forces that are not of a divine nature, leads to amphitheism (or ditheism) and on to polytheism. In showing the unity of the whole of nature, Monism points out that only one God exists, and that this God reveals himself in all the phenomena of nature. In grounding all the phenomena of organic or inorganic nature on the universal law of causality, and exhibiting them as the outcome of 'efficient causes,' Monism proves that God is the necessary cause of all things and the law itself. In recognising none but divine forces in nature, in proclaiming all natural laws to be divine, Monism rises to the greatest and most lofty conception of which man, the most perfect of all things, is capable, the conception of the unity of God and nature."

The book closes with these words and a quotation from Goethe. It had opened with a quotation from Goethe. Goethe runs through the whole of the two energetic volumes like an old and venerable anthem. The stalwart fighter not only traces his whole Monistic philosophy to Goethe: not only owes to him the very idea of morphology. In front of the second and more strictly Darwinistic volume he has a dedication "to the founders of the theory of evolution," and between Darwin and Lamarck we find the name of Goethe. It was Haeckel's firm conviction that Goethe not only believed in the unity of God and nature, but literally in the natural evolution of the various species of animals and plants from each other. In this conviction, which claims Goethe explicitly for Darwin, he has never been shaken, although his own friends and convinced evolutionists (Oscar Schmidt, for instance) have often opposed him on the point.

Much has been written since the days of the *General Morphology* both for and against this Goethe-Darwin theory, but I cannot see that we have got much further with it. I still find that a candid study of some of Goethe's smaller writings, such as the *History of my Botanical*

Studies, the criticism of D'Alton's *Sloths and Pachyderms* (which is very important), and several others, compels us to think that Goethe really believed, in a strikingly Darwinian way, in a slow transformation and evolution of animal and plant species in virtue of purely natural laws; and that he always laid great stress on this idea of his as an original notion, far in advance of the professional science of his time. We not only have several clear passages, but the whole point of his argument really rests on this idea. Hence, apart altogether from the pedantry that tries to make a cabalistic mystery out of Goethe's works, and always reads B for A and C for B, it does seem that there was truth in Haeckel's first view of the matter, in spite of all the ink that has been shed over it and the vast amount of word-splitting exegesis. Darwinism has, in a certain sense, its German side, even apart from all that Haeckel has done for it.

. . . .

This was the book, then, that the deeply afflicted author wrung from himself as his "testament." It was written and printed with unprecedented speed. When the first copies were issued, the author had a feeling that he had nearly "done for himself." He could not sleep. The state of his nerves gave great concern to his friends, who were watching him most anxiously. With a stolid fatalism, as if nothing mattered now, he yielded to their pressing advice, and decided to travel for a time. Far away on the blue Atlantic, at the gate to all the glories of the tropics, there is an island, Teneriffe, that was counted one of "the isles of the blest" in the old Roman days. A huge volcano rises from it, and on its flanks we find all the zones of the geography of plants, as in a model collection. Humboldt has given us a splendid description of it, as the first station of his voyage to the tropics. "The man who has some feeling for the beauty of Nature," he says, "will find a more powerful restorative than climate on this lovely island. No place in the world seems to me better calculated to banish sorrow and restore peace to an embittered soul." Haeckel went there.

It was not an expensive journey, but it came as a fresh greeting from Nature. It was a new ocean after the long studies on the Mediterranean. What might it not afford in the way of medusæ and other zoological prizes when the general beauty of the landscape, that had enchanted Humboldt, had been fully enjoyed. With a mingling of his overflowing passion for Nature, and the gloomy fatalism that told him this would be his "last voyage" after his "last book," he asked permission to leave Jena in the autumn of 1866, when the printing of the *Morphology* was completed, and set out. It was no more to be his last voyage than the *Morphology* to be his last testament. Although still subdued with resignation in his inner life, he came home in the spring of 1867 with a new elasticity of body and mind, restored by the influence of the palms and bananas and spurge, and braced for the great struggle of his life that was now to begin in earnest.

The voyage had really two aims. To see the volcano above a palm-clad coast, with the Atlantic Ocean bringing its medusæ; and to work for Darwin.

A personal connection between the two had already been formed as a matter of course. Darwin, almost confined for years to his isolated home at Down owing to his constant ill-health, had received a copy of the *Radiolaria*, and the correspondence had begun. The work had as yet met with little encouragement from the ranks of exact scientists. It cannot have been a matter of indifference to Darwin personally that so distinguished a work, a real model of professional research, had come over to him. Proofs of the *Morphology* were sent over to Down before the book was ready for publication. Darwin read German with difficulty, but in this case he was stimulated to make an unusual effort. At last Haeckel himself made his appearance at the master's home. It seemed as though he had to visit him in person to receive his blessing. It was, at all events, a happy moment in the history of Darwinism when the two men first met whose names will be inseparable in literature.

This was in October, 1866; Darwin had sent his carriage to bring Haeckel from the station. A sunny autumn morning smiled on the homely and beautiful English landscape with its bright woods and golden broom and red erica and evergreen oaks.

Haeckel has described their first meeting. "When the carriage drew up before Darwin's house, with its ivy and its shadowy elms, the great scientist stepped out of the shade of the creeper-covered porch to meet me. He had a tall and venerable appearance, with the broad shoulders of an Atlas that bore a world of thought: a Jove-like forehead, as we see in Goethe, with a lofty and broad vault, deeply furrowed by the plough of intellectual work. The tender and friendly eyes were overshadowed by the great roof of the prominent brows. The gentle mouth was framed in a long, silvery white beard. The noble expression of the whole face, the easy and soft voice, the slow and careful pronunciation, the natural and simple tenor of his conversation, took my heart by storm in the first hour that we talked together, just as his great work had taken my intelligence by storm at the first reading. I seemed to have before me a venerable sage of ancient Greece, a Socrates or an Aristotle."

They were delighted to meet each other, for they were like natures, in their best qualities. Darwin had more passion in him than he ever expressed, and behind all Haeckel's impetuosity there was the naïve and yielding temper of the child. He poured out his anger against the stubborn and bewigged professors who still held out against the luminous truth of the theory of evolution. Darwin put his hand on his shoulder, smiled, and said they were rather to be pitied than blamed, and that they could not keep back permanently the stream of truth. At heart, however, he was delighted with his fiery pupil. They were to fight their battle shoulder to shoulder for seventeen years. During all those years there was never the slightest disturbance of their friendship. Darwin knew well what an auxiliary he had in Haeckel. It is true that he wrote him a wonderful letter occasionally, in which he used the right of a senior to warn Haeckel not to deal so violently with his opponents. Violence only had the effect of making onlookers side with the party you attacked. We must be careful not to be too hasty in setting things up as positive truths, as we see every day people starting from the same premises and coming to opposite conclusions. But he was generally at one with Haeckel, and had the good spirit to acknowledge it openly. When Haeckel's *History of Creation* raised up the most extreme parties, and started the cry that a distinction must be drawn at once between Darwin's real scientific ideas and Haeckel's desperate excursions into natural philosophy, Darwin said, in the *Descent of Man*, which he had begun much earlier, but did not publish for some time, that he would never have written his book if he had then known Haeckel's *History of Creation*. Haeckel had anticipated so much that he wished to say. And when Virchow attacked Haeckel in 1877, Darwin spoke very severely of the opponents who would make the eternal freedom to teach the truth dependent on the accidental conditions of a modern State. Haeckel visited him twice at Down. On February 12, 1882, he sent Darwin his congratulations on his seventy-third birthday from the summit of Adam's Peak in Ceylon. This was his last greeting. Darwin died two months afterwards. There was a touch of romance in this last communication of the two great warriors. On the summit of the mountain, almost as sharp as a needle, and 2,500 yards above the Indian Ocean, a tiny temple of Buddha hangs like a stork's nest suspended by chains. Buddha is believed to have left his footprints on the rocks here. The Mohammedan tradition, however, says it was done by Adam as he stood on one foot and bemoaned the loss of Paradise. In front of this holy trace, a depression in the rock about a foot long, Haeckel made a speech to his travelling companions, and they broke the neck of a bottle of Rhine wine to Darwin's health. It is no little stretch of humanity's pilgrimage, from Adam to Buddha and on to Darwin.

In October, 1866, Haeckel had a companion in a teacher from Bonn, Richard Greeff (afterwards professor of zoology at Marburg). They took ship from London to Lisbon, where they were long detained for quarantine, though the annoyance was somewhat relieved by the discovery of an interesting medusa in the brackish water of the Tagus. They then went to Madeira and Teneriffe, not right into the tropics, but where they might get a breath of it, as it were. Two of Haeckel's pupils, who both became well known afterwards,

Ernst Haeckel and his assistant Miklucho-Maclay at Lanzarote, in the Canaries, 1867.

To face p. 244.

THE "GENERAL MORPHOLOGY" 245

Miklucho-Maclay and Fol, were with them. Greeff has given a full account of the journey in a whole volume (published at Bonn, 1868), and Haeckel has written of it in two articles, one of which (in the fifth volume of the *Zeitschrift der Gesellschaft für Erdkunde*, Berlin, 1870) is a perfect masterpiece of narrative and description of scenery. After a long search they chose as the best station for studying marine animals, especially the medusæ, the little island of Lanzarote, instead of one of the chief islands. Here they fished and drew, in the manner taught by Johannes Müller, for three months, from December, 1866, to February, 1867. It is not exactly an ideal place. "Imagine yourself dumped down on the moor!" Haeckel said afterwards in his description of it. A piece of arid land that looked like a strip of the Sahara in the middle of the ocean. There is hardly any water, and the vegetation is correspondingly meagre. Across the middle of the island stretches a chain of volcanic craters, and old lava-fields run down from them as far as the coast. Everything of zoological interest in the place was to be found in the sea. There they found abundance. As in Messina, certain local currents drove the rich animal plancton together until there were literally rivers or streets of tiny animals. One had only to dip in one's nets and glasses, and bring up whole shoals with every drop of water.

Haeckel had come chiefly to study the medusæ. But this led him on much further to a great zoological problem. In his *General Morphology* he had expounded his brilliant ideas on the subject of individuality, and now he encountered in the flesh one of the greatest marvels of animal individuality. He had shown how the higher individual is always made up of a community, a kind of state, of lower individuals. In the simplest instance there are the cells. Each of them is an individual. Millions of these individuals, banded together with division of labour for great collective operations, make up the human frame, and therefore the human "individual." In the same way others form a beetle, a snail, or a single medusa. Sometimes, however, these higher individuals enter in turn into social combinations to form still higher communities. Human beings form social commonwealths, with division of labour among the individuals. Bees and ants form their communities in the same way. But in the latter cases the texture of the community seems to be much looser than in the preceding one. It is not so easy for the imagination to grasp a human commonwealth or a colony of bees as a real "over-individual." It is, therefore, extremely instructive to find that at least one animal community of this kind is of so firm a texture that even on the most superficial examination it is recognised at once as an individual. This is found in one of the groups of the medusæ, the siphonophores, or social medusæ.

A number of single medusæ, each of which

corresponds to what we regard as the individual man, combine and form a new body, a social individual. As citizens of this new state they have introduced the most rigid division of labour. One medusa does nothing but eat, and it thus provides nourishment for the rest, as they are all joined in one body. Another accomplishes the swimming movement; another has been converted entirely into a reproductive organ. In a word, the whole has become a "unity" once more, equipped with its various organs like any large body. Sometimes thousands of separate medusæ enter into the structure of one of these wonders of the deep. And as each of the medusæ is generally a very pretty, flower-like creature, the social groups with their charming colours look like floating garlands of flowers made of transparent and tinted crystal. Their beauty would soon fix Haeckel's attention, but their bearing on his theory of individuality would give them an even greater value. For several years he had searched most attentively in the animal world for these "over-individuals" of the highest class. In the morphology he had had to be content with an old illustration of something of the kind, the star-fish. It was supposed to be a combination of vermalians. In this case the hypothesis has broken down, though there was a good deal to be said for it at first, and it was abandoned by him afterwards. But now, when he saw enormous numbers of siphonophores in the animal streams at Lanzarote, he entered upon a decisive study of

series at London, as the 28th volume of the *Zoology of the Challenger*, 1888. The voluminous work is illustrated with fifty masterly plates, some of them coloured, by Haeckel himself. The most important part of the text was also published in German at Jena, with the title, *System of the Siphonophoræ*. There is a good popular account of the siphonophore question in his lecture on "The Division of Labour in Nature and in Human Life" (1869). A few of these beautiful forms are also given on coloured plates in his illustrated work, *Art-forms in Nature*. Every thoughtful man ought, whatever his position is as regards Haeckel's ideas, to glance at this material that he has so vigorously and clearly presented.

While he was conducting this research into the embryonic development of the siphonophores, Haeckel made certain experiments on phenomena that have lately been made the subject of a special "experimental mechanical embryology" by some of his pupils, particularly Professor Roux, of Halle. He cut up siphonophore ova into several pieces at the commencement of their development, and saw an incomplete social medusa develop from each fragment.

Thus the journey, like the earlier one to Messina, brought the indefatigable student into touch once more with a "philosophical animal." This alone would have made it well worth the trouble. How many more of the kind the future might still have in reserve for him! In the quiet months at Puerto del Arrecise, on Lanzarote, he was gradually restored to his spiritual balance. Nature had taken much from him, but she offered him an inexhaustible return. His elasticity and vigour of frame had been restored before he left Teneriffe. In a twenty-two hours' tour, only interrupted by two hours' sleep, he had climbed to the highest summit of the Peak, in such an unfavourable season (in the November snow) that the native guides would not go any further in the end; all those who were with him except one stopped short a little way from the top. The short rest at the summit (4,128 yards above the sea-level, on the icy edge of the crater) was greatly enjoyed by him. He could see over a distance of 5,700 square miles, as much as one-fourth of the whole of Spain. "The extraordinary range and height of the horizon gives one a vague idea of the infinity of space. The deep unbroken silence and the consciousness that we have left all animal and vegetal life far behind, produce a profound feeling of solitude. One feels oneself, with a certain pride, master of the situation that has been secured with so much trouble and risk. But the next moment one feels what we really are —momentary waves in the infinite ocean of life, transitory combinations of a comparatively small number of organic cells, which, in the last resort, owe their origin and significance to the peculiar chemical properties of carbon. How small and mean at such moments do we find the little play of human passions that unfolds itself far below in the haunts of civilisation! How great and exalted in comparison does free Nature seem, as it unrolls before us, in one vast picture, the whole majesty and splendour of its creative power!" Thus he himself describes the moment. Something of that feeling of exalted solitude entered into his life. He stood firm and undazed—come what might.

CHAPTER VII

GROWTH OF IDEAS

AT Easter, 1867, Haeckel returned to Jena through Morocco, Madrid, and Paris. He spent a few of the pleasant spring weeks at the Strait of Gibraltar and in the South of Spain. In the fine bay of Algeciras (opposite to Gibraltar on the west) the current of the Strait brought swarms of interesting medusæ, siphonophores, and other "plancton-animals" into his net. In his solitary walks through the mountain forests of Andalusia, in the incomparable Moorish palaces and the cathedrals of Seville and Cordova, Granada and the Alhambra, he gazed on that wealth of Spain in treasures of Nature and Art which had excited his boyish imagination in the vivid pictures of Washington Irving.

With his return home a crisis occurred in his career, from our biographical point of view, such as we find at one point or other in the lives of all great men. Up to the present the course of his life has advanced steadily onward, so that the simple chronological order afforded the most natural thread for our narrative. With this crisis his activity broadens out more. His ideas, almost all of which are presented in the *General Morphology*, form a great and continuous stem, which throws out a large or a small flower on one side or other, according to the stimulus received. His life crystallises about Jena; however many journeys he makes, he always feels that he will return to his centre at Jena. Nothing in his later career ever shook him from this ideal and personal base.

In the summer after his return to Jena, 1867, he married Agnes Huschke, daughter of the distinguished Jena anatomist. He shares the happiness of this second marriage down to the present day. Of their three children, the son is now a gifted artist at Munich; the elder daughter is the wife of Professor Hans Meyer, proprietor of the Leipsic Bibliographical Institute, who is particularly known in science by his ascent of the Kilimandschars; the younger daughter is still at home with her parents.

He never leaves the University of Jena—and it never abandons him. It is a kind of spiritual marriage. In 1865, when the sky was still free from clouds, he was invited to take a position at Würtzburg, his old school-place. He declined the invitation, and was then appointed ordinary professor at Jena. Then the evil days came. The conclusions of his *Morphology* were popularised by himself, and went out far and wide amongst the masses. People opened their eyes to find that this audacious scientist was making " war upon God " out of his zoology. At length the difficult question arises whether a mind of that type can be retained in the honourable position of official professor. The Philistines are in arms. The quiet, stubborn group, that has vegetated unchanged, like a demoralised parasitic animal, from Abdern to Schilda, through thousands of years of the free development of the mind, boycots the professor and his family for a time. The Philistines appeal from their safe corner to the authorities to intervene. Once, towards the close of the sixties, the situation threatened to become really critical. The head of the governing body of the university at the time was Seebeck, a distinguished man who by no means shared Haeckel's views, but had a just feeling of Haeckel's honourableness and mental power. In the middle of the struggle Haeckel approaches him one day, and says that he is prepared to resign his position, a sacrifice to his ideas. Seebeck replied, "My dear Haeckel, you are still young, and you will come yet to have more mature views of life. After all, you will do less harm here than elsewhere, so you had better stop here." At Jena they still tell a similar story that happened on another occasion. A stern theologian presented himself in person at the chateau of Karl Alexander, Grand Duke of Weimar, and begged him to put an end to this scandal of the professorship of Haeckel, the arch-heretic. The Grand Duke, educated in the Weimar tradition of Goethe, asked, "Do you think he really believes these things that he publishes?" "Most certainly he does," was the prompt reply. "Very good," said the Grand Duke, "then the man simply does the same as you do."

Haeckel remained a professor at Jena; and when the current subsided a little, he was not insensible of their liberality. He remained faithful to Jena, though even Vienna, amongst other places, offered him a position (1871). Under his guidance "zoological" Jena flourished like a poor orphan that has suddenly been enriched. At one stroke the university was lifted to the position of an intellectual metropolis for the whole of the young scientific generation of the last quarter of the century. The best of the younger men that fill the biological positions in Germany to-day (and many others) were educated under Haeckel. Many of these pupils became opponents of his eventually, but they all went through his system. He had a further satisfaction. He not only attracted the young men to Jena, but he conjured up as if by magic the financial resources for improving the external advantages of the place for teaching and working. His style of "zoology," which was at the same time "natural philosophy," brought people to his assistance who would never have been won by a narrowly technical zoologist, no matter how learned he was. Twice men were induced "for his sake"—that is to say, induced by the magnetic force of his charming personality—to leave large legacies to be spent on the university under his direction; once it was the Countess Bose, another time Paul von Ritter of Basle.

Ritter alone gave sufficient to found two professorships at Jena for the express purpose of teaching the science of phylogeny that Haeckel had created.

All through the period of his long stay at Jena that followed we trace a series of continual holiday journeys. In these journeys he used to collect the best material for his professional research, following the method he had learned from Müller at Heligoland, and had practised at Messina and Lanzarote. At the same time these travels were, like the earlier ones, the bath of eternal youth and health for "the other soul in his breast"; the artist, the lusty wanderer, I might almost say the inveterate Bohemian in him, was then allowed to have his spell of song and gaiety. In Jena he took deeper and deeper root as time went on. There was something in him in this respect of a Persephone impulse, an alternation of winter and summer in his life. When the days of hard and wearing work were past, he would have to rush away into the free air, down to the blue sea, to far and happy Nature. "Here I am a man—dare be a man." The duty of the zoologist of Müller's school to go down to the sea to work came to his rich temperament, which included so much more than mere "professional reasons," with a splendid sense of Persephone-life: half his time in the cold North studying animal skeletons and dead bones by the burning lamp, the other half in the glare of the sun of reality, in living nature at its best. I will only quote summarily a few dates of these travels. In 1869 he spent the autumn vacation in Scandinavia. In 1871 he was in the island of Lesina in Dalmatia, where he, the arch-heretic, lived in a monastery with a jolly abbot. From beautiful Ragusa he made an interesting excursion to Cattaro and Montenegro. In 1873 he went to Egypt and Asia Minor, visiting Athens, Constantinople, Brussa, and the Black Sea. The culmination of this journey was a visit to the splendid coral banks of Tur, in the Red Sea. The Khedive, Ismail Pacha, put a Government steamer at his disposal for the journey. The excursion has been superbly described by Haeckel himself in the little volume, *The Corals of Arabia* (1876). The same volume contains the first specimens of his landscapes in water-colour. He spent the spring of 1875 in Corsica and Sardinia. On that occasion Oscar Hertwig discovered, in his presence, the process of fertilisation in the sea-urchin; his discoveries will long remain a turning-point in the history of our knowledge of sexual generation (one of the deepest mysteries in nature). In the autumn of 1876 he was at work on the coast of Great Britain, and reached as far as Ireland. In the spring of 1877 he was at Ithaca and Corfu; in the autumn we find him on the Riviera. In 1878 he went first to Fiume and Pola on the Adriatic, and afterwards on an Atlantic excursion to Brittany, Normandy, and Jersey. In the autumn of 1879 he was in Holland and Scotland.

In 1881 he made the second longest journey of his life. He secured permission to absent himself from the university for six months, and went to Ceylon. He left Jena on the 8th of October, and did not return until April 21, 1882. The traveller and æsthete in him revelled in this first plunge into the tropics. How he was taken to the enchanted land of India in the Lloyd steamer *Helios*, a pretty reminiscence of the "heliozoa" (sun-plants), a name he had himself invented; how he greeted his beloved medusæ in their beautiful tropical forms of the Indian Ocean; how he lived in the execrable but thoroughly tropical and interesting Whist-Bungalow at Colombo, where mysticism and an unholy joy in card-playing occupied him until philosophic zoology came to crown and redeem everything; how he set up his zoological laboratory far from the world at the Cingalese village of Belligemma (which he interpreted *bella gemma*, the "pretty jewel"), and fished with his Müller net for radiolaria, medusæ, and siphonophoræ, for six whole weeks, to the intense bewilderment of the naked children of the palms; how he at last penetrated into the wildest virgin forests of Ceylon, where one heard the heavy tread of the elephant and the roar of the panther —all this he has described in his *Visit to Ceylon*, the freshest expression of his temperament, which belongs utterly to the free, artistic half of his life, when Persephone has her summer days in the land of flowers.

He himself regarded this journey, happy and favoured to the very last minute, as a crown and conclusion of his travels that could never be surpassed. But many a long hour was to be spent in travel after that, and he was to make one journey that left Ceylon far behind him in the Indian Ocean. In the spring of 1887 he made a pilgrimage to the "Holy Land," Jerusalem and the Dead Sea, Damascus and Lebanon. On this journey he spent a delightful month on the island of Rhodos. In 1889 he had a pleasant time on the beautiful island of Elba. In 1890 he visited Algiers, where his innocent sketches and his anatomical knife brought suspicion on him; they arrested him and threatened to shoot him as a spy. He has described the incident in his genial way in his *Algerian Reminiscences* which is, unfortunately, lost in a back number of some magazine or other, like so many of the sketches of his travels. In 1897 he travelled over the whole of Russia, from Finland to the Caucasus, and visited Tiflis, Colchis, and the Crimea. In the autumn of 1892 he accompanied Sir John Murray, of the *Challenger* expedition, on a small deep-sea investigation on the coast of Scotland. In the spring of 1893 and 1897 he was at work once more in his beloved Messina, where he was now honoured as a world-famous guest. In the autumn of 1899 he climbed the Sabine and Corsican hills. As the second decade after his first journey to the tropics came to an end, he seemed to regard all he had done so far as a small payment on account. In his sixty-sixth year he felt the "home-sickness" for the tropics once more with such intensity that he quickly made up his mind to go as far as the equator. He left Jena on

August 21, 1900, and (after a brief visit to the exhibition at Paris) took ship at Genoa, on September 4th, for Singapore. His beloved Italy had provided part of the cost of the journey. In the previous year the Royal Academy of Science at Turin had awarded him the Bressa-prize (consisting of 10,000 lire) on account of his *Systematic Phylogeny*. Once more the tropics revived the great impression made on him in his earlier visit. This time he spent only a few hours in Ceylon, and sailed further south. He landed at Singapore on September 27th, and sixteen days afterwards went on to Java, and thus crossed the equator at last. He enjoyed to the full the charms of the landscape with its volcanoes and virgin forests, during his stay with Treub at Buitenzorg, at Tjibodas, and during his long journey across the greater part of the island. At Tjibodas he celebrated the close of the nineteenth century [German calculation] by painting a fine water-colour of the smoke-canopy over the summit of the volcano Gedeh, touched and gilded by the east rays of the sun on the last day of 1900. On January 23, 1901, he went from Batavia to Sumatra, crossed the Sunda Strait in sight of the famous volcanic ruins of Krakatoa, and spent six weeks in Padang on the south-west coast of Sumatra. This delay was largely involuntary, and due to an injury to his knee, caused by stumbling over a rail during a visit to an engineering establishment; but the time was by no means lost in the middle of such glories. On March 31st he landed in Europe (at Naples) once more, after a safe voyage. The notes he made during his journey yielded another charming work, *Letters from the East Indies and Malaysia* (1901). His spirit of enterprise is inexhaustible, and still continues.

.   .   .   .   .

Within this frame of his career we have now to study a growth of ideas and a continuance of research that tell of vigour, consistency, and success in every line. It unfolds logically like a great work of art.

The *General Morphology* stands at the parting of two ways. It afforded a programme of an infinite amount of fresh technical research—the elaboration of his studies in detail, of promorphology, of his theory of individuality, and of the phylogenetic system of living things; and the strengthening of the laws of evolution, especially the great biogenetic law. On the other hand, there was the purely philosophic work to be done: the gathering together of the general threads that ran through his work, and the building of a new philosophy of life, based on a new story of creation, from the atom to the moneron, from the moneron to man, and the whole to be comprised and contained in God. In a word, he might proceed in either of two ways from the *Morphology*: he might construct academic zoology afresh, or he might write a work on the new God.

When he came home from Lanzarote, the two ways seemed to coincide in front of him; his work had, indeed, opened them out as one. But external circumstances intervened. As things are, it was only his academic colleagues that had any right to the new biology. A new book on God and creation would go out to "the publicans and sinners." Interest must be lit up amongst the people at large, where there was as yet only the faintest spark. It appeared, moreover, that most of his academic colleagues in 1867 had no wish to enter on the new path he had opened out. A new generation would have to grow up first. The *Morphology*, from which Haeckel on his travels had expected at least a revolution, met at first with an icy silence. There was hardly any discussion of it, and no excitement whatever. Haeckel quickly made up his mind. He must turn in the other direction. Gegenbaur consoles him. He has given too much—twenty dishes instead of one. He must serve up the best part of the work on one dish, and it will be taken. Haeckel agrees with him to some extent, but his heavy technical artillery cannot be simplified so easily as that. The only possible thing to do is to give an extract of it, which will make the broad lines of the system clear. But as soon as that is done, he sees that the extract is still only the general philosophical part of it, and will not appeal to the general public.

It was such reflections as these that led to the writing of his *History of Creation*, a popular work.*

The chapters of this work were first delivered

* Translated into English with the above title. Literally, the title is: *The Story of Natural Creation.*

orally to students, in the form of lectures, and formed a kind of introduction to morphology. The lectures, retaining their lighter form, were then combined to make the book. It was published in 1868, a small volume in a very primitive garb. The success of the work was unprecedented.

Zoology and botany were treated philosophically in the *Morphology*. That did not suit the professional scientists, who (as I said) crossed themselves when they saw "natural philosophy." In the *History of Creation* the great problems of philosophy are dealt with successively on Darwinian lines, from the zoological and botanical point of view. It was like the sinking of a deep well amongst general thoughtful readers. People felt at last what a power science had become. The old riddles of life were studied in a new light with the aid of this book. There was no predecessor in this field. Haeckel was absolutely the first to appeal to the general reader in this way. It is true that what he gave them was, strictly speaking, only an extract from his own *Morphology*, especially the second volume. But as he now arranged his matter chronologically, he converted his outline of a world-system into a "world-history"—a real "history of natural creation." In the "Pictures of Nature" in the first volume of his *Cosmos* Humboldt had tried to bring the natural world before his readers as a great panorama, to be taken in at one glance. But he strictly confined his study of nature to the things that actually exist; how they came to exist was not, he intimated, a subject of scientific inquiry. Haeckel proceeds to this further task. His panorama of nature does not stand out rigidly before us; it develops, under the eyes of the observer, from the formless nebula to the intelligent human being. Even on the surface this was seen to be a prodigious advance. Very plain, but very attractive, it makes its way by the force of its convincing dialectic, and places no reliance on the fireworks of rhetoric. The subtle power of it lies in the arrangement of the facts, which suddenly assume the form of a logical chain instead of being a shapeless chaos. Even if all the main ideas of the work were false, we should be compelled to regard it as one of the cleverest works that was ever written, from the dialectical point of view. But the essence of this cleverness is the way in which the grouping of the facts is made to yield the philosophic evolution, which is the thoughtful basis of the work. As the world proceeds in its natural development from the nebular cosmic raw-material until it culminates in the ape and man, the reader finds himself at the same time advancing along a series of general philosophic conclusions with regard to God, the world, and man. If at the end he has retained the whole series of what are to him more or less new scientific details, he is bound to find himself caught in a strong net of philosophic conclusions.

In view of all this we can easily understand the different reception that the book met with from friend and foe. People who had already assented to the main issues of the work on general grounds of probability, were delighted to find these issues decisively established by the plain facts of science. On the other hand, those who would have none of Haeckel's philosophy now felt compelled, in view of this dreadful work, to call these alleged facts of science themselves into question. In face of this hostility it was some disadvantage that the *History of Creation* contained a vast amount of technical material (such as the genealogical trees, the Darwinian laws, the explanation of the facts of embryology, &c.) that could only be presented summarily in it, while the proper technical description and justification of them was buried in the thick volumes of the *Morphology*. Haeckel said, over and over again, that a certain thing had been so fully established by him scientifically in the other work that he was now at liberty to take it as a fact; and he accordingly built it up as such without prejudice into the compact structure of the popular work. Readers who wanted to go further into the discussion of these facts had to look up the relevant passages in the larger book. But the great bulk of his opponents—amongst whom we must count even many professional scientists—had never read the two volumes of the *Morphology*. They merely took the brief statement in the *History of Creation*, which was really little more than a reference, and made a violent attack on the " fact " it was said to convey.

This led to a great deal of confusion. As in this case a controversy over some petty zoological detail was always a "struggle about God," and so agitated the opponent down to the most secret folds of his philosophy, the usual consequences did not fail to put in an appearance. Haeckel was branded and calumniated personally. There has never been any apostle in the world that some sect or other has not decried as a rogue and evil-doer, simply because he was an apostle. Wherever Haeckel has made use of any material that did not seem to be absolutely sound in every respect, he was not simply accused of making a mistake, not even of ignorance, but the whole thing has been put down at once to dishonesty and the worst type of bad faith.

One should bear in mind how very generally pioneer work of this kind is liable to err. Further, in the *History of Creation* there is the danger involved in the popular presentation of the results of scientific research. Any man who has written popular works, or delivered lectures to the general public, knows what this means. There is little common measure between them. The truths of science are in a state of constant flux; it is of their essence to be so. To fish out a piece from this stream, fix it, and magnify it for the public with a broad beam of light, really amounts in principle to an alteration of it; it is putting a certain pressure on things, and giving them an arbitrary shape. The work of popularising truths is so holy a thing in its aim that this risk has to be run. We must take things as they are. We have two alternatives: either not to popularise at all, or to take the apparatus with all its defects. We can diminish these according to our skill; but there is a subjective limit to this skill in all of us.

The first edition of the *History of Creation*—Haeckel's first attempt at popularising—had a good deal of inequality in this respect. To begin with, the book had the air of an extempore deliverance. Its success was very largely due to its being cast in this form. But there was a good deal that could be improved here and there, and was improved in the later editions of the work. In the tenth edition, as we now have it, it is a splendid work in regard to the illustrations, for instance. But the first edition was merely provided with a few very crude woodcuts in outline. Some of them were very clumsy. In comparing different embryological objects the same blocks were used sometimes, and this would give rise to misunderstanding in the mind of the reader. For instance, there was question of demonstrating that certain objects, such as the human ovum and the ovum of some of the related higher mammals, were just the same in their external outlines. This fact is quite correct and established to-day. If I draw the outline, and write underneath it that as a type it is applicable to all known ova of the higher mammals, including man, there is no possibility of misunderstanding. But if I print the same illustration three times with the suggestion that they are three different mammal-ova, the general reader is easily apt to think, not only that they are identical in the general scheme of this outline, but also in internal structure. He imagines that the ova of man and the ape are just the same even in their microscopic and chemical features. This leads to a contradiction between the illustration and what Haeckel expressly says in the text. We read that there is indeed an external resemblance in shape between these ova, but that there is bound to be a great difference in internal structure, since an ape is developed from the one and a human being developed from the other. It would have been better if the general reader, who is not familiar with these outline pictures, had been more emphatically informed in the text below the illustration that even the outline is to be taken as a general and ideal scheme. In this sense we must certainly admit that the illustration was bad, since it would lead to a misunderstanding of the clear words of the text. But what are we to say when the opponents of Haeckel's views viciously raise the cry of "bad faith" on the ground of a few little slips like this, and suggest that he deliberately tried to mislead his readers with false illustrations? Amongst the general public, in so far as it was hostile to Haeckel, the charge blossomed out into the most curious forms. Some declared that the whole story of a resemblance between man's ovum and embryo and those of other animals was an invention of Professor Haeckel's; others—we even read it now and again in our own time—went so far as to say that the human ovum and embryonic forms only existed in Haeckel's imagination. All these wild charges are of no avail. The human ovum, which corresponds entirely in its general scheme to that of the other higher mammals, was not discovered in 1868 by the wicked Haeckel, but in 1827 by the great master of embryological research, Carl Ernst von Baer. The considerable external resemblance, at certain stages of development, between the embryos of reptiles, birds, and mammals, including man, was decisively established by the same great scientist. These really remarkable stages in the development of the human embryo, during which, in accordance with the biogenetic law, it shows clear traces of the gill-slits of its fish-ancestors, and has a corresponding fin-like structure of the four limbs and a very considerable tail, can be seen by the general reader at any time in the illustrated works of His, Ecker, and Kölliker (Haeckel's chief opponents) or in any illustrated manual of embryology, and their full force as evolutionary evidence can be appreciated. Any man that constructs his philosophy in such a way that, in his conviction, it stands or falls with the existence of these embryonic phenomena, is in a very delicate position, apart altogether from Haeckel. His philosophy will collapse, even if the *History of Creation* had never been written.

These curious discussions did not seriously interfere with the success of the book. In thousands and thousands of minds, in 1868, this little work proved the grain of seed that led on in time to serious thought. From that time onward Haeckel knew that he had not only scientific colleagues and academic pupils, but a crowd of followers. When he made an excursion into the northern part of the

Sahara, as far as the first oasis, twenty-two years afterwards, he met an artist there. They talked philosophy, and the man, not knowing Haeckel, naïvely recommended him to study the *History of Creation* as likely to give him most help. The little incident shows us something of the great pioneer work done by the volume, something of its spiritual circumnavigation of the globe.

.   .   .   .

Thus the spiritual nucleus of the *General Morphology* is introduced, with great ability, to a much wider circle than Haeckel had dreamed of when he gave the *Morphology* to his colleagues. But the agitation gradually spread into academic circles. On the whole the Darwinian ideas pressed in everywhere by their own irresistible weight. Haeckel's more particular concern, however, was to secure the recognition of one single point in the larger group of ideas—the great biogenetic law. This was for many years the pivot on which almost all the discussions with him and about him turned.

He himself did not at first conceive his law as a matter of controversy, but as a method that must be brought into a position of practical utility. An opportunity to do this arose immediately.

While he was at Lanzarote he began to take an interest in a second group of lowly animals besides the siphonophores, namely the sponges. When the general reader hears the word "sponge" he must modify his ordinary ideas a little. In the present instance he must not think of the plants, belonging to the fungi-group, such as the morel and cognate forms, that are often called "sponges" in common parlance. He must think rather of the sponge he uses in his bath. The bath-sponge is a structure made up of very tough, elastic, horny fibres. This structure is originally the skeleton, as it were, of certain animals that are known as "sponge-animals" or, briefly, sponges; they have nothing to do with the spongy mushrooms I spoke of. At the same time these socially-living sponges are such curious creatures that it was disputed for a long time whether they were real animals or not. There was a second controversy in regard to them as to where the "individual" began—what was a single animal, and what a co-operative colony of animals. The latter point alone would have been enough to direct Haeckel's attention to this group after he had, in the case of the siphonophores, gone so deeply into the mystery of combined individuals, forming a new "state-individual." His own opinion eventually was that as a matter of fact in the majority of cases the whole sponge is a stock or colony of separate sponge individuals closely connected together. They had not, indeed, anything like the ingenious method of division of labour that we find in the social medusæ; in fact, the sponges are in all respects much more lowly organised animals than the medusæ. But they were certainly true animals. And in the middle of his efforts to prove this Haeckel travelled into an entirely new field of research, lying far beyond the theory of individuality.

As there is an enormous number of different sponges, he had confined his studies from the first to a single group of them that might be taken as typical. He chose the calcispongiæ (calcareous sponges), which had been the least studied up to that time. As the name obviously implies, these sponges form their internal framework or skeleton, not of elastic horny fibres like the common bath-sponge, but of solid calcareous needles or spines. They secrete these out of the soft substance of their bodies just as the radiolaria do their pretty siliceous houses. Haeckel was engaged for five years, from 1867 to 1872, in a profound and careful study of the natural history of the calcispongiæ. Then he published the results in his *Monograph on the Calcispongiæ*, consisting of two volumes of text and an atlas of sixty fine plates.

The first result was that the calcispongiæ afforded a splendid proof of the impossibility of drawing sharp limits between species in the perpetually developing animal world. In their case the different varieties passed constantly out of each other and back into each other in a way that would have made a classifier of the old type distracted. But Haeckel had travelled far beyond the position of his boyhood, when he had timorously concealed the bad species that would not fit into the system. He said humorously that in the case of the calcispongiæ you had the choice of distinguishing one genus with three species, or three genera with 239 species, or 113 genera with

Ernst Haeckel, 1874.

To face p. 272.

591 species. All this confusion was saved by the Darwinian idea of not setting up absolutely rigid classes, families, genera, and species. But even this was not yet the essential point.

As he had done in the case of the siphonophores, Haeckel endeavoured to derive as much information as possible from the "ontogeny," or embryonic development, of the calcispongiæ. He established in some cases, it seemed to him, that a single calcisponge-individual at first and up to a certain stage developed from the ovum in the same way as a medusa or a coral or an anemone. The fertilised ovum, a single cell, divided into two cells, then several, and at last formed a whole cluster of cells. In this cluster the cells arranged themselves at the surface, and left a hollow cavity within. Then two layers of cells were formed, like a double skin, in the wall of this vesicle, and an opening was left at one spot in the wall of it. Thus we got a free-swimming embryo, with a mouth, an external skin, and an internal digestive skin or membrane. Then the creature attaches itself to the floor of the sea and becomes a real sponge, partly by developing along its characteristic lines, and partly (in most cases) by producing other sponges from itself in the form of buds, like the siphonophore, and so forming an elaborate colony, to which we give collectively the title of "a sponge." These facts led to the following reflections.

This original development from the ovum, first into an embryo with the form of a small globe or, more correctly, an oval body consisting of two layers of cells and having a hole at one pole—in other words, a creature with nothing but skin, stomach, and mouth—was found, curiously enough, in other animals besides the medusæ, corals, and sponges. We have the same course of development in representatives of the most varied groups of animals. There are worms, star-fishes, crabs, and snails that develop in the same way. In fact, it was proved in this very year (1867) that the lowest of the vertebrates, the amphioxus (or lancelet), develops in the same way. And this was not all. In the ontogeny of all the higher animals right up to man (inclusive) we find a state of things that most closely resembles the same development. At all events, the fertilised ovum gives rise in all cases to a cluster of cells; this cluster forms something like a flattened or elongated vesicle with a single-layered wall; the single layer of cells is doubled, and in the building up of the body one half makes the external coat or skin and the other half the internal lining or membrane. Haeckel reflected on the whole of the facts, and drew his conclusions. This very curious agreement in the earlier embryonic forms must be interpreted in terms of the biogenetic law. In the case of the higher animals the forms have been profoundly modified by cenogenesis. In the lower animals they are almost or altogether a pure recapitulation of the real primitive course of the development of the animal kingdom. In the earliest times animals were evolved in something like the following way. First, the primitive unicellular protozoa came together and formed crude social bodies, clusters of cells that kept together, but had no special division of labour. As all the members in the cluster pressed to the surface, in order to obtain their food, they came to form, not a solid mass of cells, but a hollow vesicle with a wall of cells. Then the first division of labour set in. Certain cells, those that were situated at the anterior pole, and so were better placed to receive the floating food as the animal moved along, became the eating-cells of the group; they provided nourishment for the others, as the nutritious sap circulated through all the cells in the cluster, as we find in the case of the siphonophores. As these feeding-cells multiplied rapidly at the fore part of the animal, a depression was formed at that pole of the body. In the end the ball or vesicle was doubled in upon itself, until it came to have the form of a cup with a double-layered wall. Externally were the cells in the skin that effected movement and feeling, and afforded protection; inside, forming the internal wall, were the eating- or stomach-cells. An opening remained at the top—the opening of the cup or vase-like body. The food entered by it: it was virtually the "mouth." Thus was formed a primitive multicellular animal with division of labour. If we imagine it attaching itself to the bottom by its lower pole, we can see that it would easily become a sponge of the simplest kind, a polyp, a coral, or, detaching itself once more, a medusa. If we imagine it swimming ahead in the water or creeping along the ground in such a way as to assume a bilateral symmetrical structure, like a tube, with right and left, back and belly, and an anus behind, we have a worm. This worm developed, under the action of the Darwinian laws, into a star-fish in one case, a crab or insect in another, a snail or mussel in another, and lastly into the amphioxus, which led on through the vertebrates to the human frame. But the mysterious series of forms always remained in the development of the individual from the egg, pointing more or less clearly to the earlier stages: ovum, cluster of cells, ball, two cell-layers in a cup-shaped form, skin, stomach, and mouth. All animals that exhibit this primitive scheme belong to one great stem. It was not until this skin-stomach-mouth animal was formed that the tree branched out—evolving into sessile, creeping, swimming, and other forms. Let us give a name to this phylogenetic (ancestral) form, which stands at the great parting of the ways in the animal world, as embryology proves. Leaving aside its innumerable relatives in the primitive days, it must have differed essentially from all other living things at the time—all the protists and the plants—by its possession of a skin, stomach, and mouth. *Gaster* is the Greek for stomach. Let us, therefore, call this primitive parent of all the sponges polyps, medusæ, worms, crustacea, insects, snails, mussels, cephalopods, fishes, salamanders, lizards, birds, mammals, and man, the *gastræa*, the primitive-stomach or primitive-gut animal. The corresponding embryonic form may be distinguished from it as the *gastrula*. There are still many living species of animals that are very little higher in organisation than the gastræa-form. The *Pemmatodiscus gastrulaceus*, discovered by Monticelli in 1895, corresponds entirely to it. And the gastrula is found, as I said, with astonishing regularity in its precise gastræa-form in representatives of all the higher groups of animals.

That is an outline of the famous gastræa-theory, that Haeckel discovered when he was engaged in studying the calcisponges. It was first published in his large *Monograph on the Calcispongiæ* in 1872, elaborated in his *Studies of the Gastræa-theory* in 1873, 1875, and 1876 (published in one volume in 1877), and generally expounded, together with the biogenetic law, in (amongst other works) his polemical essay, "The aims and methods of modern embryology" (1875). This discovery, in Haeckel's opinion, now made the biogenetic law a real search-light in the exploration of the obscure past. It indicated a third critical point in the great genealogical tree. Already we had the root (the monera) and the crown (man); now we had the point from which the various real animal stems radiated like the umbellate branches of a single large bloom. Through it the Darwinian system had been converted into the greatest practical reform of animal classification. If this gastræa-theory was correct, it was an incalculable gain for zoology. The difficulty of it, on the other hand, lay in the infinite modifications of the embryonic processes in detail that had been brought about by cenogenesis; almost everywhere this had more or less obscured the original features. On the whole it gave rise to the greatest and most far-reaching discussion that has taken place in zoology for the last thirty years, apart from the Darwinian theory itself. To-day, at the close of these three decades, there are only two alternatives. One is that there is still an absolutely mysterious and hidden law of ontogeny, that compels countless animals over and over again to pass through these embryonic forms and assume a likeness to the gastræa. After all the eagerness with which the whole school of embryologists opposed to Haeckel have sought, up to our own day, to establish such a direct law, we have not yet got the shadow of a clear formulation of it. The other alternative is that Haeckel is right in believing that he has discovered the correct formula in his phylogenetic interpretation of embryonic processes in accordance with the biogenetic law. If that is so, the gastræa-theory is the crown of all his labours in technical zoology proper. Let us wait another thirty years.

The scientific controversy over the gastræa-theory was in full swing when Haeckel entered upon another bold experiment in the direction of the biogenetic law. He thought it would be useful, instead of framing wider hypotheses, to take one single instance of one of the highest animals, and trace the whole parallel of its embryonic and ancestral development down to its finest details. It would serve as an excellent object-lesson. He would take it, not from some remote corner of the system, such as the sponges or medusæ, but from the very top of the tree, where palingenesis and cenogenesis seemed to have culminated in an inextricable confusion. But what example could be more appropriate and effective than the most advanced of all living things—man. He would write a monograph on man on an entirely new method; would show ontogeny and phylogeny confirming each other down to the smallest detail. It was another great enterprise. And this particular subject was so interesting that it would appeal strongly to the general readers of his *History of Creation* as well as to the academic scientists. Man was a subject of such obviousness and importance to the layman that in this case there was really no professional limitation of interest at all. Every detail in the most technical treatment of the subject would be taken into account, and evoked his strongest sympathy.

When Haeckel had fully matured this plan, he produced his *Anthropogeny*.* The word, founded on the Greek, means the "genesis" or "evolution of man."

The work is a very able combination of two

* The fifth edition is translated into English, with all the plates and illustrations, under the title of *The Evolution of Man*. [Trans.]

different aims. On the one hand it affords the technical student the outline of a wholly new and distinctive manual of human embryology (up to a certain extent) and general anatomy; and this is intimately bound up by his method with a kind of historical introduction to general anthropology. At the same time the book forms a second part of the *History of Creation*. It builds up the most important chapter of the later work, from the philosophical point of view, namely, that which deals with the origin of man, into a fresh volume; and it represents the first popular treatment of embryology on broad philosophic lines—a thing that had never been attempted before. Springing up from this double root, the work is certainly one of the most successful things in the whole of Haeckel's literary career. Moreover, it is not merely a compendium of a larger work, like the *History of Creation*. In spirit and form it is an original work, and gives his very best to the reader. As far as its general effect is concerned, the double-address of the work has had its disadvantages. The academic students who were hostile to it have once more selected for attack certain excrescences and gaps that were merely due to the exigencies of popular treatment. On the other hand, the general reader found it, in spite of the popular form, on which Herculean labour had been spent—one has only to think of the details of embryology—a book that was not to be "read" in the ordinary sense of the word, but studied. The first edition appeared in 1874. A fifth edition has now been published, equipped with the finest illustrations, both from the artistic and the scientific point of view, that have ever appeared in a popular work on embryology. We find in the *Anthropogeny* all that the nineteenth century has learned or surmised with regard to the ancestral history of mankind. Even the gastræa-theory—the gastræa belonging to man's direct ancestry—is dealt with in popular fashion as far as this was possible.

When the *Anthropogeny* was published Haeckel's public position became more stormy than ever. In professional circles a number of the embryologists had taken up an attitude of opposition to him; the most heated of them attacked his popular works continually on the ground that he was popularising, not the real results of official science, but his own personal opinions. There was a great deal of truth in that. The only question was, which would stand best with the future, his or their personal opinion? It does not alter the subjectivity of opinions that a few people here and there combine and pretentiously constitute themselves into a "science." Posterity will deal coolly enough with their collective decisions. It will take every man of science as an individual, and merely ask which of them came nearest to the truth. The name, the official science, will pass into the grave with many titles and decorations. All that will remain in men's minds is the star of the personality in its relation to the great constellation of contemporary human truth. However, as regards the particular embryological attacks of these opponents, it seems to me to-day especially characteristic that such people are more and more abandoning the idea that it is only a question of contesting certain particular deductions of Haeckel's *within* the limits of Darwinism. They find themselves increasingly compelled to throw Darwinism overboard altogether. Instead of its attempts to explain phenomena they are putting forward a confused claim of "direct mechanical explanations," or relying on the sonorous old phrase, started in 1859, an "immanent law of evolution," or retreating into a despairing attitude of "I don't know." These clearer divisions will make it very much easier for posterity to pass its judgment on the situation.

After the embryologists we have a considerable group of opponents on the anthropological side. The objections of these anthropological critics have in the course of time narrowed down to the single argument that no transitional form between man and the ape has yet been discovered. And for many years now this position has not been held on serious scientific grounds, but rather on ingenious and strained hypotheses. Because we now have, in the bones found at Java by Eugen Dubois in 1894, the remains of a being that stands precisely half-way between the gibbon and man. Hence what is called the anti-Darwinian and especially anti-Haeckelian school of anthropology to-day is mainly distinguished for its preference of more risky and more subtle hypotheses instead of plain conclusions from obvious facts. Finally, there is the theological opposition to Haeckel that increased with every book in which he put his ideas before the general public and helped them (in their boundless professional wisdom) to realise the danger of the situation.

The year 1877 was a critical one in this respect. In the middle of his struggles Haeckel retained all the simplicity of his nature. He saw that the idea of evolution was triumphing over all obstacles and rapidly securing the allegiance of the best men of the time. On the 18th of September, 1877, he spoke of this with unrestrained delight at the scientific congress at Munich. He described the theory of evolution as "the most important advance that has been made in pure and applied science." Then Rudolf Virchow delivered a speech at the same congress.

There is no doubt whatever that in the period since Virchow had indicated a neutral field in 1863, in which science might effect "its compromise," Haeckel had boldly invaded that province. In the previous year he had published a little work called *The Perigenesis of the Plastidules, or the Generation of Waves in Vital Particles*. It was delivered in lecture-form at the medical-scientific congress at Jena in November, 1875, and then printed on the occasion of Seebeck's jubilee, May 9, 1876. Possibly it is the least known of all Haeckel's works, though in my opinion it is one of the most valuable in regard to the prophetic breadth of its intuition. It essays to establish a theory of heredity. In dealing with this deepest mystery of life psychic factors are pressed into service without reserve. Not only is the cell-soul put into prominence, but the cell in turn is resolved into a number of smaller units, the plastidules. Each plastidule is then conceived as a psychic unity. The souls of the plastidules are endowed with memory; that is the root of heredity. They learn; that is the psychological expression of adaptation. The little work offers a suggestion of a psychology of Darwinism that may very well become the nucleus of the whole Darwinian structure in the twentieth century. But at the time it was quite obvious that a man with such ideas as these was breaking with lusty fist through the sacred net that spread before Virchow's reserved province. The hour had come, therefore, for Virchow to feel that he must expel the idea of evolution from the whole field of science, and not merely from embryology and anthropology.

It is very instructive to note how Virchow shifted his position a little in accordance with the time. In his judgment science *had* to make peace. It had to make concessions in certain directions. In 1863 he had spoken of the "ruling Churches." Now, in 1877, he speaks of the freedom of science in the "modern State." The great *Kulturkampf* had set in. The Church was for the time being powerless in face of the State. Hence Virchow now plays off the State as the guardian of his tabooed province. This time Darwinism is supposed to be threatening the virgin field in which we exact scientists make our peace with the State. At the right moment he adroitly points out that the Social Democrats have taken to Darwinism. Every man on deck, then. That must not go any further. At the bottom it was the old contest. If one lays down as a general principle that the scientific pursuit and presentment of truth has to respect neutral provinces and make concessions, every change in current affairs will demand a fresh application of it. To-day it is some Church or other, to-morrow a State, the next day the momentary code of morals, and lastly some bumbledom or other that renews the prohibition to dissect corpses, because our dissecting knives disturb the peace of mind of our Philistine neighbours. Haeckel published a sharp reply to Virchow (*Free Science and Free Teaching*, 1878), in which he sought to show amongst other things, taking his stand on his political principles, that Socialism and Darwinism have nothing to do with each other.

I will not go more fully into the controversy here. If one province of knowledge is to receive light from another at all, we must admit that there is only one general truth. All stationary or reactionary political interest is irreconcilable with the theory of evolution. That is clear from the very meaning of the words. As to the direction in which we must seek real political and social progress opinions are bound to differ very considerably; it may be shown that the laws of evolution which have selected the various species of plants and animals can only be used very sparingly and cautiously for the promotion of human progress. But I believe that is quite an immaterial point in this matter of Virchow's attack. The real influence of Darwinism on political questions is not the chief question. The principle we have to determine is whether the freedom of scientific research and the teaching of what the individual student believes he has discovered to be true are to have "external" restrictions or not. The question is whether inquiry and teaching are to be regarded merely as things "tolerated" and interfered with at will amongst the various elements of modern life; or whether they are not to be considered the very bed-rock of civilisation, and every agency that has power for the moment is not doomed whenever it comes into collision with them.

In this momentous duel of the two men who were regarded at the time as unquestionably the most distinguished scientists in Germany it seemed to most people for a time that Haeckel had gone off altogether into general and public questions with regard to the aim of research and philosophy. He seemed to lend colour to the belief as he published, in quick succession, a number of new popular lectures (*Cell-souls and Soul-cells*, 1878, and *The Origin and Evolution of the Sense-organs*, 1878), and at the same time published a collected volume of older and recent *Essays on the Theory of Evolution* (one part in 1878, a second in 1879, and a new and enlarged edition in 1902). As a matter of fact, we find him in these years occupied with a small but particularly well-lit field of his whole work. It was not merely that in a few years he buried himself in the primitive forests of Ceylon, in order to pursue his special studies far removed from all civilisation for months together. Just at this date appeared the great monograph on the medusæ, which he had at length concluded. The first volume (*The System of the Medusæ*, with 40 coloured plates) was published in 1879, and the second (*The Deep-sea Medusæ of the Challenger Expedition and the Organisms of the Medusæ*, with 32 plates) in 1881. And while these splendid volumes showed his academic colleagues that he had no mind to remain entirely on the outer battlements as a philosophic champion, he plunged up to the ears in a new special study of a range that would have made even the most enthusiastic specialist recoil.

From December, 1872, to May, 1876, the English had conducted a peaceful enterprise that will be for ever memorable. A staff of distinguished naturalists had gone on the ship *Challenger* to explore the depth, temperature, and bottom of remote seas. With the aid of the best appliances specimens of the mud from the floor of the ocean (sometimes more than a mile in depth) were brought up at 354 different spots. It was known from earlier deep-sea explorations that this slime on the floor of the ocean, from a certain coast-limit into the deepest parts, is composed for the most part of the microscopically small shells of little marine animals. The living creatures that form these shells swim in the water of the ocean, partly at the surface and partly at various depths beneath it. When they die the little hard coat of mail sinks to the bottom, and as there are millions upon millions of them living in the sea, thick deposits are gradually formed at the bottom that consist almost entirely of these microscopic shells. The animals in question are primitive little creatures consisting of a single cell, of the type that Haeckel has called "Protists." Even in Ehrenberg's time it had been noticed that amongst the shells in the deep-sea mud there were, besides chalky shells, a number of graceful flinty coats that clearly pointed to the radiolaria. The *Challenger* expedition now made the great discovery that vast fields at the floor of the ocean, especially of the Pacific, were covered almost exclusively with these flinty shells. It was seen at once that the few hundred species of radiolaria that had hitherto been described by Haeckel and others were only a very small part of the masses of radiolaria found in the ocean. The specimens of the deposits which were carefully preserved and brought home by the *Challenger* contained such an immense number of unknown species with their flinty shells faultlessly preserved, that it was necessary to reconstruct the whole of this wonderful group of animals. And who could be better qualified for the work than the man who had already made a name by his study of the radiolaria, Haeckel?

When the English Government came to publish the results of the *Challenger* expedition in a monumental work (of fifty volumes), he was entrusted with the work on the siphonophores, the corneous sponges, and all the radiolaria in the collection. For ten years, from 1877 to 1887, Haeckel devoted every available hour to the work of selecting the radiolarian shells with his microscope from these specimens of the deep-sea deposits, and naming, describing, and drawing the new species. When he began his task 810 species of radiolaria were known to science. When he came to his provisional conclusion, ten years afterwards, though his material was not yet exhausted, there were 4,318 species and 739 genera. They are described in the splendid work that he wrote for the *Challenger* Report. It consists of two volumes of text (in English) with 2,750 pages and 140 large plates, with the title, *Report on the Radiolaria collected by H.M.S. Challenger*. In the preparation of these plates (and in the illustration of all his later works) he had the very valuable assistance of the gifted Jena designer and lithographer, Adolph Giltch. A good deal of new information with regard to the living body of the radiolaria had come to light since 1862. In particular it had now been settled beyond question that they consisted merely of a single cell. There was, therefore, a good opportunity of reconstructing the *Monograph* of 1862 with the new and more comprehensive work. The chief contents of the English work (with a selection of the plates) were then published in German, and appeared in 1887 and 1888 as the second, third, and fourth parts of the *Monograph on the Radiolaria*. A sort of supplementary essay on the methods of studying the radiolaria and cognate "plancton" animals was published separately with the title of *Planctonic studies* (1890). Though it was a moderate and tactful criticism of the methods of some of his colleagues in this kind of work, it was "refuted" by them in a way that it would be difficult to qualify—in other words, it was fruitlessly assailed with charges of the most general but most unpleasant character. In the English Report we find two other volumes afterwards from Haeckel—the volume on the siphonophoræ in 1888, and the *Report on the Deep-sea Keratosa collected by H.M.S. Challenger* in 1889; these again opened up new chapters in zoology. The *Challenger* work is the crown of Haeckel's studies as a specialist. To some extent the conclusion of it closes an epoch in his life.

We will only touch briefly on what he has done since. It has not yet passed into the region of history.

The latest years in Haeckel's constructive work are characterised mainly by *one* idea. He had often been pressed to work up afresh the material of his *General Morphology*. He has not done so in the form that was expected, but chose a form of his own. In the first place he took the systematic introduction to the second volume, which had been the first able attempt to draw up the genealogical tree of the living world, branch by branch, and, with the material that had accumulated in the subsequent thirty-four years, built it up into a separate work. It had consisted formerly of 160 pages: now it formed three volumes of 1,800 pages. There were forty years of incessant study embodied in it. It had the title *Systematic Phylogeny*:* "a sketch of a natural system of organisms on the basis of their stem-history." The first volume (dealing with the protists and plants) appeared in 1894; the second volume (dealing with the invertebrate animals) in 1896, and the third (dealing with the vertebrates) in 1895. Closely connected with it is his special systematic study of the stem-history of the echinoderms (star-fish, &c.), with particular reference to paleontology (*The amphoridea and cystoidea* in the *Work in Commemoration of Karl Gegenbaur*, 1896).

His academic colleagues had hardly begun to master this new phylogeny when Haeckel once more roused a general agitation by working up the philosophic nucleus of the *Morphology* in a more general form than he had done in the *History of Creation*. This new work was *The Riddle of the Universe*, "a popular study of the Monistic philosophy." † It was, he declared, his philosophical testament. In a few months 10,000 copies of the work were sold, and a later cheap popular edition

* It has not been translated into English. A recent reviewer in *Nature* pronounced it to be Haeckel's best work. [Trans.]

† Literally, the title is "World-Riddles," or "World-Problems." [Trans.]

ran to more than 100,000 copies. It has also been translated into fourteen different languages. The controversy it excited has not yet died away. Already a supplementary volume, *The Wonders of Life*, has followed it (1904). Haeckel had been working in this department with great vigour for many years. He only made one appearance at a German scientific congress since the Virchow affair. That was on September 18, 1882, in quiet and uncontroversial form. A little excitement was caused amongst those who saw their salvation in keeping the gentle Darwin far apart from the impetuous Haeckel when he read a rather free philosophical confession of Darwin's. Their tactics broke down as the deceased Darwin passed into an historical personality and disappeared from the struggle of contending parties. In 1892 Haeckel wrote with great vigour in the militant Berlin journal, the *Freie Bühne*, on the new alliance of the Church and political parties in Germany, criticising the political situation on general philosophical principles, and in opposition to Virchow's spirit of compromise. In the same year he delivered at Altenburg a lecture on " Monism as a connecting link between religion and science." In this he took a conciliatory line, and showed how his philosophic views could be reconciled with any really sincere pursuit of truth, whatever aim it professed to have. The address closed with the words: " May God, the spirit of the good, the beautiful, and the true, grant it." However, both his criticism and his attempt at conciliation only led

Ernst Haeckel, 1896.
From a photograph by Gabriel Max.

to further and more bitter attacks in certain quarters. His only reply was to bring out the first numbers of a fine illustrated work—a work that came from a quite different depth of his rich personality. This was the *Art-forms in Nature* [not translated], a collection of beautiful forms of radiolaria, sponges, siphonophores, &c., for artists and admirers of the beautiful. It was a work such as he alone could produce. "In the storm didst thou begin: in the storm shalt thou end," he might have said to himself, in the words of David Strauss. The storm never left him. In its mood was flung off with ready pen the *Riddle of the Universe*. "Up, old warrior, gird thy loins!" as we read in Strauss.

* * *

The biographical sketch of a living man does not close with a stroke, but with three stars. They glow still, these stars. Under their influence much may yet happen—much struggle, much peace. In view of the general situation of our time there is little hope that the last stretch of this extraordinary career will be spent in peace, though behind it all lies the peace-loving soul of an artist. But if Haeckel's career is to be one of struggle to the last hour, he may console himself with the noble words of Goethe :—

> "And when at length the long gray lashes fall
> A gentle light will broaden o'er the scene,
> In whose effulgence our remoter sons
> Will read the lineaments of yonder stars,
> And in the loftier view to which they rise
> Of God and man a loftier image hold."

CHAPTER VIII

THE CROWNING YEARS

[By Joseph McCabe]

WHEN Professor Bölsche closed his biographical sketch in 1900 with the three stars that "still glowed," he had little suspicion how widely they would yet flame out before they passed from the firmament of biography to that of history. As it has proved, Haeckel was then only entering upon the period of vast popular influence which forms the closing part of his remarkable career. He had in 1900 a few thousand thoughtful readers in several countries beside his own. To-day he is read by hundreds of thousands in Germany, England, France, and Italy, and the fourteen different translations of his most popular work have carried his ideas over the whole world. To-day the thoughts of this professor of zoology in an obscure German town are discussed eagerly by bronzed and blackened artisans in the workshops of London, Paris, and Tokio, as well as throughout Germany. The reader will have noticed in the earlier chapters that the most dignified and disdainful of Haeckel's opponents have been the academic philosophers. In the year 1905 a Berlin professor of philosophy, a stern critic of his system, devotes a long special section of his *History of Philosophy since Kant* to Haeckel and his long-contemned speculations. Why? Because, to quote his concluding sentences, " the far-reaching impulse that Haeckel has given will never more die out. He has become a sower of the future. The glad echo that his words have found in a hundred thousand breasts must stir every representative of ruling power in Church and Science to make a closer self-examination, a closer scrutiny of received ideas. Does not the thought press irresistibly upon us that somehow or other we have entered upon the wrong path in our modern development?" *

In an earlier chapter Professor Bölsche tells the moving story of the writing of the *General Morphology*: the young man making his masterly appeal to the scientists of Germany, which he thinks they will read over his grave. There is a singular parallel to this in Haeckel's attitude at the time when Bölsche closed his work. Haeckel had just written another "last will and testament," another proud and defiant utterance of what he felt to be the truth about God and man and nature. Once more he seemed to see the marble gates at the close of his career, and his sombre glance fell round on a

* Dr. Otto Gramzow's *Geschichte der Philosophie seit Kant*, p. 503.

world that was, he thought, sinking into reaction. This time he appealed to the people. The five years that have followed have witnessed an extraordinary response on the part of the people. With the speed of a popular romance his work has flown through Europe. He has received a hundred proofs that, at all events, the ideas he thinks to be fraught with salvation for humanity are being considered and discussed in wide circles that had never before known that there was a "riddle of the universe." He has been urged in the heart of the Sahara to read his own works. He has met, as he travelled on an Alpine railway, cultured nuns who told him they had learned evolution from "Professor Haeckel's works." He has looked down with mingled feeling on the wild applause of a gathering of thousands of Socialists. He has been immortalised—strangest and last of all apotheoses—in an academic history of philosophy!

The present chapter will tell the story of these five stirring years. It will aim at conveying to the English reader, by plain presentment of facts, a full picture of the activity that has attracted or distracted the attention of so many in the last few years. If Dr. Gramzow is right, if through these five years of indefatigable labour the aged scientist has become a "sower of the future," it is well for friend and foe to understand him.

There is only one respect in which one's personal feeling may be allowed to tinge such a narrative as this. For good or evil Haeckel's great influence on our generation is a reality. It is the biographer's duty to record and measure it: the reader's to appraise it. The future historian of the dramatic course of humanity's ideals must be left to interpret it in cosmic perspective. Do the stars exult, or do they grow thinner and colder in their light, over this great stirring? The far-distant generation, that will have reached the summit of the hill, will know. We who, with narrow horizon, are cutting our fond paths up the slope, have but the poor luxuries of faith and hope. Yet there is one aspect of Haeckel's recent life that makes us almost forget the cosmic issues. These five years have been, in literal truth, "crowning years" of his aims. For all the slights and insults that have been showered on the grim worker he has had a rich recompense of honour and love. Even if his ideas are to fade and wither like his laurel crowns, it will be something for a future historian to record that a gentler and more genial light fell about his closing years. As Gramzow says: "He *tried* to give us his best."

An event that Professor Bölsche has only briefly alluded to in his last crowded chapter was a fitting inauguration of the last decade of Haeckel's career. On the 17th of February, 1894, his sixtieth birthday was celebrated at Jena. The lover of nature and of the silent study passes uneasily through such functions, but the student of Haeckel's life must dwell on it. Jena had for some years realised that world-fame somehow attached to the straight, smiling figure that it saw passing daily to the Zoological Institute. It had witnessed the grave procedure of the boycot in the sixties. It had heard distinguished leaders of Churches, like Professor Michelis, brand his works as " a fleck of shame on the escutcheon of Germany," " an attack on the foundations of religion and morality," " a symptom of senile marasmus." It saw all these unworthy attacks sink into confusion, and a new era begin. It heard of greater universities competing for their professor and his refusal to leave them. It saw Bismarck fall on his neck and kiss him repeatedly when, in 1892, he headed the deputation to invite him to Jena; and it noted how the Prince absolutely refused to drive through their town " unless Haeckel comes with me" in the carriage. It gave his name proudly to one of its fine new streets.

In February, 1894, Jena witnessed a remarkable celebration—remarkable not only to those who had lived with him in the sixties. A marble bust of Haeckel was unveiled by Professor Hertwig, with noble speech, in the Zoological Institute. A festive dinner, such as Germans alone can conduct, was held in the famous Luther-Hostel. More than a thousand letters and telegrams poured in from all parts of the world, and scores of journals awoke the interest of Germany. I have before me the privately-published report on the celebration, autographed to " Agnes Haeckel."

Two lists in it catch the eye. One is a list of Haeckel's publications. Apart from his long and numerous articles in scientific journals he has written forty-two works (13,000 pages, frequently quarto) in thirty-three years. All but two are pure contributions to science: some of them are classical monographs of original research; most are beautifully illustrated by himself. The second list gives the names of those who have contributed towards the marble bust by Professor Kopf, of Rome. It is worthy of science. It includes five hundred university professors and heads of academic institutions in all parts of the world, from Brazil and the States to Algiers and Egypt and India. In their name Professor Hertwig greeted Haeckel as one "who has written his name in letters of light in the history of science." From Italy the Minister of Public Instruction sent the following telegram: "Italy, that you love so much, takes cordial part in all the honours that the civilised nations of the earth are heaping on you in commemoration of your sixtieth birthday. In the name of the Italian Universities, which love you so much and so much admire your undying work, I send you a heartfelt greeting and wishes for a long and happy and active career." Dr. Paul von Ritter gave 75,000 marks [shillings] for the erection of a monument to Haeckel at Jena when the hour comes. He had previously given 300,000 marks to be spent in the furtherance of Haeckel's scientific views.

The story so vividly unfolded by Professor Bölsche has explained how the estrangement arose between Haeckel and so many of his scientific colleagues in Germany. It is not a little gratifying to find the names of some of his critics amongst the subscribers to his festival. The personality, the aim, the self-sacrifice of the man, no less than his distinguished special contributions to science, had won a superb recognition.

In the years 1894-6 Haeckel published the *Systematic Phylogeny*. "We may differ," says Professor Arnold Lang of it, "as to the value of special or even fundamental opinions in it, but we must stand before this work in astonishment and admiration: astonishment at the vast range of his knowledge—it would seem that one head could contain no more: admiration of the intellectual labour with which the various phenomena are connected and the gigantic mass of material is reduced to order." The Royal Academy of Science at Turin judged the work the best that had been published in the last four years of the nineteenth century, and awarded its author the Bressa prize, a sum of 10,000 lire.

In August, 1898, he made a further visit to England. The International Congress of Zoology met at Cambridge, and Haeckel was invited to deliver an address. He chose his ever-present theme—the evolution of man. The long lecture, or essay, has been translated by Dr. Gadow under the title, *The Last Link*. The title is somewhat misleading, as only a page or two are devoted to

HAECKEL AND A GROUP OF ITALIAN PROFESSORS.
HOTEL BRISTOL, GENOA, 1904.

Pavona. Cattaneo.   Ariola. Berninzo. Potto. Jocchi. Andres.
Monti. Issel.   Maggi. Haeckel. Morselli. Cattaneo.
Orlando. Penzig.

To face p. 300.

"the last link." Otherwise the little work offers students a most excellent summary of " our present knowledge of the evolution of man," the title which Haeckel gave it.

But the last period of Haeckel's career is associated chiefly with, and is really inaugurated by his now famous *Riddle of the Universe*, published in 1899. To understand that work, to avoid the extremes of praise and censure that have been lavished on it, one must put oneself in Haeckel's position at the close of the last century. Mr. Wells has given us a forecast of the coming social order in which the intellectual few are separated by a wider and deeper gulf than ever from the workers and the women of the world. That keen-eyed and judicious social writer has already modified his forecast, but there were symptoms enough of the possibility of such an issue a few years ago. In Germany the signs were ominous to a man like Haeckel. The older Liberalism to which he belonged by tradition and conviction seemed in danger of being ground to dust between the upper and the nether stones of the new political mill—the increasing strength of Social Democracy and the increasing and consequent alliance of Conservative Kaiserism with the still powerful Catholic Church. Haeckel distrusted the power of Demos much as Renan did when he wrote his sombre dialogues in the seventies; and a political alliance with the Vatican opened out to him the grim prospect of a return to the Middle Ages. The freedom of research and teaching for which he had fought with unsparing vigour was, he thought, imperilled by the new alliance, no less than the very existence of culture was endangered by the triumph of Social Democracy. His academic colleagues remained in that isolation which he had ever bitterly resented.

In face of this situation, which seemed to grow more sombre as the last years of the century dragged on, his zeal for truth and progress had but one outlet. He must appeal to the people. He must take the conclusions he had so laboriously worked out in his *Systematic Phylogeny*, and translate them from scientific hieroglyphics into a demotic tongue. He must nail his theses with his own hand on the cathedral door, like the great monk whose work seemed in danger of perishing. The partial success of his *History of Creation* was encouraging, though that work had only penetrated into the first circle beyond the sacred academic enclosure, and was still unknown to the crowd. Gathering his strength for what he believed to be his final effort, he blew a blast that would reach the far-off shop and factory. It must be no gentle note, no timid suggestion that the scientific work of the nineteenth century had thrown doubt on current religious notions. He was quitting the stage. He believed these things were true, were established. The world must listen to them, must discuss them; and then the twentieth century would pass its informed verdict over his grave.

So he wrote a vigorous, an irritating, an awakening book. It must be read in this context. The charge of "dogmatism" so often hurled at it is not without humour. It is generally raised by men who in the same breath hold their truths so dogmatically that they resent his very questions. They forget, too, that the chief conclusions of the *Riddle* are references to the larger work in which, soundly or unsoundly, they are provided with massive foundations of scientific material. In England there is some excuse, as the larger work is untranslated and unknown; though one may resent the critic who charges Haeckel with egoism for his constant references to his other works and then proceeds to ridicule the slenderness of the foundations of his theories. Further, it is too often forgotten that Haeckel opens his work with a rare warning to the reader that his opinions are very largely "subjective" and his command of other subjects than biology is very "unequal." In fine, his constant and exaggerated allusions to the opposition he encounters from his scientific colleagues is, for any candid reader, a sufficient corrective of "dogmatism."

The work lit up at once a flame of controversy that has hardly yet diminished in Germany. Students have told me how, when some professor dropped the well-known name in the course of his lecture, the class would split at once into two demonstrative sections. Ten thousand copies of the library edition of the work were sold within a few months, and it quickly ran to eight editions. This remarkable success irritated his opponents, and the wide range of the subjects touched in the work gave them opportunities. Germany was deluged with pamphlets of offence and defence. Some of Haeckel's pupils replied to his opponents, but the master himself smiled through the storm. His chief critics were men with no competence in biology, and he was not minded to comply with their stratagem of withdrawing attention from the substantial positions of the work. Dennert, the philologist, swept together all the hard sayings about Haeckel that the fierce struggle of the preceding twenty years had produced—Paulsen and Adickes, the metaphysicians, poured philosophic scorn on his pretensions to construct a theory of knowledge. Adickes, in particular, met him with a vigorous fusillade of pure Kantism. It is a curious commentary on this long philosophic disdain to find Haeckel awarded a prominent place amongst "the philosophers since Kant."

Two points in this connection are noteworthy. Haeckel's first sin against the ruling metaphysic of the nineteenth century was his " naïve realism." He had dared to think he could break beyond the charmed circle of our states of consciousness. He had dreamed that a real material world lay here in space before the human mind came into existence; that a living, palpitating humanity, not a bloodless phantasm in the mind, called for our most solemn efforts. Where the ordinary reader saw a truism the metaphysicians recognised a deadly sin, and laughed Homeric laughter. To-day we have, both in England and Germany, a strong claim arising amongst the metaphysicians themselves for a return to a realist basis. Haeckel's second and chief sin was his claim to have thrown light on the evolution of consciousness and his disdain of all study of mind that was not grounded on evolution. To-day Gramzow writes: "The criticism which he makes of Kant's theory of knowledge from the evolutionary point of view is the greatest advance that philosophy has made in that branch since Kant's time."

The most violent critics of the *Riddle* were the theologians. It would be improper here to enter into the controversy, and indeed Haeckel has paid little attention to his critics of late years. Some time ago a German religious magazine was sent to me in which one of his leading critics had written a shameful article with the aim of alienating him from me. I at once wrote to him, and received a letter brimming over with his hearty laughter at the idea that he might have taken any notice of what they said. The eminent ecclesiastical historian, Professor Loofs, made a ponderous attack on his incidental reference to the birth of Christ. As Loofs himself denied the divinity and supernatural birth of Christ, Haeckel felt little inclination to enter on a serious argument about the human parentage. The theologian was so much hurt that he used language, as far as was consistent with a broad view of the theological dignity, that came within legal limits, and then quoted to Haeckel the page and letter in the German code on which he might take action!

But a great counterpoise to these bitter attacks—attacks that forgot, as Gramzow says, that "there is an ethic for the critic as well as for the man of science"—had now been provided. Men like Dr. Schmidt, Dr. Breitenbach, Professor Bölsche, and Professor Verworn rallied to their master, and conveyed a juster image of him and his work to the public. The ominous silence of the great biologists was felt to mean that his views were, in substance, no heresy to them. The man's warm and enthusiastic zeal for truth and humanity, his earnest efforts to pierce the barriers that shut off the treasures of science from the mass, could not be ignored. A cheaper edition of his work was demanded, and it was soon in the hands of more than 150,000 readers. Country after country imported his "gospel of Monism," the stirring agitation spread to France, England, America, Italy, and on until it reached Australia and Japan. To-day fourteen translations of the *Riddle* bear his teaching to the ends of the world.

Little need be said here of the Haeckel controversy in this country. I remember well the day when the German work was submitted to me with a view to publication. It did not seem to have the stuff of a conflagration in it. I hazarded a guess that it would sell a thousand copies, and thought that it contained so valuable a description of the evolution of mind that it should be published.

It has sold, with rather less than the usual advertising, with no special machinery for pressing it such as is at the command of religious works—it has sold about 100,000 copies. The success of the work astounded us. While we were being accused of "thrusting it down people's throats" we could not have arrested its circulation, had we wished, without positively refusing to republish it. Indeed, the last library edition has long been out of print, though still in frequent demand. It has made Haeckel's a familiar name in circles where even Spencer has been heard to be described as "a great balloonist." Clergymen have written to their journals saying how they heard the Monistic philosophy discussed by groups of paviors. Sir Leslie Stephen told me, on his death-bed, but with a momentary flash of his old humour, how an Orkney clergyman had written to him for consolation, as it was circulating amongst the fishers of that *ultima thule*.*

From the seething agitation he had aroused Professor Haeckel cheerfully withdrew in the autumn of 1900 to make his long journey to Java.

* The reader who desires a summary of the criticisms passed on the work may consult Dr. Schmidt's *Der Kampf um die Welträthsel* for Germany, and my own *Haeckel's Critics Answered* for England. The only biologist of competence who has written on it in this country is Prof. Lloyd-Morgan (*Contemporary Review*, 1903), but his reply is indirect. Sir Oliver Lodge has recently dealt with it at length in his *Life and Matter*, but the distinguished physicist's conception of life is in extreme and general disfavour with the biologists of England.

He now lived under the public eye, and amusing constructions were put on his movements. American journalism arrived, by its peculiar methods, at the knowledge that he had gone in quest of bones of the "missing link." A few bones of a half-human, half-ape form had been discovered on the south coast of Java a few years previously, and the trained American imagination quickly constructed a theory, which as quickly crystallised into fact. Haeckel had been heavily subsidised by an American millionaire to discover more bones of the ape-man of Java. Not to be outdone, other journals added a rival subsidy (from the American Government) and a rival search. The sober truth was that Haeckel had used his Bressa prize fund, with a subsidy from the Ritter fund at Jena, to make a study of botany and marine life in the tropics. He was within a hundred miles of the spot where Dubois had found his interesting relics, but made no effort to go further. For him the evolution of man rested on too massive a foundation for a few bones to increase its solidity. Once more he brought home huge cases of preparations, a large number of sketches (some of them touched up by Verestchagin, who was returning on the boat from China), and material for the inevitable book. *Aus Insulinde* is a charming and finely illustrated work of travel, but has not been translated.

Before he left Jena he had, with his characteristic urbanity and diligence, given personal replies to about a thousand letters he had received apropos of his *Riddle of the Universe*. The epistolary flood rose higher than ever on his return. The struggle had spread to England and France. He had returned to a cauldron of controversy. He quietly resumed his teaching at the university and attacked his still formidable literary programme. Day after day the aged scholar—he was now in his sixty-seventh year—briskly stepped up to the podium at the Zoological Institute and delivered his lectures, drawing his objects with a few quick strokes on the board or exhibiting the plates prepared by Giltsch. He noted with a quiet gleam of satisfaction that a few ladies now ventured into the "Materialist" circle. The new century had begun.

In 1902 he issued the cheap edition of the *Riddle*, of which 180,000 copies have been sold in Germany, with a reply to its critics. "The great struggle for truth," he wrote to his friend, Dr. Breitenbach, "grows fiercer and fiercer, the more my work is attacked by the clergy, the metaphysical schoolmen, and the erudite Philistines. I am continually receiving lively and sometimes enthusiastic letters of congratulation from all parts of the world." In the meantime he was engaged upon two important works, which he published in 1903.

The earlier edition of the *Anthropogeny*, of which Professor Bölsche has written, was undergoing a thorough revision. New evidence was pouring in every year in support of his sketch of the genealogy of humanity. Dubois had discovered what is now admitted to be an organism midway between the highest ape and the earliest prehistoric man.

Selenka had published wonderful studies of the anthropoid apes. Friendenthal and others had shown the literal blood-relationship of the higher apes and man by a series of beautiful experiments. He must once more gather together the enormous mass of facts, and marshal them with his old command. For six months he worked incessantly on the new edition. A hundred pages of matter were added to it, a hundred fresh illustrations. Great and exacting as the task would have been for a younger man, the work appeared in 1903 in a form that silenced criticism. I need only quote a sentence from the notice of it that was published in the *Daily Telegraph* by one of our leading literary critics, when it was issued in this country. "It is a grand conception, this of the great physiologist, that every man, in the brief term of his prenatal development, should go through these successive changes, by which man has, in countless ages, been evolved from the primitive germ-cell; and it is triumphantly vindicated in *The Evolution of Man*. It is impossible to do justice in words to the patience, the labour, the specialised skill and industry involved in the preparation of this monumental work." And one has only to compare this latest edition with the previous one to see at a glance the complete transformation, and realise the freshness and force of mind of the aged biologist.

In the face of such a work, with its towering structure of proof from embryology, comparative anatomy, and paleontology, one must look leniently on some of Haeckel's references to fellow-anthropologists like Virchow. It is not many years since the great pathologist declared emphatically at a scientific congress that "we could just as well conceive man to have descended from a sheep or an elephant as from an ape." When a leading anthropologist could say such things in 1894, a strain is laid on our charity. Darwin's words, written in a letter to Haeckel, press on us once more : " Virchow's conduct is shameful, and I trust he will one day feel the shame of it." Professor Rabl has lately contended that his deceased father-in-law (Virchow) admitted the evolution of man in private. We cannot wonder if Haeckel merely retorts : "So much the more shame on his public utterances." Such things must, at least, be borne in mind when one reads Haeckel's severe judgment on some of his great contemporaries.

The *Evolution of Man* not only offers the complete proof of its thesis—a proof accepted by every prominent biologist in England and by many prelates (such as the Bishop of London and the Dean of Westminster)—but affords also interesting proof of Haeckel's artistic gifts. Some of the best plates in the work are executed by him. But in the same year, 1903, he gave a more popular evidence of it. In detached numbers he published the large and beautiful volume of his *Art-forms in Nature*. In this work he depicts with remarkable success hundreds of the most beautiful forms that his long study of marine life had brought before him. A fine expression of the man's dual nature, the work appeals with equal force to the æsthete and the scientist. And during the long hours that he was peering into his microscope and sketching the delicate and graceful forms, the din and roar of the mighty controversy he had aroused was breaking in with every post. By the end of the year he had received more than 5,000 letters in connection with the *Riddle of the Universe*. Scurrilous letters and idolatrous letters, sober letters and fantastic letters, flowed upon the Zoological Institute, where he worked with pen and pencil, and were duly read. He merely defended himself by posting to each correspondent a printed form that he would soon issue a new work in which the further questions would be answered. He had given his life to science and humanity, and would not withdraw for the well-earned rest. And from a thousand pulpits over Europe and America the aged and self-sacrificing worker was being denounced and caricatured to audiences who had not the remotest knowledge of his aims and his work. A friend of mine heard a minister in an important Glasgow church assure his congregation from the pulpit that "Haeckel was a man of notoriously licentious life;" he had heard it "from a friend of Haeckel's." At the very time when Haeckel was buried in his splendid artistic work, the *Christian World Pulpit* was issuing a sermon in which Dr. Horton was explaining "the personal factor" in Haeckel. "He is an atrophied soul, a being that is blind on the spiritual side," the popular preacher declared.

From the turmoil Haeckel withdrew once more

to his beloved Italy. There was another reason for his flight. His seventieth birthday was approaching. He had declared at the banquet given in his honour on the occasion of his sixtieth birthday, that if he lived for the seventieth he would "bury himself in some dark corner of the Thuringian forest, far away from all festivities." Strenuous and exacting as the ten years had been, he now found himself on the threshold of his eighth decade of life. His wife, also, was ailing, and they both proceeded to the Italian Riviera at the beginning of the winter. Few of his friends were informed where he was. "I want," he wrote to me, " to pass my seventieth birthday in peace." He settled at Rapallo, and at once commenced his favourite fishing for the tiny inhabitants of the Mediterranean. The "cloistral quietness" of the little town, the daily prospect of the blue Mediterranean, "the solitary walks in the wild gorges of the Ligurian Apennines, and the uplifting sight of their forest-crowned mountain-altars" restored his freshness of spirit. Once more a vast labour lay before him. He had promised a work that would answer all biological questions addressed to him in the 5,000 letters of his correspondents. He had all the queries, all the criticisms of his views, all the latest literature of the subject, to digest into a compact volume. The result was a new work of 557 pages, *The Wonders of Life*, a remarkable summary of his zoological and botanical knowledge, with excursions into psychology, suicide, lunacy, ethnography, theology, and ethics. Its twenty solid and well-arranged chapters were written in four months.

"Promptly at 5," he wrote in December, "I am awakened by the bells of the church hard by. I write continuously until 12. After a frugal lunch and a short rest, the afternoon is devoted to a walk or to water-colour sketches. The longer days allow me to sit and paint in the open air until five. Our quiet evenings, from 5 to 10, are spent in reading and in writing letters. The interruption for dinner, from 7 to 8, gives us an opportunity to exchange jokes over our 'cloistral life.'" Thus the veteran naturalist, of "notoriously licentious life" (the words of the Glasgow preacher were spoken at this very period), approached his eighth decade of life—of work.

He remained at Rapallo until the birthday had passed, but his address had meantime become widely known, and the miniature postal arrangements at Rapallo were severely taxed. Letters, telegrams, flowers, and other gifts—mostly spontaneous expressions of gratitude from "unknown readers of the *Riddle of the Universe*"—reminded him of the larger world that now appreciated him. A still larger number of letters and gifts reached Jena from all parts of the world. Hundreds of German journals and periodicals devoted long and generous articles to the distinguished worker, and little festive commemorations were held at many of the universities. At Zurich, Professor Conrad Keller and Professor

Arnold Lang delivered speeches which have since been published. Jena sent a deputation consisting of a number of its professors to visit the hero in person at Rapallo. Reflecting on these remarkable demonstrations and the extraordinary correspondence that continually reaches Haeckel, one is disposed to repeat of him the phrase applied to a great heretical teacher of the Middle Ages, Peter Abélard: "Never was man so loved—and so hated."

A feature of the commemoration that peculiarly gratified him was the special festive number of the German students' lively periodical, *Jugend*, published at Munich. On February 16th it appeared as a "Haeckel number," full of sprightly anecdote and generous appreciation, and bearing on its cover a striking reproduction in colour of the Lenbach portrait. His letter of thanks to the journal shows that the repose and the beauty of Italy, and the outburst of affection his birthday has provoked, have set him perfectly atune to life once more. "Ah! Prithee stay, thou art so fair," he almost says in the Goethe phrase, as he "hails the moment fleeing." He goes on to deprecate the effort to make "a learned man" of him. "That, alas, I am not. We have in Germany many professors and teachers who are more learned, and have read far more books than your poor Jena schoolmaster. But from my earliest youth, since I tore up flowers and admired butterflies in my fourth year, I have yielded to the inclination of my heart and studied incessantly one great book—

Nature. This greatest of all books has taught me to know the true God, the God of Spinoza and Goethe. Then as physician I saw human life in all its heights and depths, and in my many travels through half the globe I learned the inexhaustible splendour of the earth. And I have honestly tried with all my modest powers, to reproduce with pen and pencil a part of what I saw, and reveal it to my fellows. I have had to fight many a hard fight, and in my hatred of lies and hypocrisy and decaying traditions I have at times struck a sharp note. But I trust, dear *Youth*, that thou wilt not judge all that harshly in so old and storm-tried, a warrior, and that thou wilt go on to stand with me, shoulder to shoulder, fighting for the spiritual progress of humanity, fighting in the cause of the great trinity of the true, the good, and the beautiful."

The work he had composed in four months at Rapallo, *The Wonders of Life*, was issued on his return. It has not had the stormy success of its predecessor. The fact is instructive. This work contains a fuller proof of the chief scientific positions of the *Riddle*. It is, therefore, more technical and more difficult to read. Amongst other matters, it contains a fine summary of those speculations on the mathematical forms of organisms and the idea of individuality of which Professor Bölsche has written so appreciatively. It must be recognised that Haeckel has fulfilled a duty in thus providing the general reader with a fuller biological proof of his theses. If that estimable person, the general reader, betrays less eagerness for the fuller proof, we must remember that for ages he has been taught to disregard such a thing as "proof." It is the general reader that makes Haeckel didactic. It is Haeckel's opponents who made the general reader. However, the great bulk of *The Wonders of Life* is true to its title. It is an intensely interesting summary of biological facts. For the rest, if it contains speculations that run beyond the evidence (though based on it) who is better qualified to open up these new paths than men with the enormous range of knowledge that Haeckel has? "I agree with you," one of the first biologists in England wrote to me recently, "that Haeckel is one of the first living biologists. There are not any others who have the same wide knowledge and experience and consequent 'point of view.' He knows his zoology, botany, physiology, and pathology, also geology, and has travelled, and has a keen interest in and knowledge of no small degree of philology, archæology, and ethnography."

Haeckel was in Italy once more in the autumn of 1904, and although he did little quiet travel and no fishing for radiolaria it is probable that no visit to the country ever afforded him such satisfaction. One great shadow lay over the beautiful land and its genial race whenever he visited it—a gross and almost impenetrable superstition. Turn off the great routes of Italy, with their splendid cathedrals, and visit the small towns and villages. See the scum of Naples tearing the clothes from each other to kiss the "blood of St. Januarius." Peer into the abysses of vice and grossness that are covered effectually by this formal and unlovely practice of religion. Haeckel had seen all that with sad eyes for many a year.

In 1904 a little institution that called itself "The International Congress of Freethinkers" announced that it would hold its annual gathering at Rome. The pope — the new pope, friend of the royal house—lodged a feeling protest with the authorities. The priests poured inflammatory rhetoric over their people until violence seemed inevitable. The Italian Government's only reply was to grant the heretics all the privileges that were ever given to the great Catholic pilgrimages: to put at their disposal its finest institution, the Collegio Romano, and to send its Minister of Public Instruction to open the Congress. Veteran warriors such as Haeckel, Berthelot, Salmeron, Sergi, Denis, and Björnsen, gladly announced their adhesion. Paris sent a thousand delegates; Spain nearly a thousand; Italy her thousands. Whole municipalities in Italy and France (even that of Paris) took part. The Latin world was aflame with rebellion. We met, seven thousand strong, in the heart of Rome, and Rome—the jade—smiled prettily as we marched up the Via Venti Settembre, as it had smiled once on processions of Cybele, and then on processions of Catholics.

Haeckel was greeted with a wild demonstration as he stepped on to the platform in the great *Cortile* of the College. Straight and proud, white with age but pink with more than the freshness of a young man, he adjured them in futile German, in his thin, inaudible voice, to form themselves into a new Church, the great Association of Monists. Few heard and less understood him, but his name was on every heart and his reception superb.

A week afterwards I picked up a London journal in an Italian hotel, and read—as hundreds of thousands had done—that a miserable Freethought conference had been held at Rome : that its rowdy proceedings had disgusted the scholars who had, in a misguided moment, lent their names to it. Thus are we informed at times. I remembered Sergi's enthusiastic comments at the close. " E magnifico, e magnifico," was all he could gasp. I remembered Haeckel's exultation as we walked home to his Albergo Santa Chiara, and Berthelot's deep joy. The same scholars, except Bjornsen, took part in the Congress at Paris, in 1905, when 100,000 of us were nobly received by the Conseil Municipal. But Haeckel was too unwell to come. Nature has laid her hand on him at length, and bade him hang his weapons on the wall. He can but hope to remain a passive spectator for a few years more of that vast stirring of the Latin peoples which he has so much contributed to bring about.

His last active effort was the delivery of three lectures at Berlin in the spring of 1905. He has always avoided public lectures as much as possible. His poor voice and comparative nervousness make the work unattractive. A severe attack of influenza sapped his strength in the winter of 1905, and he has been unable to eliminate its unpleasant consequences. But the opportunity of enforcing his gospel in the capital of the Empire, where the Virchows and Du Bois-Reymonds had ruled so long made him deaf to the counsels of prudence. He chose as his theme the controversy in regard to evolution, and gave three spirited lectures. The changed world came home to him vividly enough. A vast and enthusiastic gathering of admirers in one of the finest halls in Berlin: outside, at the very door, his clerical opponents distributing handbills that offered a choice selection of the most venomous attacks on his person and work. The lectures are now available in English under the title of *Last Words on Evolution*.

The present state of Haeckel's health forbids him to hope that he will do any more active work. As I write, he lies in his villa, in "Haeckel Street," overlooking the handsome Zoological Institute, which he raised, and the little university town that he has made known to the world. Beyond the graceful hills that cradle it, he sees the dark waves tossing that he has worked so hard to set in motion. In Germany the alliance of the Emperor with the Catholics saddens him, but—the Jesuits are accepting evolution, over the fresh grave of Virchow. Abroad his ideals, even his ideas, are making triumphant progress. He thinks of the vast changes that have taken place since he stood out, almost alone, reckless of all but honour and truth, at the Stettin Congress in 1863. "Das Leben ist schön," he still repeats. What will men say of *him* when the lines of history draw in, and the critic will have the proper perspective? I believe no great worker ever thought less about it. Through inexorable labour, through constant sacrifice, through storms of painful obloquy, he has lived his ideals, if he has made mistakes—been mortal. Those ideals are an enduring contribution to the good. The first, the motto of his young days, was *Impavidi progrediamur*—"Let us march on fearlessly." The second, the motto of his later years, was: "The good, the true, and the beautiful, are the ideals, yea the gods, of our Monistic philosophy."

Bibliography

THE following is a list of the works by Professor Haeckel that have been translated into English :—

"The History of Creation." Translation (in two vols., edited by E. Ray-Lankester) of the *Natürliche Schöpfungsgeschichte*. 1876. [4th edition, 1892.]

"Freedom in Science and Teaching." Translation (with preface by T. H. Huxley) of the *Freie Wissenschaft und Freie Lehre*. 1879.

"Report on the Deep-sea Medusæ dredged by H.M.S. *Challenger*." Zoology series, vol. iv. [330 pp. and 2 plates.] 1882.

"The Pedigree of Man." Translation (by E. B. Aveling) of the *Gesammelte Populäre Vorträge*. 1883.

"A Visit to Ceylon." Translation (by Clara Bell) of the *Indische Reisebriefe*. 1883.

"Report on the Radiolaria collected by H.M.S. *Challenger*." Zoology series, vol. xviii. [2,000 pp. 4to and 140 plates.] 1887.

"Report on the Siphonophoræ collected by H.M.S. *Challenger*." Zoology series, vol. xxviii. [380 pp. 4to and 50 plates.] 1888.

"Report on the Deep-sea Keratosa collected by H.M.S. *Challenger*." Zoology series, vol. xxxii. [92 pp. and 8 plates.] 1889.

"Planktonic-studies." Translation (by S. W. Field) of *Plankton-studien*. 1891.

"The Confession of Faith of a Man of Science." Translation (by J. Gilchrist) of *Monismus*. 1894.

"The Last Link." Translation (by Dr. Gadow) of the Cambridge Lecture on Evolution. 1898.

"The Riddle of the Universe." Translation (by J. McCabe) of *Die Welträthsel*. 1901. [6th edition, 1905.]

"The Wonders of Life." Translation (by J. McCabe) of *Die Lebenswunder*. 1904.

"The Evolution of Man." Translation (by J. McCabe) of the 5th edition of the *Anthropogenie*. [905 pp., 512 illustrations, and 30 plates.] 1905.

"Last Words on Evolution." Translation (by J. McCabe) of *Der Kampf um den Entwickelungs-Gedanken*. 1906.

COMPLETE LIST OF PROF. HAECKEL'S WORKS

(EXCLUSIVE OF ARTICLES IN SCIENTIFIC PERIODICALS, ETC.)

"De telis quibusdam Astaci fluviatilis." Dissertatio inauguralis histologica. [48 pp. and 2 plates.] 1857.

"De rhizopodum finibus et ordinibus." Diss. pro venia legendi impetranda. 1861.

"Die Radiolarien (*Rhizopoda radiaria*)." [Vol. i., 572 pp. fol.; vol ii., 35 plates.] 1862.

BIBLIOGRAPHY

"Beiträge zur Naturgeschichte der Hydromedusen. Die Familie der Rüsselquallen (*Medusæ Geryonidæ*)." [204 pp. and 6 plates.] 1865.

"Generelle Morphologie der Organismen." [Vol. i, xxxii and 574 pp. and 2 plates; vol. ii., clx and 462 pp. and 8 plates.] 1866.

"Natürliche Schöpfungsgeschichte." [568 pp. and 9 plates.] 1868. [10th edition, 1902.]

"Uber die Entstehung und den Stammbaum des Menschengeschlechts." 1868.

"Zur Entwickelungsgeschichte der Siphonophoren." Crowned by the Utrecht Society of Art and Science. [124 pp. 4to and 14 plates.] 1869.

"Uber Arbeitstheilung in Natur und Menschenleben." 1869.

"Das Leben in den grössten Meerestiefen." 1870.

"Biologische Studien." [184 pp. and 6 plates.] 1870.

"Die Kalkschwämme (*Calcispongiæ*)." [Vol. i., xvi and 484 pp.; vol ii., 418 pp.; vol. iii., 60 plates.] 1872.

"Anthropogenie, oder Entwickelungsgeschichte des Menschen." [xviii and 732 pp., 12 plates, and 210 woodcuts.] 1874.

"Arabische Korallen." 1875.

"Die Perigenesis der Plastidule oder die Wellenzengung der Lebenstheilchen." 1876.

"Studien zur Gastræatheorie." [270 pp. and 14 plates.] 1877.

"Die heutige Entwickelungslehre im Verhältnisse zur Gesammtwissenschaft." 1877.

"Freie Wissenschaft und Freie Lehre." [106 pp.] 1878

BIBLIOGRAPHY

"Das Protistenreich." [104 pp., 58 woodcuts.] 1878.

"Gesammelte populäre Vorträge aus dem Gebiete der Entwickelungslehre." [181 pp., 50 woodcuts.] 1878.

"Das System der Medusen." [xxx and 672 pp. and 40 plates.] 1879.

"Gesammelte populäre Vorträge." Vol. ii. [164 pp. and 30 woodcuts.] 1879.

"Das System der Acraspeden." [312 pp. and 20 plates.] 1880.

"Metagenesis und Hypogenesis von *Aurelia aurita*. [36 pp. and 2 plates.] 1881.

"Die Tiefsee-Medusen der Challenger-Reise und der Organismus der Medusen." [205 pp. and 32 plates.] 1881.

"Indische Reisebriefe." [380 pp.] 1882.

"Die Naturanschauung von Darwin, Goethe, und Lamarck." 1882.

"Grundriss einer allgemeiner Naturgeschichte der Radiolarien." [248 pp. 4to and 64 plates.] 1887.

"Die Acantharien oder actipyleen Radiolarien." [32 pp. and 12 plates.] 1888.

"Die Phæodarien oder cannopyleen Radiolarien." [32 pp. and 30 plates]. 1888.

"Plankton-studien." [112 pp.] 1890.

"Der Monismus als Band zwischen Religion und Wissenschaft." 1892.

"Zur Phylogenie der Australischen Fauna." 1893.

"Die Systematische Phylogenie." [3 vols., 1,800 pp.] 1894.

"Die Amphorideen und Cystoideen." 1896.

"Ueber unsere gegenwärtige Kenntniss vom Ursprung des Menschen." 1898.

"Die Welträthsel." [473 pp.] 1899.

"Aus Insulinde." [260 pp., 80 illustrations.] 1901.

"Anthropogenie." [5th edition, 991 pp., 30 plates, and 512 illustrations.] 1903.

"Kunstformen der Natur." [100 large coloured plates and text.] 1904.

"Die Lebenswunder." [567 pp.] 1904.

"Ernst Haeckel's Wanderbilder." [Series of prints of his oil-paintings and water-colour landscapes.] 1905.

"Der Kampf um den Entwickelungs-Gedanken." [112 pp. and 4 plates.] 1905.

Index

A

Adam's Peak, Haeckel on, 244
Adaptations, embryonic, 228
Adaptation to environment, 119
Adickes, Professor, 304
Adriatic, visit to the, 257
Æsthetic element in Haeckel, 83
Affinities of animals, 283
Agassiz, 229
„ on creation, 128
Alexander, Karl, Grand Duke of Weimar, 254
Algeciras, Haeckel at, 252
Algiers, Haeckel arrested in, 259
Allmers, Hermann, 85
Alpine salamander, the, 221
America, the discovery of, 20
Amphioxus, the, 274
Amphoridea and Cystoidea, the, 291
Angelo, Michael, paintings of, 15
Anthropogenie, the, 279, 309
Anthropological critics, Haeckel's, 283
Arabia, coral-fishing in, 257
Archeopteryx, the, 167, 223
Arctic hare, the, 119
Art and mathematics, 216
Art-forms in Nature, the, 26, 293, 311

Artificial selection, 117
Artistic gifts of Haeckel, 83-4
Asia Minor, travels in, 257
Aspects of Nature, 46
Association of Monists, 319
Athletic festival, Haeckel at the 173
Atom, the, 212
Aus Insulinde, 308

B

Bacilli, the, 206
Bacteria, the, 180
Basedow, 32
Belligemma, 258
Berlin, Haeckel's criticism of, 30
„ , lectures at, in 1905, 319
Berthelot, 318, 319
Björnsen, B., 318, 319
Bible, the, 126
Biogenetic law, the, 219
Bird, evolution of the, 223
Birth of Haeckel, 29
Birthday, celebration of Haeckel's sixtieth, 297
Birthday, celebration of Haeckel's seventieth, 314
Birthdays, real determination of, 102

Bismarck, esteem of, for Haeckel, 298
Bleek, Professor, 37
Bose, Countess, liberality of, 255
Botany, Haeckel's early love of, 36
Braun, Alexander, 52
Bressa prize, the, 300
Bronn, 128
Bruno, Giordano, 16
Butterfly, development of the, 227

C

Calcispongiæ, the, 272
„ , embryology of the, 273
Calumniation of Haeckel, 266, 268
Cambridge, Haeckel at, 300
Canaries, voyage to the, 240
Catastrophic theory, the, 108
Catholicism in Germany, 301
„ , lower features of, 134
Cell, discovery of the, 56, 65
„ , nature of the, 178
Cell-soul, the, 161
Cell-souls and Soul-cells, 286
Cell-state, the, 57
„ , man as a, 160
Cell-theory, the, and Darwinism, 178
Cenogenesis, 231
Ceylon, Haeckel's life in, 33
„ , visit to, 258
Challenger expedition, the, 287
Chromacea, the, 180
Chrysaora, 176
Classical studies, 35
Classification, Haeckel's reform of, 233-4
Colombo, Haeckel at, 258
Columbus, 16, 20
Compromise, Virchow advocates, 163-171
Congresses, founding of scientific, 144

Consciousness, Virchow on, 163
Copernicus, 16
Corals of Arabia, the, 257
Craw-fish, study of the, 77
Creation, difficulties of, 98
Crystal, life of the, 203
Cuvier's theory of creation, 107
Cyanea, 176

D

Dalmatia, visit to, 257
Darwin's condemnation of Virchow, 311
Darwin, Haeckel's intercourse with, 241
„ in South America, 103
„ on botany, 39
„ , physiognomy of, 146
„ , reasoning of, 117-20
„ , theism of, 124
Darwinism accepted by Haeckel, 133
"Dead" matter, 203
Death of Haeckel's wife, 184
Deep-sea Medusæ, the, 287
Degree, dissertation for the, 77
Dennert, Prof., 304
Descent of Man, the, 243
Design, abandonment of, 169
Desmonema Annasethe the, 186
Dissection, 55
Division of labour, essay on, 249
Doctorates held by Haeckel, 24
Dogmatism, alleged, of Haeckel, 23, 218, 303
Dohrn, Anton, 59
Down, Haeckel's visit to, 241
Dubois, Eugen, 167, 309
Du Bois-Reymond, E., 135

E

Education, Haeckel on elementary, 34
Egypt, visit to, 257

INDEX

Ehrenberg, 78, 96
Elective Affinities, the, 45
Embryonic diagrams, Haeckel's early, 268
Embryology, 57
,, and evolution, 170
,, in Haeckel's works, 268, 280
Embryology of the Siphonophoræ, the, 248
Emotional character of Haeckel, 186-7
Engelmann, 173
Erica cinerea, search for the, 37
"Ernst Haeckel Street," 43
Essay, Haeckel's first, 71
Essays on the Theory of Evolution, 287
Evolution, internal law of, 130
,, of species, 114
Evolution of Man, the, 279, 310
"Exact" scientists, 131, 132, 164
Extinct species, 107
Extinction of species, 112, 119

F

Family of Haeckel, the, 253
Filippo de Filippi, 76
Fish, nature of the, 219
FitzRoy, Captain, 103
Flora Hallensis, contribution to the, 37
Fol, 245
For Darwin, 230
Force and Matter, 201
Forms, science of, 190-2
Form-unities, 207
Free Science and Free Teaching, 285
Freedom of research, 75, 156
French rule in Prussia, 25
Freytag, Gustav, 21, 29
Friedenthal, 310

Frog, the, 219
,, , evolution of the, 222

G

Galapagos Islands, Darwin in the, 116
Galileo, 16
Gandtner, 37
Gastræa, the, 276
Gastræa-theory, the, 278
Gastrula, the, 277
Gegenbaur, Karl, 62-4
Genealogical tree of organisms, 149, 152, 226
Generelle Morphologie, the, 188
Genius, 102
Geology, 108
,, and evolution, 167
Geryonidæ, the, 177
Gill-slits in the human embryo, 269
Giltsch, Adolph, 289
Glyptodon, the, 113
Gneisenau, 29
God, Haeckel's conception of, 133-5, 236
,, , the new conception of, 19
Goethe, 17
,, , evolution in works of, 238
,, on morphology, 190-1
Goethe's influence on Haeckel, 41-6
Gramzow, Otto, on Haeckel, 295
Greece, visit to, 257
Greeff, Richard, 244
Greek, Haeckel's knowledge of, 36
Green Henry, 45
Gryptotherium, the, 113
Gude, Karl, 37

H

Haeckel abandons theology, 75, 133
,, , æsthetic element in, 83, 185
,, , ancestry of, 21

Haeckel and Darwin, 127, 241
,, ,, Gegenbaur, 62
,, ,, Müller, 69
,, ,, Virchow, 163, 284
,, as a physician, 80
,, ,, traveller, 256
,, at Down, 241
,, at Stettin, 146
,, , birth of, 29
,, , boyhood of, 31-3
,, , early education of, 34-50
,, embraces evolution, 137
,, , family of, 253
,, , first marriage of, 100
,, goes to Jena, 100
,, , honours awarded to, 10, 298, 300
,, in Heligoland, 69
,, in Italy, 82
,, in the Canaries, 240
,, , medical training of, 76
,, , parents of, 28
,, , personal charm of, 146
,, , political views of, 301
,, , recent popularity of, 295
,, reconstructs zoology, 181
,, , religion of, 230
,, , second marriage of, 253
,, , university training of, 54
Haeckel, Councillor Karl, 29, 32
,, , Walter, 83
Haeckel's Critics Answered, 307
Heine, 21
Heligoland, the first journey to, 69
Heliosphæra, the, 141
Heliozoa, the, 258
Heredity, a theory of, 284
Hertwig, Oscar, 257
Hertwig, R., 189
Histology, 56
History of Creation, the, 262
History, unity of, 44
Holy Land, travels in the, 259
Horton, Dr., on Haeckel, 312

Hüffer, Hermann, 21
Humboldt, 46, 144
,, foundation, the, 31
Huschke, Agnes, 253
Huxley on the origin of man, 180

I

Illustrations, charges against Haeckel's, 267-8
Imagination in science, 200
Independence, Haeckel's early sense of, 31
Indische Reisebriefe, the, 261
Individuality, nature of, 207, 211
,, , stages of, 209
Infusoria, the, 78
International Congress of Freethinkers, the, 316
Irene, 176
Ischia, journey to, 87
Italy, appreciation of Haeckel in 299
,, , Haeckel's first visit to, 82

J

Java, ape-man of, 167, 308
,, , voyage to, 260, 308
Jena, 42
,, , Haeckel's first visit to, 50
Jugend, Haeckel number of, 315
Jump, Haeckel's record, 173
Jurist, Haeckel as a, 22

K

Keferstein, Professor, on Darwinism, 148
Keller, Gottfried, 45
Kepler, 16
Kölliker, Albert, 56
Königsberg, Congress at, 99
Kopf, Professor, bust of Haeckel by, 299
Kükenthal, 43
Kulturkampf, the, 284

INDEX

L

Lamprey, the, 181
Lancelet, the, 181
Lang, Professor A., on Haeckel, 300
Lange, F. A., 154
Language, evolution of, 150
Lanzarote, Haeckel at, 245
Last Link, the, 300
Last Words on Evolution, the, 320
Latin, Haeckel's knowledge of, 36
"Law of development," 129
Law, training for the, 23
Lawyers in Haeckel's family, 22
Lemur, the, 181
Leydig, Frantz, 56
Lichtenstein, Professor, 71
Life, earliest forms of, 151
„ , origin of, 124
Linné, classification of, 105
Literary production of Haeckel, 299
Lizard, evolution of the, 222
Lizzia Elizabethæ, the, 185
Lloyd-Morgan, Professor, 307
Lodge, Sir Oliver, 307
Loofs, Professor, 305
Love of nature in Haeckel, 31
Lyell's reform of geology, 109

M

Macrauchenia, the, 112
Mammoth, the, 106
Man, creation of, 126
„ , evolution of, 180–1, 279
Man's genealogical tree, 181
Marine animals, study of, 60
Marriage, Haeckel's first, 100
„ „ second, 253
Mastodon, the, 112
Materialism and idealism, 83, 154
Mathematical types of form, 214
Matter, potentialities of, 204
Mechanical embryology, 249
Medical studies of Haeckel, 72
Medusæ, the, 174, 246

Megatherium, the, 106, 112
Merseburg, 30
Messina, 90
Metaphysics, Haeckel's views on, 304
Method, analysis of scientific, 200
Meyer, Frau, 253
Microscope, beauty in the, 92
Miklucho-Maclay, 245
Miracles in modern Italy, 134
"Missing link," the, 308
Mitrocoma Annæ, the, 185
Moleschott, 83, 154
Monera, the, 179
Monism, 73, 203, 217
Monism as a Connecting Link, the 292
Monograph on the Calcispongiæ, the, 272
Monograph on the Medusæ, the, 185
Monograph on the Monera, the, 182
Monograph on the Radiolaria, the, 100, 138
Monophyletic theory of life, the, 158
Morphology, the science of, 190
„ , history of, 199
Mosaic story of creation, 105, 108
Mottoes, Haeckel's, 321
Mouth, the primitive, 275
Müller, Fritz, 230
„ , Johannes, 65–8
„ „ , death of, 80
Müller-net, the, 69
Munich, Haeckel and Virchow at, 157, 283
Murray, Sir John, 259

N

Naples, Haeckel at, 87
Natural law, relativity of, 232
„ philosophy, 48

Natural selection, 119-120
Nature and God, 20
Naturalist's Voyage round the World, 46
Nausicaa phæacum, the, 185
Nineteenth century, work of the, 18
Nomenclature, scientific, 185
Nucleus, the, 179

O

Oken, L., 144
„ on embryonic development, 224
Ontogeny, 231
Optimism of early Darwinians, 166
Origin and Evolution of the Sense-organs, 286
Origin of Species, the, 122
Over-individuals, 247
Ovi di mare, 93
Ovum, the, 268, 273
„ , discovery of the, 58

P

Paleontology, 149
Palingenesis, 231
Pampas, fossil remains in the, 112
Paris, Freethought Congress at, 319
Pathology, Virchow's reform of, 57
Paulsen, Professor, 304
Peak of Teneriffe, Haeckel climbs the, 250
Pelagic sweepings, 70
Pemmatodiscus gastrulaceus, the, 277
Persephone-impulse, the, in Haeckel, 256
Philosophy and observation, 156
„ and science, 202
Philosophy, Haeckel's work in, 305
Phylogeny, 231

Physician, Haeckel as a, 80
„ , qualities of the, 53
Pithecanthropus, the, 167, 308
Plankton, 70
Plankton-studies, 290
Plant or animal, priority of the 205
Plastidules, 284
Political views of Haeckel, 301
Polyps, 175
Popular works, why written, 262
Potsdam, Haeckel's birthplace, 30
Private teacher, Haeckel as, 100
Profession, choice of a, 53
Professor of Zoology, Haeckel appointed, 100
Progressive evolution, 168
Promorphology, 215
Protestant religion, character of the, 134
Protists, the, 206
Protistology, 206
Puerto del Arrecise, 250
Pupa, the, 227

R

Rabl, Professor, 311
Radiolaria, the, 93, 289
„ , shells of the, 95
„ , system of the, 140
Rapallo, Haeckel at, 313
Realism of Haeckel, 304
Report on the Deep-sea Keratosa, the, 290
Report on the Radiolaria, the, 289
Riddle of the Universe, the, 22, 291, 301-7
Ritter, Paul von, donation of, 255, 299
Riviera, marine study on the, 76
Rocks, formation of the, 109
Roederer, 25
Romance nations, religion of the 134

INDEX

Rome, Freethought Congress at, 316
Roux, Professor, 249
Russia, travels in, 259

S

Scandinavia, visit to, 257
Schiller, 42, 43
Schleiden, M. J., 47
Schleiermacher, 27-8
Schmidt, Dr., 307
School-days at Merseburg, 34
Schopenhauer on Darwinism, 132
Schwann, Theodor, 65
Scientific method, variations of, 48
Scilla bifolia, search for the, 51
Scotland, visit to, 257, 259
Sea-urchin, fertilisation of the, 257
Seebeck refuses Haeckel's resignation, 254
Semon, 43
Sergi, Professor, 319
Sethe, Anna, 81, 100
" , Bertha, 26
" , Christian, 21, 22
" , Christoph, 21, 25
Siphonophores, the, 246
Social Democrats, the, 285, 301
Soul, unity of the, 161
Spain, Haeckel's visit to, 252
Specialism in science, 48
Species, early difficulties about, 37-8
" idea of fixity of, 105
Sponge, nature of a, 271
Sponges, Haeckel's study of the, 270
Spontaneous generation, Haeckel's early opposition to, 77
Spontaneous generation, possibility of, 136
Stereometric structures, 215
Stephen, Sir Leslie, 307
Stettin, Congress of, 145

Stocks, animal, 211
Strauss, 83
Struggle for life, the, 119
Studies of the Gastræa-theory, the, 277
Sumatra, Haeckel in, 260
Superstition in Italy, 315
System of the Medusæ, the, 287
System of the Siphonophoræ, the, 249
Systematic Phylogeny, the, 291

T

Tadpole, the, 220
Teeth in young parrots, 223
Teneriffe, 240
Terminology created by Haeckel, 36
Theological critics of Haeckel, 298, 305
Theology, Haeckel's rejection of, 75-6
Tiara, 176
Tierra del Fuego, 103
Tissues of the Craw-fish, the, 77
Tjibodas, 260
Training, early, of Haeckel, 32
Transformism, 111
Translations of Haeckel's works, 294
"Travel Pictures," 84
Travels of Haeckel, 256
Tree-frog, the, 119

U

Unicellular animals, 94, 98
Unity of nature, the, 235
Unnucleated organisms, 180
Utrecht Society of Art and Science, 248

V

Venus of Milo, the, 191
Vienna, medical studies at, 80

Villefranche, fishing at, 76
Virchow, Rudolf, 56, 72
,, at Stettin, 153–171
,, Haeckel's conflict with, 74
,, on the evolution of man, 311
Visit to Ceylon, the, 259
Vital force, the, 135
Vogt, 83, 154
Volger, Otto, 167

W

Wallace, A. R., and Darwin, 123
Weimar, Grand Duke of, 254

Wonders of Life, the, 292, 313
Works, number of Haeckel's, 299
Worm, evolution of the, 276
Würtzburg, Haeckel at, 54
,, invitation to the University of, 253

Z

Zipangu, 20
Zoological Institute, the, 42
,, philosophy, 194
,, Station at Naples, 59
Zoology, reconstruction of, by Haeckel, 24
,, the old and the new, 60

Milton Keynes UK
Ingram Content Group UK Ltd.
UKHW040046180324
439604UK00006B/1038